CONTESTED TERRAIN

RECONCEPTUALISING SECURITY IN THE PACIFIC

CONTESTED TERRAIN

RECONCEPTUALISING SECURITY IN THE PACIFIC

STEVEN RATUVA

Australian
National
University

PRESS

PACIFIC SERIES

ANU PRESS

Published by ANU Press
The Australian National University
Acton ACT 2601, Australia
Email: anupress@anu.edu.au

Available to download for free at press.anu.edu.au

ISBN (print): 9781760463199
ISBN (online): 9781760463205

WorldCat (print): 1117322426
WorldCat (online): 1117322368

DOI: 10.22459/CT.2019

Cover design and layout by ANU Press

Contents

Preface

The world is confronted with multiple issues of security challenges, and how we understand these challenges is often based on parochial prisms that serve our own political, ideological and economic interests. This self-centric framing of security is part of the challenge that we must confront. This book is an attempt to address some of these challenges by exploring how the use of multiple lenses could help enrich our understanding of the interconnected layers of security thinking and practices. Although the case studies used are from the Pacific, the broader conceptual narratives have universal resonance. In a world where security issues are linked to socioeconomic, political, ethnic, ideological and environmental issues, unpacking these connections in a way that makes analytical and policy sense is imperative.

The book is a result of data accumulated over three years of research (both field and archival), conferences, workshops and seminars. It is one of four books I have written that were funded by a New Zealand Marsden Fund research grant. Like any other book in social science, it is a kind of 'work in progress', in the sense that, by the time the book is published, it will already be overtaken by continuously unfolding security issues. Hence there is a temptation to update either by producing another edition or even a separate follow-up volume. But this is not the intention, at least for the time being.

Security by its very nature is contested, and the debate about regional security in the Pacific is multidimensional and reflects the transforming and precarious nature of global security. What constitutes security is subject to multiple discourses, and to privilege one set of security variables over another, as is often done by researchers and policy-makers, can be unwise given the multifarious factors that shape our security environment. The book attempts to weave together both conceptual analysis and applied narratives in a symbiotic way, where one informs and shapes the other.

It has an interdisciplinary approach and is meant to be used by academics, researchers, policy-makers, security experts, regional and international agencies, civil society organisations and the public at large.

Ultimately, it is hoped that the book will contribute to understanding some of the deeper issues of conflict that continue to fracture communities with the hope of finding lasting solutions for a peaceful Pacific and a peaceful humanity.

The book is a result of invaluable contribution by a number of people and institutions. The funding for this research was generously provided by the Marsden Fund of the Royal Society of New Zealand. This is one of the four books that benefited from the Marsden funding. I also acknowledge the support of the Faculty of Arts at the University of Canterbury and other project collaborators on Pacific regional security, including the United Nations Development Program and United Nations regional office in Fiji, Department of Pacific Affairs (The Australian National University) and other individuals and organisations who were represented in a series of conferences and seminars that were part of the Marsden project on regional security. I also acknowledge the proficient role of the anonymous reviewers and Fulbright New Zealand for providing me the opportunity in 2018 to complete parts of the manuscript while based at UCLA, Duke University and Georgetown University as a Fulbright senior fellow. My special thanks to the numerous groups and individuals around the Pacific, especially Fiji, Tonga and Solomon Islands, who participated in various direct or indirect ways in the project.

A number of individuals need special mention. My sincere thanks to Professor Stewart Firth of The Australian National University for his professional advice and contribution to editing and arranging the publication logistics. I also extend my hearty thanks to John Moriarty, who worked hard on editing the first draft, and Cathryn Game for her meticulous work on copy-editing the manuscript. Last but not least, I thank my wife Mere for her moral support on this incredible journey.

1

Introduction: Interconnected and multifaceted security

We must concentrate not merely on the negative expulsion of war, but on the positive affirmation of peace.

Martin Luther King

The few months I spent in the United States in 2018 as a senior Fulbright scholar at University of California, Los Angeles (UCLA), Duke and Georgetown reinforced in my mind some of the contradictory manifestations of security in our contemporary era. Here was a country so militarily, politically and economically powerful, yet so insecure and paranoid about its own sense of identity, being and security. Here was a country that prided itself in being a hub of multiculturalism, yet there was so much division, tension and anxiety. Here was a country that marketed itself as the richest in the world, where the 'American dream' was a divine destiny, yet I witnessed so much poverty, homelessness and economic insecurity as I wandered the streets of Los Angeles and other major US cities.

This situation of contested narratives of security reflects the philosophical backdrop to this book. An experience of 'security' in one context may be the basis for 'insecurity' in another. Contending notions of security define the shifting prisms through which we socially construct our lived experiences and the dramatically changing world around us.

The concept of security is often contested, given the different normative and empirical approaches as well as the different conceptual emphasis used by scholars (Baldwin, 1997). The normative differences can be a result of varying methodologies used and competing political, gender and cultural assumptions as well as different ideological outlooks, which may colour how security is conceptualised in everyday life or operationalised in policies (McLeod, 2015). The same can be said of Pacific security, where discussions have been wide-ranging with different authors emphasising different discourses and priority areas. One of the latest Pacific regional security agreements, the Boe Declaration on regional security endorsed by the Pacific leaders in September 2018, emphasised the primacy of climate change as 'the single greatest threat to the livelihoods, security and well-being of the peoples of the Pacific' (Pacific Islands Forum Secretariat, 2018: 10). Others see political security and conflict as central issues that need greater focus, given some cases of instability in some Pacific countries in the past (for instance, see Henderson & Watson, 2005). The point is that while the selective emphasis may appear to help desegregate and simplify issues, it tends to prioritise and privilege some approaches while undermining the significance of some. At the same time, it has the potential to conceal the social synergies and historical connections between issues.

This book attempts to contribute to discussions on Pacific security using the analytical eclecticism approach, which selectively recombines different strands of discourses and focuses on connecting abstract theorisation with applied analysis and policies (Sils & Katzenstein, 2010). Within this broad parameter, the book weaves together different discourses in an interdisciplinary way to examine various dimensions of security and their connecting synergies, including their policy implications. The use of multiple prisms could help in enriching our understanding of the complex interconnections between the different aspects of Pacific security, some of which are more visible and some of which are more subtle. Each aspect, whether, political, economic, sociocultural, environmental or psychological, is interconnected in both manifest and latent ways. In doing so, the book attempts to provide a critique of some paradigms often used in analysis of Pacific security and raises questions about their reliability in the context of a fast-changing and complex region. In this regard, the book deliberately sets out to combine both theoretical discourse and empirical analysis of case studies. The first three chapters are heavily conceptual and attempt to unpack some of the philosophical assumptions and sociological debates about the nature of security at the global and regional spheres, which are often overlooked, and these are followed by three empirical chapters that draw their conceptual narratives from the theoretical discussions.

The book does not in any way claim to provide definitive answers to the myriad of security questions in the Pacific but rather to raise some critical questions about some of the existing security assumptions and discourses and how they are articulated and operationalised in the context of competing paradigms and contested methodologies. While the use of multiple conceptual prisms provides us with a broader picture of unfolding realities, the use of comparative case studies (Fiji, Tonga and Solomon Islands) is equally important to enable us to understand the unique historical experiences of Pacific Island Countries (PICs). The Pacific is not a homogeneous and generic entity, which is easily generalisable, but consists of diverse countries and communities that have undergone different forms of security experiences that have influenced their political, social and economic developments.

Context and approach

The notion of security is multifaceted and is constructed differently in varying contexts, depending on the theoretical, ideological, cultural and political prisms deployed to make sense of particular circumstances (Brooks, 2010). The questions of what constitutes a security problem, what is a risky situation, what and who poses threat to our lives, have been part of humanity's self-exploratory journey since time immemorial as we construct and adapt our identities and define our social boundaries. As globalisation incorporates disparate societies into a collective hegemonic embrace, security becomes fundamentally ethical in nature as we attempt to make sense of the diverse manifestations of threat at different levels—global, regional, national and local (Burke, Lee-Koo & McDonald, 2016). Many of these security issues will continue to haunt humanity in the future as long as the basic causes are insufficiently addressed or even ignored.

Threats posed by terrorism, climate change, socioeconomic inequality, political marginalisation, hunger, racism, environmental degradation, war, crime, violence, poverty and gender discrimination are not isolated phenomena with distant roots but are bred by the very conditions of which we are an integral part. Furthermore, they are manifestly or latently interconnected in complex ways and manifest themselves in different degrees (Xuetong, 2009). They represent in multiple ways humanity's social tendency to dominate, accumulate, appropriate and transform at the cost of others. Competition over resources, grabs for power and a desire for influence have left many threatened by powerlessness, marginalisation and oppression, in turn often creating a chain reaction of resistance and counter-resistance. Many security issues, such as poverty, terrorism and climate change, are 'glocal', meaning that they manifest themselves locally while having a global character and impact. This is indeed a challenge of significant proportions. How can these security issues be addressed simultaneously at the local and global levels to ensure a reasonable, sustainable and effective way of containing them without further contributing to their escalation? This book is a modest attempt to explore some of these issues. However, to avoid being swallowed up by the huge chorus of security narratives, the book focuses on selected security issues in the Pacific and how they articulate themselves uniquely in different island countries.

When American sociologist C. Wright Mills coined the term 'sociological imagination', he was referring to how humans, as agents of social consciousness and transformation, are able to expand their analytical faculty to connect and make sense of seemingly disparate issues, whether local or global, in a coherent and meaningful way (Mills, 1959). With this idea of interconnectedness and encompassment in mind, this book is an attempt to make sense of the complex relationships between various aspects of security at the global, regional and local levels, focusing on the PICs, in particular Fiji, Tonga and Solomon Islands, as case studies. In a broad way, the conceptual narrative used to capture this diversity is 'analytical eclecticism', which refers to consciously addressing and selectively recombining the theoretical and applied approaches of different theoretical schools to understand the multidimensional and complex issues related to security in different situations (Suh, Katzenstein & Carson, 2004). Due to the multifarious nature of security, the idea is to move away from the parochial obsession with deploying a single theoretical position to narrowly frame a multilayered and shifting phenomenon such as security to embracing a more multidimensional approach that allows for theoretical flexibility and adaptation. The singular approach tends to privilege particular ideological and analytical narratives over others and often leaves gaps in analysis. Different conceptual prisms such as the securitisation theory, postcolonial discourse, human security, constructivism, realism and liberalism, to name some, have something to offer, although some more vigorously and inspiringly than others. Theories are not meant to impose a near-divine blueprint for constructing social reality, but rather they need to be treated as dispensable tools to help illuminate one's path in the exploratory journey towards enhancement of knowledge. Thus the use of the analytical eclecticism approach in the book is really an acknowledgement of the multiple ways in which one can make critical discursive inroads into the issue of security without having to be limited by the confinements of singular theoretical dogma.

As a generic concept, security has universal relevance, but as a social construct it manifests itself differently when seen through different political, ideological or cultural lenses. We examine this in more detail in Chapter 2 when we analyse some of the contending discourses on security and their assumptions. There is a natural tendency to define security parochially in relation to threat to one's immediate social environment and thereby ignore other levels of threat deemed remote and therefore irrelevant, such as the global aspects. This is understandable given the way security is intimately linked to people's collective sentiments, identity as a group, shared notion of nationalism and sense of being and belonging. We can no longer ignore the fact that globalisation has connected the world in diverse ways; therefore societies that once saw themselves as 'isolated' are now drawn into the whirlpool of neoliberal values, overwhelmed by the hegemonic effects of Hollywood imagery, absorbed into unhealthy cravings for McDonalds and Coca Cola, or captured by the culturally transformative addiction of cyber-technology (Stiglitz, 2002). Pacific societies are no exceptions and, as part of these complex changes, their security challenges also go through a process of transformation and rearticulation (Lockwood, 2003).

Challenges in defining security

In everyday use, the term security seems to be quite straightforward and easily understood because it relates to people's sense of safety and well-being. However, it becomes more complex as we probe more deeply into the levels of epistemological genesis, ontological essence and social manifestations (Buzan, Wæver & de Wilde, 1998). Different schools of thought define security not from the vantage point of a universalised principle but from specific ideological, political and cultural prisms.

This lack of consensus is not abnormal in academia and is often a result of competing narratives of history, geopolitics, human psychology and environment. For instance, as we shall see in Chapter 2, the securitisation theory, which emerged from the post–Cold War paradigm shift, moved the focus from the realist mainstream 'hard' security position towards a more constructivist prism, where conceptual constructions and words framed notions of security (Buzan, Wæver & de Wilde, 1998). In contrast, the postcolonial theorists framed security in relation to power differentiation as responses to Western hegemony (Ayoob, 1995). Central to the postcolonial position were the notions of domination and subalternisation and the need to invert the hegemonic colonial perceptions using subaltern gazes (Green, 2011). Deconstructing and even decanting colonial hegemony and its security apparatus (institutional and ideological) is often a challenge because of the way in which it has been deeply intertwined with our contemporary lives (Ashcroft, Griffiths & Tiffin, 2013). On the other hand, the human security project (with origins in the early 1990s), which saw security through multiple disciplinary lenses, was a response to the increasing diversity and interconnectedness of the world (Chandler, 2012). In some ways, it muddied the water further with its boundless and nebulous representation of security by declaring almost every aspect of life as being security related. The feminist approach was closely linked to the postcolonial approach in terms of the centrality of power and inequality in the discourse, but goes further by critiquing the inherent masculine-oriented framing of security. These differences in approach should not be seen as invalidating and neutralising the term 'security', but rather should alert us to the fact that it reflects the multidimensional, transformative and adaptive nature of the term, as we shall see in Chapter 2.

'Security' is no doubt one of the most high-profile issues in contemporary political, economic and social discourse, across nations and cultures, because of people's obsession with self-preservation and perpetuity in the face of emerging threats and challenges to individuals, social groups, states, regions and the global community generally. Nevertheless, there is no consensus in terms of how it is experienced and perceived. Hence what may be experienced and perceived as a security 'threat' by one group may be different from the experience and perception of another. Different circumstances and conditions create different security situations, and people's responses may also differ. Any attempt to frame a common conception is increasingly thwarted by the array of political, cultural, economic, psychological and social variables associated with security in response to diverse issues such as war, poverty, human rights abuse, terrorism, genocide, internal conflicts, global geopolitical tension, global financial crisis and gender violence, just to name a few.

The horizontal and vertical configurations of security create an even more complex situation, especially when it comes to identifying and isolating individual security variables for study. Security can be assessed in relation to its 'horizontal' configuration (referring to the different types of security situation) as well as its 'vertical' configuration (referring to the different security contexts in a stratified way) at the levels of the individual, family, community, cultural group, nation, region and global community. It is very much a contextual construction as people frame their sense of fear, anxiety, safety and well-being individually or collectively in situations that they consider to be a 'threat'. The source of a threat can be seen and felt directly or it can be 'perceived' (i.e. the source of fear may be imagined). Regardless of whether a threat is 'real', the psychological and social impact on an individual or group can be deep and long lasting. Identifying the sources of threat can be cumbersome and controversial because what might be a threat to an individual or a group might not be so to another. Threats, and responses to threats, can be constructed by some groups to suit their specific purpose at particular historical moments. For instance, stereotyping a group as a source of threat could be used as justification for the vilification or even annihilation of that target group, and this might serve the interest of some other groups. The opposing and incompatible construction of security images, paradoxically, can itself nurture security threats. For instance, competing groups casting each other as terrorists can escalate hatred and violence and entrench the spiral of violence.

The use of the term 'security' itself is often aligned to specific power interests. For instance, the term 'national security' has many faces, depending on the context and the underpinning political, ideological and cultural interest of those who define it. In the context of war between two countries, national interest is often defined in relation to protection and preservation of sovereign territory, people and state against foreign intrusion. However, this definition changes in times of internal strife, when national security could mean the safety of the citizens, and it could also strongly imply the protection of the elites in power. Often, as Pierre Bourdieu (1977) suggests, it is a means of mystification and legitimisation of the interests of powerful groups who falsely articulate it as universally representing the interest of the entire society.

Because of the breadth and diversity of the subject, studies of security have largely been selective and based on specific research interests, political and social agenda, ideological orientation or policy demands. For instance, those studying global security may be interested in a range of issues such as big power rivalry, nuclear weaponry, terrorism, transnational crime or global peace; those studying national security may be interested in civil–military relations, state repression, social control or social movements; while those studying human security may be interested in a whole bundle of issues revolving around people's sense of well-being, ranging from poverty to environmental degradation.

Security as leverage: Justification and legitimisation

Because of its multiple levels of expression, meaning and appeal, the term 'security' is readily deployed to frame foreign, economic, immigration, development, food and environmental policies and strategies. It is also used as a convenient justificatory device for xenophobia, genocide, ethnonationalism, anti-immigrant policies and religious intolerance. Ethnic, cultural and religious stereotypes are often constructed around security, especially in situations where cultural diversity intersects with other factors such as resource distribution and contestation over political power. This connection is made more explicit and sharper in times of crisis and, as the crisis deepens, this relationship becomes more intense and often assumes a cyclic and symbiotic pattern, where security becomes inseparable from everyday issues. It is common for certain actions, behaviour, ideas and groups to be cast as threatening to justify a response—and often these responses provoke another cycle of insecurity.

The construction of 'threat' is a political act that enables a group or institution—whether state, religion, political organisation or ethnic community—to legitimise the exercise of moral or physical coercion on another group. In some cases, it can be a way of inducing and extracting political or economic advantage. For instance, the US military–industrial complex, which is critical for the US economy, needs the construction of a broad climate of regional or global threat, and even identification of specific threats, to sustain itself through arms sales. Subtler than this is how the military–industrial complex, under the guise of national security, engages in latent militarisation of society through Hollywood, cyber communication and other means (Turse, 2008).

A direct consequence of threat identification is the creation of policies and practices aimed to contain a particular group. Trump's attempt to create an immigration policy targeted at certain Muslim countries is linked to the broader climate of Islamophobia associated with the 'war on terror'. Security is often inflamed through identification or construction of a threat or perceived threat, whether from within or outside a society. The source of threat is usually constructed and defined using the prism and security variables selectively chosen by the 'threatened'. The circumstances in which this threat takes place have a profound bearing on the intensity and urgency of the threat. How imminent the threat of war is, for instance, is dependent on the level of tension, the preparedness of the two sides and the existence of certain factors such as provocation, media intimidation and propaganda, which would heighten the possibility of a war. However, as in the Cuban crisis, when a full-blown military confrontation was thought to be imminent, interfering variables such as the decision of a Soviet submarine commander to disregard the order to fire, could quickly mitigate and even invalidate the threat. The collective sense of threat is a shared psychological state of anxiety, which can be readily provoked and heightened, and sometimes this can be quickly dispersed when favourable circumstances prevail.

Sometimes, identification and realisation of threat can be a long-term process, as in the case of climate change. The issue of climate change is socially and environmentally complex and involves a relatively long period. Climate change deniers, many of whom are supporters of the fossil fuel industry, use this long span of time to throw ambiguity and doubt into the scientific arguments on the global climate data and even reinterpret scientific evidence to support their arguments, against the opinion of the majority of scientists. The climate change debate shows that a diversity of factors, such as economics, ideology and political interests, have an influence on defining the nature of the threat. Debates on whether a phenomenon is a security threat may heighten or reduce the perceived threat level, depending on the persuasive discursive power of a particular position. Again, as in climate change, a generic threat may be directly or indirectly associated with other forms of threat. For instance, climate change is associated with displacement resulting from sea level rise and erosion and destruction of properties, plantations and livelihood by cyclones, floods and droughts. It is also associated with exacerbated poverty, child malnutrition, conflict over land and scarce resources as people migrate, and reinforcement of gender inequality as women tend to be the ones more at risk than men, because of their culturally defined subordinate role in the domestic sphere looking after children and family subsistence.

In the same vein, responses to a perceived political threat have the potential to provoke more threatening situations, as we saw in the invasion of Iraq. Justified by the invented myth of Saddam Hussein's weapons of mass destruction, that action led to a series of destructive events, including the sectarian civil war between Sunnis and Shiites that destabilised the country and created more threats than expected. The resulting chaos and destruction spawned the rise of the Islamic State (ISIS), whose expansionist intent spilled over into Syria, another country going through a civil war, thus plunging the already volatile region into an abyss of destruction and suffering, creating refugee problems and prolonged instability. The threat is further internationalised by the involvement of the United States and Russia, which have deeply embedded economic, political and strategic interests in the Middle East.

The Israeli/Palestinian conflict raises the important relationship between security and legitimacy. The issue of legitimacy is central to many conflicts around the world as competing groups construct philosophical, legal, cultural, political or historical narratives to give credibility to their claims and actions to defend those claims. The Israelis use the apartheid Zionist ideals for a separate Jewish state, based on the biblical myth of the 'chosen people' and 'promised land' to stamp their claims on what used to be the state of Palestine. On the other hand, Palestinians, whether Christian or Muslim, justify their claims on the basis of immemoriality; that is, they have always been there, and Palestine as a state was a legal and sovereign entity before being overwhelmed by Jewish immigrants. Israel sees Palestinians, whether youth, women and even children, fighting against Israeli occupation, domination and displacement, as 'Islamic terrorists' while Palestinians frame the Israeli military as agents of 'Zionist terrorism'. The cycle of violence and counter-violence, justified by the negative framing of the other, fuels the burning fire of conflict. Both have competing historical memories to stake their claim on a common territory as their respective 'motherland'.

The multidimensional approach

The book approaches security from a multilayered vantage point, through a comparative study of three PICs: Fiji, Tonga and Solomon Islands. The first layer of analysis examines some of the global discourse on security and the way security has been defined and articulated over the years. The second layer of analysis provides a wide panoramic view of Pacific regional security, and the third layer focuses on the case studies on the ground, drawing on some of the strands of discourses in the first two layers. The idea is to construct an interconnected epistemological structure that links knowledge of the local, regional and global in a dynamic and coherent way. Our framing of security is enhanced by acknowledging that security is not a static construct but a dynamic phenomenon that oscillates between different layers of articulation.

The broad global security narrative

The general theoretical prisms that frame security discourses, as we shall see in Chapter 3, range across academic disciplines and are informed by varying ideological positions, from Samuel Huntington's 'clash of culture' position, which helped shape and justify the neoconservative political rubric of world politics, to Edward Said's 'orientalism' discourse, which has inspired generations of postcolonial thinkers and activists; from the securitisation school's emphasis on the post-structural action-based value of language, to the human security framework initiated by the United Nations. The list goes on. It is important to note that the general theories of conflict are based on multiple interpretations of history and human society, broad assumptions about power and institutions and, in some cases, responses to some existing modes of explanation that are deemed either theoretically unacceptable or empirically untenable.

Despite dramatic changes in the world in recent times, some modes of analysis remain unchanged, as adherents cling to vestiges of past thinking that are supposedly universal in terms of time and space. Some theories are more flexible and adaptable to the changing contours of events as they unfold, and some, like Francis Fukuyama's 'end of history' thesis, which was meant to celebrate the triumph of capitalism, are quickly overtaken by events and then die a quick death. Some theories, especially those that are supported by a deeper and broader panorama of history and human culture, are able to survive in different forms, despite dramatic social transformations. For instance, Antonio Gramsci's theory of hegemony, although unrefined in its original form, influenced the way security has been defined by generations of left-wing scholars and postcolonial writers in the fields of sociology, anthropology, development studies, media studies, indigenous studies, cultural studies and literature. Two of the most prominent discourses of the Gramscian tradition are Noam Chomsky's idea of manufacturing consent and Edward Said's orientalism.

As Chapter 2 shows, the book avoids being caught in the narrow confines of a mechanical and one-dimensional dictionary definition. The term 'security' is not defined in any one universally relevant theoretical narrative or applied schema, but the concept is left open to theoretical contestation to allow for a critical examination of how the term is defined in different contexts from different vantage points.

Regional discourse

The book's focus on regional analysis in Chapter 3 is significant in two major ways. First, it frames the most immediate geopolitical and sociocultural context for the case studies and, second, it provides some common political, economic, cultural and environmental characteristics on which the case studies draw and that help to define some of their shared commonalities. Although the Pacific, in which more than a thousand languages are spoken, is the most culturally diverse region in the world, the PICs themselves have much in common in terms of the security threats they face. Many of these threats, such as vulnerability to the dictates of the global neoliberal agenda, are externally generated, whereas many others, such as political tension, are internally induced. There are many that are, in equal measure, shaped and affected by both internal and external forces.

The region is going through dramatic transformation, and many of the emerging security issues, such as inequality, poverty, environmental degradation, climate change, crime and land disputes, to mention only some, affect these PICs differently, depending on their capacity to respond to change, the availability of resources, the level of expertise available and political will. The scattered PICs are linked through regional institutions such as the South Pacific Commission (now called the Pacific Community), Pacific Islands Forum and a number of other educational, environmental, sporting, religious, civil society, developmental and professional organisations. In the midst of global power dynamics, PICs find common solace in regional cooperation as a means to ensure that their collective voices are heard and their interests are recognised at the United Nations and other international forums. The regional security analysis this book presents tries to link, in a critical way, the different security narratives and historical strands to make sense of the complexities and challenges of security in the small island states, separated by thousands of miles of open sea. This provides the backdrop for the three case studies.

Local comparative case studies

The approach to the case studies of Fiji, Tonga and Solomon Islands in Chapters 4, 5 and 6 is based on the diverse variable method where, instead of using the same template for every case study, the approach for every case study differs in terms of method and emphasis. Using the same template and variables for comparative purposes tends to be mechanical and static, and effaces the uniqueness of the case studies. Each case study is different, and the idea is not to compare and contrast one against the other but to showcase each country's own unique historical, political, social, cultural and economic realities. Fiji, Tonga and Solomon Islands are very different, and it would be both analytically flawed and theoretically unsound to make superficial comparisons, as certain variables would favour one case study over the others. Each case study is examined in the context of what, in my opinion, are the most pressing sociopolitical security issues. The three countries were chosen because they have all experienced major security upheavals in recent years in the form of internal political conflict, from which they have barely recovered. It is of interest to determine what lessons we can learn from them in terms of the broader regional security agenda.

Chapter 4 is focused on Fiji and emphasises the power contestation and ethnopolitical conflict and the ramification of these for Fiji's multicultural society. The chapter broadens the panorama of security lenses and links major security issues of the precolonial, colonial and postcolonial era. A historical reflection reveals that some aspects of precolonial political culture continue in various forms and in some cases contributed to ethnopolitical conflict in latent ways during the colonial and postcolonial eras. Fiji's security issues are complicated by intracommunal loyalties, religion, culture and socioeconomic inequality, which in some instances tend to intersect with ethnicity. The role of the military has become increasingly pronounced since the first coup in 1987 and is now seen as both a stabilising factor in times of potential turmoil and a usurper of democracy. The chapter looks at various attempts to address the multidimensional security situation in Fiji, including the formal constitutional process, civil society peace initiatives and community-based conflict resolution mechanisms.

Chapter 5 provides an assessment of the political power contestation in Tonga, in particular between the ruling monarchical class and the pro-democracy commoner movement. Of all the Pacific countries, Tonga is probably the most hierarchical and certainly has the most rigid political and class structure, consisting of the monarch, nobles (*nopele*), who act as feudal lords, below whom are the commoners, the equivalent of the serfs. The internal contradictions have been well concealed through various means, including the appeal to culture and divinity. The tension built up over the years erupted into violence in the form of riots and burnings in Nukualofa, the capital, in 2006. This changed the complexion of Tongan politics in a significant way as the military, untested in local situations, began to build up its capacity to respond more effectively to internal security conditions.

The focus on the Solomon Islands in Chapter 6 is principally on the historical conditions and dynamics that helped to create conditions that built up to the 1999 violent conflict, the worst in the history of the country. Multiple factors contributed to the conflict, and many of them were rooted in the colonial history of Solomon Islands and how these shaped the economic, political and ethnic landscape. British colonialism was half-hearted, patronising and exploitative and pitted the locals, who wanted greater autonomy, against the colonial hierarchy, which was directly controlled from Fiji, the main British colonial base in the Pacific. Development was minimal, and the state infrastructure was embryonic. The inequality and incompatibility between the colonial state and the local population became a security issue. Anti-colonial resistance was viciously suppressed as the British sought to use local police against their own people. The British recruited local cheap labour, principally from Malaita Island, to work in plantations in various parts of Solomon Islands, especially Guadalcanal, and this contributed to land disputes and tension. A combination of land disputes, inequality, resource appropriation, corrupt leadership and lack of a unifying political culture helped to inflame the conflict. In a paternalistic way, Solomon Islands also became a laboratory for peace-building in the form of the Regional Assistance

Mission to Solomon Islands (RAMSI), in which international agencies, academics and civil society organisations tried new methods of conflict resolution to serve their particular agenda.

The different approaches of the following chapters provide us with multiple prisms and angles of analysis that focus on aspects of conflict unique to those countries. Although the PICs may be geographically small and isolated, they must not be considered insignificant just because of this, but rather the rest of the world must learn from some of their successful ventures into peace-building. At a time when conflict pervades every corner of the globe and when world leaders, international organisations and countries (torn by wars and destruction) are looking for solutions to the plight of millions of people, the PICs can provide some lessons for humanity: lessons of peace. Conflict in the PICs seems to be short-lived because solutions are deeply entrenched in their culture and in their way of seeing conflict and the world. State intervention in the form of formal institutions of the law and politics might have a role, but expressions of resilience, hope and endurance among the communities, which have been part of culture for centuries, need serious attention.

2

Exploring the contours of threat: Competing security discourses

There are very few people who are going to look into the mirror and say, 'That person I see is a savage monster;' instead, they make up some construction that justifies what they do.

Noam Chomsky

As mentioned in Chapter 1, the analytical eclecticism approach deployed in this book requires one to be cognisant of the diversity of theoretical positions in the area of security, their strengths and their weaknesses, and how they might inform one's formulation and application of relevant concepts in a constantly changing world. Disentangling the continually morphing and increasingly turbulent security sphere is a herculean task in its own right due to the multiplicity of factors involved and the range of discourses used to frame security across disciplines. This is made even more complex by the ever-changing nature of global and local security situations, the diverse responses to these and how these responses are understood and framed by states, international institutions, local communities, political organisations, scholars and other groups in society. The ensuing security debates revolve around a number of interrelated questions: What does security entail? Whose security is at stake? What or who is the source of insecurity or threat? Which factors contribute to, enhance and shape insecurity? The notions of security and insecurity belong to opposite sides of the same coin because, as the adage goes, the security of one is the insecurity of another. Certainly, in the Pacific, these questions need to be asked much more overtly as the local, regional and global security environments change.

With this in mind, this chapter attempts to critically examine five discursive narratives of security, which have been chosen because of their prominence in recent years. This is far from being an exhaustive foray into this multifaceted area of debate but is, rather, an attempt to draw out selected strands of arguments to inform our understanding of global, regional and national dynamics of current thinking and practices related to security. This will provide a theoretical backdrop to the study of Pacific regional security in Chapter 3 as well as the case studies on Fiji, Tonga and Solomon Islands in Chapters 4, 5 and 6. It should be noted at the outset that some aspects of the security discourses might be applicable, directly or indirectly, to situations in the Pacific and some might not, as this depends very much on how the concepts are defined, interpreted and applied in varying circumstances. Security has a multidisciplinary flavour, and this is because of the growing interest in the subject by scholars in different academic discourses. This is increasingly so given the consciousness about the interconnectedness of contemporary issues such as terrorism, racism, political instability, crime, wars, refugees, inequality, militarisation, poverty and climate change, which have influenced people's sense of anxiety. The framing and experience of security have become inescapable parts of our being as a global community. Thus, as the world becomes more globalised, security also becomes a globally shared concern at a time when local threats readily become globalised and global threats readily become localised in a complex symphony of symbiotic relationships.

Security is more than just a political concept. It can be construed to cover virtually every aspect of life, including the economic, cultural, psychological and spiritual domains, as long as there is realisation of an element of risk and threat that could affect people's lives and well-being. However, it is often constructed in relation to specific contexts. Thus, as we will see later, particular definitions of security that claim to possess universal appeal and validity are in danger of being irrelevant in particular historical, cultural and political contexts. This is why it is important to have an open mind and to attempt to understand a particular security discourse using relativist, contextual, eclectic and even arbitrary lenses. In other words, what might be a security situation in a particular conceptual sphere, time and space might not be so in another. Security has to be located within the ambit of 'habitus', or contextual configuration of human activities, norms and interests, as Pierre Bourdieu (1990) reminds us.

The chapter begins by looking at the multidisciplinary nature of security and critically examines some classical theories of security as well as some theoretical implications and some of the dilemmas posed in relation to policy-making. While security has been traditionally associated with some mainstream 'political' disciplines such as political science, international relations and political sociology, in recent years it has become a convergence zone for a whole range of disciplines, including economics, psychology, management, law and even mathematics. The chapter then examines the notion of securitisation, especially the way it has been framed by postconstructivists as a means of moving the argument away from the realist and formal statist position. Central to this is the work of the Copenhagen School, which has been instrumental in redefining the post–Cold War security debate.

The chapter next examines the idea of human security, a concept that was popularised by the United Nations from the early 1990s and has become dominant in development and policy discourse since then. Human security extended the traditional boundaries of security thinking and incorporated virtually every aspect of human life—whether political, economic, social, cultural, environmental or psychological—as security-related. Following this is a critical analysis of human security as a conceptual schema as well as an applied developmental tool. The chapter then explores gender, an area of security that is often ignored. Historically, security has been largely defined using masculine lenses and ideological constructions. Changing this trend by incorporating a more inclusive gender lens provides us with a more nuanced reality of how security plays out in society.

The last part of the chapter examines some of the salient features of the critical security paradigm, in particular the postcolonial discourse and how it critiques and deconstructs the dominant theories of politics, society and security. In a way, a significant portion of the book's analysis will be drawn from the critical security approach, especially its analysis of the political economy of security, the power dynamics involved and how PICs find themselves in a subaltern position amid the hegemonic machinations of the big powers.

The challenge of security: An interdisciplinary and contested term

There is no consensus on the core existential features of 'security' because the term is often defined contextually and situationally, often in arbitrary ways. The diversity of the 'security' experiences of groups in different historical, cultural, political and psychological settings makes the concept a fertile ground for different disciplines to pick and choose aspects that are relevant to their particular areas of study. Security pervades all levels of human society from the private world of an individual experiencing psychological apprehension to global disputes over strategic interest and power, and including other issues pertaining to threat and risk in between. Throughout history, the perception and experience of security has influenced the conceptualisation, construction and operationalisation of human thinking and world views, cultural norms, political institutions, technological change and economic systems (Wallerstein, 1989). At the macro-global level, security is one of the largest industries in the world today. For instance, the US military–industrial complex connects a whole range of players such as large corporations, which manufacture weapons, universities, which carry out research, the state, which facilitates and legitimises the militarisation process, and the military in the United States and other parts of the world, which use the weapons (Giroux, 2007). This network is linked to wars, political instability and associated problems, such as displacement, poverty and human rights abuses in other parts of the world. Thus, not only are the different aspects and levels of security interconnected but also different conceptual approaches to the subject have brought together different disciplines to focus on security, conflict and peace studies (Webel & Johansen, 2012). Despite the different disciplinary foci, there are commonalities in terms of the need to carry out research using multiple methodologies with the ultimate purpose of creating a secure society for the future.

The division between different approaches is also ideological in nature, largely because of the influence of the Cold War when, by and large, global security was defined around two contending ideological camps: the Soviet Union, representing socialism, and the United States, representing capitalism. This established the fundamental ideological divide between the 'Left' and the 'Right', which influenced security studies. For instance, peace studies as an area of university research and teaching was often linked to academics on the Left, who saw global capitalism and US hegemony as a threat to peace. Even within the Left, there were those who saw the Soviet Union as equally as hegemonic as US imperialism. In the 'Third World', peace activism was a response to the neocolonial excesses of the major powers as well as to internal dynamics, and many of its proponents were aligned to peace groups in Western countries. Many social scientists and natural scientists were part of the peace movement and used their transdisciplinary research skills in the collective fight for 'peace', however they defined it. In the Pacific, as will be shown in Chapter 3, the Nuclear Free and Independent Pacific (NFIP) movement included a range of issues such as the environment, decolonisation, land rights, economic development, racism and militarism. These multiple issues were framed using multiple lenses, which resulted in debates even among peace activists and within academic disciplines.

At the end of the Cold War, there was renewed hope that the world had seen the worst in terms of conflict, and many security scholars shifted their focus from the 'East' versus 'West' contestation to localised intranational conflicts in the form of ethnic, religious and communal wars. This hope was exemplified in the rather over-optimistic declaration by Francis Fukuyama (1992) that the end of the Cold War heralded the triumph of liberal democracy and the 'end of history'. However, this provocative position failed to grasp the reality that, despite the end of the Cold War, liberal democracy and capitalism were facing even more menacing challenges, which saw the rise of people protests, terrorism, cyber-wars, intrastate wars, transnational crime, ethnic conflict and increasing poverty and marginalisation (Dorling, 2015). The increase in 'new wars', as Kaldor (2013) calls them, was characterised by the shift from interstate conflict to multiple levels of conflict involving a range of non-state actors, terrorism, cyber-technology and non-conventional means.

Moreover, the withering away of the Cold War bipolarity saw a reconfiguration of ideological positions and the emergence of 'non-aligned' security discourses. Among these was the 'greed and grievance' approach popularised by Oxford economists Paul Collier and Anke Hoeffler (2002). Based on particular interpretations of selected African experiences, Collier and Hoeffler argued that civil wars were caused by 'grievances' over such issues as identity, social class, religion and culture and 'greed' over economic resources such as diamonds. Institutions such as the World Bank enthusiastically adopted these ideas and used them to frame their conflict and development policies. This was a significant foray by economists into the realm of conflict and security, and many economists, even some in the Pacific, used the greed and grievance theory as a basis for understanding resource-based conflict in such places as Solomon Islands and Bougainville (Allen, 2007).

The greed and grievance theory has come under intense criticism because of its tendency to use single factors like greed to oversimplify complex situations shaped by a number of intervening and interrelated factors (Keen, 2000). The use of quantitative econometrics methods tends to undervalue the significance of subjective human feelings and perceptions, culture and politics in the conflict equation. The seemingly 'scientific' approach by the greed and grievance school is largely based on attempts at numerical quantification of incidents of conflict, and this overshadows the complex nature of society, social relations and the individual or collective propensity for conflict. The notion of greed itself tends to both moralise and psychologise the issue of competition of resources with the assumption that individual pursuit of wealth is a natural state of being, an argument that finds resonance in the biological determinist theory advocated by many psychologists (Thayer, 2004).

Another argument that makes a similar assumption is the rational choice theory, which economists have used to explain conflict over resources and power as individuals and groups attempt to maximise their gains at minimal cost and through displacement of others (Amadae, 2003). Like the greed model, the rational choice theory operates on the fallacious assumption that human behaviour is always predictable and quantifiable, as if it is predetermined by certain natural laws of human behaviour and social action.

The historical, socioeconomic and sociocultural conditions in Africa during the diamond wars of the 1990s that gave rise to the theory in the first place are hardly prominent in the PICs. The colonial histories of Africa (which were largely exploitative and turbulent) and that of the PICs (which were relatively benign) are very different indeed and cannot be connected simplistically using the same historical paintbrush (Fraenkel, 2004).

In the field of global politics and international relations, debates about the nature of security have revolved around a number of competing narratives of interstate relations. The notion of realism focuses on the Hobbesian idea of a human natural propensity for competition and violence, which is extended to self-serving interstate competition for power using aggressive means such as militarism (Snyder, 2004). The neoconservative and hawkish elements within the US political system are often seen as belonging to this school, which was probably at its height during the Mutually Assured Destruction (MAD) policies of the Cold War (Mearsheimer, 2014). Those who were critical of the realist school saw this propensity for aggression as containable within international structures and norms, whose role was to rein in pariah states as a means of maintaining global peace and order (Lamy, 2008).

In almost direct contrast to the realist school was the liberal approach, which took a much more flexible stance by arguing for the goodness of humanity and the potential for collective peaceful engagement (Copeland, 1996). In a way this approach was also linked to the 'liberal peace' movement, which assumes the possibility of creating stability through the global 'norm diffusion' of Western liberal democracy. A more radical departure was expounded by the constructivist school, which, based on the post-structuralist schema, examined security in relation to the significance of persuasive ideas, collective values, culture and social identities (Barnett, 2008). In a way, except for constructivism, these 'classical' international relations theories, while dominant in geopolitical debates, tended to be too state-centric and failed to address the dramatically changing situations where competing forces such as 'terrorist' organisations have taken 'dispersed' forms.

The critical theories (so named because of their propensity to question and offer alternatives to mainstream ideas) provided different lenses to the classical approaches mentioned earlier. For instance, the dependency and neo-Gramscian theories focused on how global politics and conflict were shaped by power dynamics and economic exploitation by dominant powers over subaltern countries and groups of people (Cox, 1996). This position was further bolstered by the rise of feminism, which added the gender dimension as resistance to the largely masculine-dominated world of politics, militarism and power (Grant & Newland, 1991). The critical approaches were transdisciplinary and were linked to scholars arguing from the standpoint of exploitation, domination and power. They were, by and large, derivatives of the more generic conflict theory in sociology, which had its genesis in Marx's philosophy of dialectical materialism. Some notable examples of the critical school were Noam Chomsky and Edward Said, whose ideas, as we shall see later, were diametrically opposed to those of Samuel Huntington, a modern-day intellectual beacon for 'conservative' thinkers and regarded as a 'prophet for the Trump era' (Lozada, 2017).

Although the brief overview of security discourses above is far from exhaustive, the point I want to make here is that the illusive, contextual and situational nature of security invokes diverse approaches. The different disciplinary approaches in their own ways offer particular insights into the vast area of security. There are strengths and weaknesses that need careful analysis, and the book will draw on some of those that might be appropriate and applicable to the Pacific. The rest of the chapter examines in more detail some influential narratives on security and how they help to inform some discussions on Pacific security in the later chapters.

The securitisation discourse

The securitisation theory has hardly been used to frame security in the Pacific in a systematic way partly because of its reputation as being too European in terms of its conceptual genesis. This is not to say that it is irrelevant to the Pacific—in fact, as we shall see later, despite some of its weaknesses, it does provide useful conceptual tools to illuminate certain aspects of security in the Pacific.

What is securitisation? In the post–Cold War era, the prevailing realist view was subjected to critical examination by those who saw human behaviour as more complex than a simple dichotomy based on the bipolar division of socialism versus capitalism. There was an emerging school of thought that security had to be seen not just in terms of structural factors but also in the context of a speech act—this was the basis of the securitisation discourse popularised by Wæver (1995) and elaborated further by Buzan, Wæver and de Wilde (1998) of the Copenhagen School.[1] The notion of securitisation provided an alternative constructivist approach to the age-old debate as to whether a threat can be understood as an objective reality or a reflection of subjective perception, by suggesting that threats are social constructions centred on speech acts. In various strands of social theory, 'speech acts' refers to the idea that verbalisation is the basis for 'doing'. An example would relate to bringing a person into existence merely through the process of naming him or her; in the same way, the act of uttering the word 'security' makes it real and various aspects of life associated with it—including the military, political, economic

---

1   The term 'Copenhagen School' is a reference to the University of Copenhagen, where the exponents of the securitisation approach were based.

and environmental issues—become threats. This intrinsic relationship between verbalisation and action was what Austin (1962) referred to as 'performative utterance' or 'perlocutionary act'.

It must be noted, however, that to ensure that the speech acts are related to securitisation, they have to be part of the rhetorical structure and process related to war and associated concepts, such as survival, urgency, threat and defence. This forms the basis of the Copenhagen School's assumptions about securitisation regarding: (a) the claim that the object in question is existentially threatened, (b) the right to take extraordinary measures to counter the threat and (c) convincing an audience that extralegal behaviour to counter the threat is justified. The idea of threat is embedded in politics itself and can be articulated in three major discursive trends: politics, action and intentionality; modern organisation of politics, spheres and sectors; politics, ethics and science (Gad & Petersen, 2011). For PICs, desecuritisation means inverting the securitisation discourse through ideas and policies that remove the threat and sense of anxiety through peace-building measures by civil society organisations or regional security initiatives such as the Biketawa Declaration (Pacific Islands Forum, 2000).

While the securitisation theory was an attempt to open possibilities of analysis beyond military affairs (Wæver, 2010), it has inspired debates, with its opponents arguing that it is too narrow and lacks universal contextual relevance. The criticisms range from constructivists, who argue for the theory's reconfiguration and fine-tuning to correspond to changing circumstances, to critical postcolonial thinkers, who declare it moribund outright. One of the flaws of the theory is that the idea of securitising any activity by a group in power can be an arbitrary act, which can be used to stifle democratic debate and which could be used as justification for suppression of alternative views. What is probably needed is not so much a focus on securitisation, which could create more harm than good, but on the reduction of threats by focusing on 'desecuritisation', which Tjalve (2011) argued should take place at the level of polity rather than policy because of the close association between power politics and threat.

Another criticism is that the securitisation theory fails to take into consideration the fact that a combination of the security speech and practice of elites may contribute to erasing the distinction between 'exceptional' and 'normal' political behaviour and security environments (Huysmans, 2006: 124–6; Williams, 2003). Furthermore, the theory is unable to recognise the significance of normal and daily operation of security issues through bureaucracies (Aradau, 2006; Bigo, 2000; Kaliber, 2005; Neal, 2006).

A major criticism of the Copenhagen School is its failure to consider the significance of the morality of securitisation. For instance, Floyd (2011: 428) made the argument that the moral righteousness of securitisation was a core aspect of its own legitimacy, and he provided three criteria of moral framing, based on the just war theory. First, there must be an objective threat that endangers the survival of the actors; second, the referent object of security must be based on human needs; and third, the response must be appropriate to the threat. Apart from the absence of morality, there was also a strong argument about the lack of interface between science and securitisation. Berling (2011) used the Bourdieusian approach to argue that scientific arguments and 'facts' were critical aspects in understanding the way securitisation was defined, articulated and applied in real life, and he questioned the adequacy of the theory in explaining the issue of context and the importance of 'practical reflexivity' for security experts.

In addition, Salter (2007) is of the view that although there has been a growing number of case studies of successful securitisation and desecuritisation processes, there is still a strong dominant tendency by scholars to hold a statist view of securitisation, whereby the emergency powers of the executive are used in response to identification of threat and acceptance of the threat by an audience. There are, according to Salter, multiple sources of security moves and at least four different types of audience and speech contexts: popular, elite, technocratic and scientific. The relationship between threat and fear is an underlying strand of the securitisation theory, especially in terms of how fear can facilitate the process of securitisation. Williams (2011) inverted this suggestion and contended, using the notion of 'liberalism of fear', that instead of facilitating securitisation, the liberalism of fear opens a new window to enable us to visualise how fear can in fact undermine securitisation; that is, the fear of fear can be a desecuritising rather than a securitising factor.

Another major methodological flaw was that securitisation research tended to be based on casual approaches and did not have much empirical basis (Guzzini, 2011) because of the subjective interpretation of threat through speech act. Thus, the reliance on post-structuralist framing and lack of empirical identification of threat weakens securitisation's importance in applied policy. Because the notions of framing and translation of securitisation are closely integrated, Stritzel (2011) made the argument that securitisation as conceived by Wæver was too traditional and essentialist and therefore there was a need to seriously review it. Along this line, Huysmans (2011) was of the view that the emphasis on the discursive and communicative aspects of securitising has overshadowed the significance of the concept of 'act', which in many ways defined the politicality of the speech act approach to security. Security practices were shaped more by political acts than by mere speeches.

Although many criticisms of the Copenhagen School by European theorists were based, as we have seen, on the need to refine securitisation theory to be more applicable, criticisms by some non-Western scholars and those from the critical security perspective were more directly dismissive, arguing that securitisation theory was not relevant to non-Western societies (Bilgin, 2011; Sheikh, 2005; Vuori, 2008). There was also a view that even desecuritisation was a conservative process that reproduced the existing liberal order (Aradau, 2004). Those using the peace studies lens made the point that securitisation had no morally defensible position on such issues as minorities and AIDS (Elbe, 2006; Roe, 2004). The theory's Eurocentric and statist nature tended to be too analytically restrictive to be of much use in unpacking the complex security situation in postcolonial societies whose historical and cultural evolution had been shaped by complex colonial and postcolonial forces.

One of the most ardent critics of the Copenhagen School and mainstream security studies generally was the Aberystwyth School, which drew from the critical lenses of neo-Marxian dialectics and the neo-Gramscian notion of hegemony, and the Frankfurt School, to make the argument that security could be meaningfully understood only in the context of social transformation and human emancipation. Two leading figures of this school, Ken Booth and Richard Jones, asserted that security was not conceptually constructed and subjectively defined, as the Copenhagen School contended, but was related to real social conditions and human needs (Booth, 1991; Jones, 2001).

European security studies generally, including the work of the Copenhagen School, since World War II, was criticised as self-serving and possessing a 'Eurocentric character' (Barkawi & Laffey, 2006: 329) because of how it misrepresented societies, cultures and security relations of the global South. One of the consequences of this misrepresentation was the characterisation of the world in the form of self-constructed

Western cultural supremacy and ignorance of historical security relations through the acknowledgement of the joint contribution of European and non-European cultures in making history (Bessis, 2003). This is a salient theoretical plank in postcolonial security discourse, which we will consider further towards the end of the chapter. While securitisation was largely Europe-focused, the rise of the human security discourse had a more global impact during the post–Cold War era, and this redefined the security debate much more fundamentally in terms of the shift from the state to society as important units of security.

Despite some of the shortcomings of the securitisation discourse, an important aspect that is useful in understanding the security environment and security psychology in the Pacific is the notion of speech act and its association with the security rhetorical structure. Let us take the case of Fiji, for instance, where, since 1987, the term 'coup' has securitised the political narrative in a psychologically influential way. Since the series of coups between 1987 and 2006, the mere mention of the term 'coup' has had the potential to invoke anxiety, fear and feelings of insecurity (Ratuva, 2011a). Although triggered largely by perception, this climate of insecurity can influence a range of behavioural and normative issues such as people's choices during elections, ethnic consciousness and relationship between cultural groups. A coup, whether real or illusory, becomes a security threat by its mere mention due to its prominence and sensitivity as part of the rhetorical structure of Fijian political discourse. The use of the terms 'riots' in Tonga (Senituli, 2006) and 'tension' in Solomon Islands (Fraenkel, Madraiwiwi & Okole, 2014) might also have a similar influence on the political rhetorical structure of the two countries.

The securitisation of the term 'climate change', through its strong association with human security, has provided a new dimension to the way we see and understand the integral connection between our environment, well-being and sense of threat (Mason, 2015). The securitisation of the term makes it political and therefore contested. For PICs, the securitisation of the climate change narrative works in their favour because it can be used strategically to access the Green Climate Fund and other facilities related to climate change. The same goes for the advent of the human security discourse in the early 1990s in the Asia-Pacific region, which saw the securitisation of almost every aspect of human life from poverty to diseases, education to religion, transportation to housing (Davies, 2017). The list goes on. As we shall see later, this universalised process of securitisation has a number of conceptual shortcomings.

In both conscious and subtle ways, securitised concepts can influence the framing of issues and policy formulation by Pacific states, civil society, policy community, regional agencies and community groups to respond to a threat, whether real or perceived. Once framed as sources of possible threats, these issues can be used to mobilise public sentiments and justification for formulation of official state narratives, policies and legislations and in the process become institutionalised security discourses (Mason, 2015).

The shift from the statal to the societal: The human security discourse

The rise of the human security discourse in the 1990s shifted the security paradigm from the centrality of the state to the centrality of society (Shinoda, 2004). In the Pacific, this has filtered into government policies on security, poverty alleviation, education, development, welfare and almost every aspect of sociocultural and economic life (Cox et al., 2017). We will see this in more detail in Chapter 3.

The significance and relevance of the traditional notion of state-based 'hard' security, often framed around the ideas of political security, national security and state security, have come under scrutiny as a result of attempts to re-evaluate the diverse conditions that threaten people's lives and well-being. This includes a multiplicity of factors—political, social, cultural, economic, environmental, spiritual and psychological—that shape, in various ways, people's sense of insecurity, fear, instability and anxiety. An array of disparate issues—including violence, exploitation, poverty, crime, climate change, education, governance, health and demographic change, to name a few—became part of the broad rubric of human security. The growing sense of insecurity and the loss of faith in the state as guardian of security contributed to this alternative analysis of security (Durodie, 2010).

The human security discourse was a response to the proliferation of new forms of security threats that could not be adequately captured within the confines of the traditional, state-centric national security paradigm. The transdisciplinary approach to human security spans a diverse range of academic and policy areas such as international relations, development studies, gender studies, environmental studies, public health, economics, human rights, public policy, foreign policy and conflict or peace studies. This new wave of security thinking has helped to inform policy-making in many 'developed' and 'developing' countries, including the Pacific Islands, in global institutions such as the United Nations, Asian Development Bank and World Bank, and in civil society organisations and corporate sector organisations (Hampson & Penny, 2008). The extent to which human security ideas are integrated to policy, the specific contexts in which this happens and the ideological justifications used vary from situation to situation, but by and large there is some agreement that human security is an inseparable and inherent aspect of development, social life and change.

The human security narrative provides for flexibility in the way security is defined as new global and local conditions change. For instance, the threats of terrorism and the impacts of globalisation and mass migration have raised serious questions about identities, politics and world views. It has been suggested that these can be understood more critically by framing human security through legal, international relations and human rights lenses, especially when dealing with refugees, migrants and displaced and stateless persons and how, conceptually and practically, human security can sufficiently illuminate the myriad challenges they face (Edwards & Ferstman, 2010).

The appeal of the human security discourse has also been amplified by the failure of hard security policies in global affairs. For instance, the failure of the US-led coalition to achieve its political and strategic objectives in the period after the terrorist attacks of 11 September 2001 was a clear manifestation of the inadequacy of the hard security paradigm and the need to broaden the analysis. Although the human security framework may be considered by some to be 'conceptually fuzzy', it still provides a more theoretically encompassing tool to examine the multiple dimensions and dynamics of the 'war on terror' (Shani, Sato & Pasha, 2007).

The war on terror was based largely on the deployment of force, consolidation of like-minded countries through the 'coalition of the willing', psychological warfare and arbitrary framing of the world in terms of the ideological binary 'West' versus 'the rest' (Scruton, 2002). The ideological fuel that inflamed and justified the wave of anti-Islamic sentiments ranged from crude propaganda through Fox News and other mainstream media to more sophisticated academic treatises such as Huntington's 'clash of civilisations' thesis. These opinions blurred the lines between empirical reality and myths and spawned irrational hysteria, religious intolerance and racial stereotyping. The complex interplay between socioeconomic factors, religion, political ideology, culture and militarism was beyond the realm of hard security.

In situations of modern conflict, human security often becomes more complex as different participants are driven by competing interests, such as corporate entities aiming to benefit financially from conflict, states who want to use conflict as a testing ground for their military power, combatants driven by claims to a historical motherland or humanitarian groups intervening to stop the conflict. Even humanitarian aid is confronted with apparently insurmountable political, legal, social and military challenges (Cahill, 2004). Creating a humanitarian space in a conflict situation is important to protect human dignity and human rights, especially the rights of the displaced, as well as contributing to peaceful reform and consolidation in the post-conflict transition period.

Another major issue of discussion is the link between human security and democracy, especially in terms of how countries can deliver social and economic rights through the broad inclusion of all citizens in decision-making and poverty reduction. This is related to how democratic practices, separation of powers, freedom of the press and guarantees of human rights enhance human security (Large, Austin & IDEA, 2006). While the opening up of a more participatory and enlightened political space can be conducive to enhancement of human security, there are other significant factors, such as institutionalised inequality, vested economic and political interests and the hegemonic role of the dominant classes and institutions, that might undermine the democratisation of citizen participation.

Simply focusing on the formal and mechanical aspects of democracy such as elections, separation of powers, freedom of the press and guarantees of human rights has the potential to overshadow the deeper structural causes of inequality and disempowerment that cannot be addressed merely through formal institutional democratisation. Formal democracy does not necessarily equate to progressive development; in fact the opposite can also be true, as evidenced by the high level of development of some authoritarian states such as Singapore and the high level of acute inequality and poverty in India, which is a democratic state.

An emerging concern in recent years is the relationship between human security and cultural socialisation, especially in the form of formal education where certain values, norms and behavioural dispositions either reproduce or undermine aspects of human security. The reproduction of various forms of behaviour and attitudes that encourage violence, including terrorism, through education is of particular concern (Nelles, 2003). The increasing international and local threats raise questions about the need for more political and pedagogic debates and policy formulation about how to use education as a means of reproducing peace values and eradicating violent behavioural tendencies. This debate needs to extend beyond formal pedagogy to involve parents who allow children to engage in 'killing games', such as in PlayStations and computer programs, and corporate institutions that create and make money from toys that simulate killing. This process requires a major, multipronged, approach geared to reforming the education system and the formulation of new foreign and domestic policy approaches based on conflict resolution at the local and global levels.

In the last 10 years or so, the issue of climate change has been dominant in the human security debate in many international forums, primarily because the phenomenon has a global impact on people's human security, although how countries are affected varies considerably. For small island states such as many of those in the Pacific, the issue is urgent because of the progressive erosion and sinking of low-lying islands like those that make up Tuvalu and Kiribati. The process of climate change raises important issues of vulnerability and adaptation as critical components of human security. People's vulnerability to naturally occurring or human-induced climate change is often mitigated by new modes of cultural and technological innovation to enable people to adapt to the deteriorating conditions in the short term, but the real test is the challenge of creating sustainable long-term responses. The global climate change debate has been influenced by the national and neoliberal economic interests of the major industrialised powers at the cost of the smaller and more vulnerable island states. The effects of climate change pose risks not so much to state security but to human security in the form of basic needs, human rights and core values of individuals and communities (Barnett, 2011). Effective mitigation of climate change must involve shifting the emphasis away from the neoliberal economic discourse to framing it in human security terms, and this should be part of the global human security paradigm.

A globalised human security paradigm provides a shift in emphasis from the confinements of national-security thinking. Such a shift entails redefining the principles of state sovereignty in a global world where threats to humanity are beyond the capacity of any one nation to address through unilateral action. This redefinition requires not only a new theoretical shift but also a change in the policy direction, capacity and roles of international agencies and civil society organisations in relation to human rights and the development of an effective intervention capacity to protect individuals from state action as well as other security threats arising from conflict, poverty, disease and environmental degradation (Battersby & Siracusa, 2009).

Moreover, achieving consensus and legitimacy for a global human security paradigm could prove problematic because of the contending political, economic, strategic and ideological interests and positions of the major global actors. For instance, President Trump's climate change denial position as opposed to the rest of the world might prove to be a major stumbling block in the fight to save our planet from the impact of climate change. Corporate and ideological interests, challenges that compromise national sovereignty and international interests and differences in the power of states undermine the growth of any consensus on a global human security agenda (Bromley, Cooper & Holtom, 2012). The primacy of national interests over global human security considerations is likely to remain a major political bottleneck in the attempt to create a global human security environment.

It has also been argued that debates over the 'narrow' and 'broad' human security frameworks have undermined the emphasis on power relationships, a theme that is central to the critical theorists we will look at later (Chandler, 2012). This is why it is important to integrate preventive human security practices to enhance resilience, to facilitate the empowerment of the vulnerable and to intervene to protect victims. These measures become more imperative in a situation where hegemonic groups use their control of state institutions to project their economic and political interests at the cost of subaltern groups. For instance, using the postcolonial discourse, d'Hauteserre (2011), in her study of colonial representation in New Caledonia, demonstrated that international tourism marketing is a political statement that constructs New Caledonia as a French enclave that relegates Kanaks to a subaltern position with minimal significance. This representation reinforced French colonial hegemony and neoliberal commodification of Kanak identity and ran counter to attempts to promote the human security of Kanaks.

The globalisation of the neoliberal philosophy, practices and policies has raised and affirmed the relevance of global justice, which has acquired new meanings in the context of the economic, social and humanitarian crisis induced by the extreme phenomena associated with climate change (Munoz, 2010). Theorising democracy and justice in national contexts might be inadequate in transnational contexts, especially when dealing with the safety of individuals and communities such as those now being affected by climate change. This requires a new framework, revolving around the notion of human safety as a way of understanding the relationship between environmental crisis, unsustainable development and conflict. A critical process here is to link the concept of global justice and the democratic mechanisms of international governance (Munoz, 2010). Relatedly, many scholars and policy-makers are critical of the liberal institutionalist values that underpin international peace-building and their emphasis on democracy, free market economics and the liberal state. The reason for that negative stance, it is suggested, is that such values undermine the importance of basic and everyday human needs while promoting externally imposed and inappropriate models of state institutions. It is argued that effective peace-building needs to be framed within the human security discourse with greater emphasis on welfare, livelihoods and local engagement to ensure legitimacy and sustainability (Newman, 2011).

To ensure effectiveness and legitimacy, human security should be part of a collective responsibility, especially in grave humanitarian crises involving genocide or ethnic cleansing. Collective responsibility relates to conceptualising the world as a community of peoples, rather than as a society of states in which other international and transnational actors operate (Peltonen, 2013). This collective realisation of common responsibility has led to the development of the Responsibility to Protect (R2P) framework. Related to this, it has been argued that the notion of shared responsibility should also extend to linking global development and human security to make sense of how countries are connected to the global economy and to defusing the social tensions and managing the security risks that can result from exposure to a turbulent international system (Picciotto, Olonisakin & Clarke, 2007). An instructive model for this is Sweden's Shared Responsibility Bill, which merges peace, security, opportunity, environmental conservation, human rights and democracy into an integrated system.

Along this line, we need to note that globalisation has strengthened the link between development and human security in the context of the changing contemporary sphere of international relations (Ştefanachi, 2011). This has especially been so since the Cold War, where the impact of the normative relationship between human development and human security policies on individuals has come under greater scrutiny. A more nuanced approach to this would require retheorising and employing alternative discourses of human security that encompass global transformation and local realities as well as multiple disciplines. The need for such a re-examination of theory and use of alternative discourses arises because the transnationalisation of threat and rolling back of state power can no longer be studied in a one-dimensional fashion but must be conceptualised from an interdisciplinary point of view, taking into account a range of interacting variables. Tadjbakhsh and Chenoy (2005) emphasise this point by using case studies from Afghanistan, Central Asia and South Asia to frame and illuminate the international importance of human security as a basis for policy thinking in response to an intellectual need.

Nevertheless, there are still gaps to be addressed. For instance, Von Tigerstrom (2007) makes the assertion that, despite the fact that the concept of human security has influenced discourse and practice, and has become the subject of vigorous debate regarding its relevance to central questions of international law, it has, until recently, received little attention from international lawyers. Human security, it is argued, provides a credible platform for the re-evaluation and rethinking of international law in terms of its ethical, normative and legal dimensions. This is especially so in relation to humanitarian intervention, internally displaced persons, small arms control and global health.

Critiques of human security

The initial enthusiasm relating to human security slowly withered away over the years as it became apparent that the concept was too broad and nebulous to be useful and, in certain cases, could not be neatly captured in policy framing. It has been described as too 'fuzzy', inconclusive and amorphous in the way it frames any potential threat in society, and while the term was initially used to escape the limitations of the hard security approach, its encompassing and holistic approach has turned out to be a liability because it 'is so vague that it verges on meaninglessness' (Paris, 2001: 102).

Its fluid character allows it to be readily subjected to arbitrary manipulation as a propagandistic euphemism by states and various groups to project self-serving positive and popular images. Like populist but fuzzy terms such as 'development', 'good governance', 'democracy', 'freedom', 'justice' and 'humanity', which invoke affirmative images, the term 'human security' has been used by scholars, policy-makers, states and civil society organisations as a panacea for almost all social ills. Aid agencies often use values such as democratic behaviour and good governance, associated with human security, as preconditions to dictate the terms of aid. Hence the danger here is that aid can become a tool to leverage ideological conformity rather than a means of addressing poverty. A classic example of this is the Cotonou Agreement between the European Union and the African Caribbean and Pacific (ACP) countries, where conformity to certain political criteria by ACP countries was required as a condition of the aid. EU aid earmarked for the reform of Fiji's sugar industry was withheld and redirected towards civil society organisations as a result of the delay in the post-2006 coup election, which was seen as a contravention of the democratic governance conditions of the Cotonou Agreement.

The association often made between human security and democracy, as if they were symbiotic, is problematic. This is partly because the concept of democracy can be used readily in a paradoxical way as justification for the violent imposition of external rule. The US involvement in Vietnam and invasion of Iraq, for instance, were justified on the grounds that the governing regimes in those countries were threats to democracy: Vietnam because of communism and Iraq because of the mythical weapons of mass destruction. Although the justifications were flawed, the fact that protection of freedom and other democratic values were used as tools of ideological mobilisation raises questions about the reliability of democracy as a viable human security concept.

In many nations of the global South, democratisation processes can be inherently conflictual because of a constant contestation over power, which sometimes leads to instability and unregulated competition for resources. Political elites, state bureaucrats and powerful corporations are usually in a position to control power and resources, and the resulting inequality has the potential to undermine human security. Often the local aspects of human security are ignored in development thinking in favour of state-based, corporate and international narratives and polices. This sometimes leads to further conflict.

One of the paradoxical situations is the potential of the human security agenda to inadvertently undermine the international human rights regime. This is because the threat to human rights, which is driven by specific conditions, is subsumed and lost under the broad rubric of human security (Howard-Hassmann, 2012). While human security is meant to complement human rights principles, it also has the potential to undermine the primacy of civil and political rights as a strategic tool for citizens to fight for their rights. The use of the umbrella human security concept has created confusion between previously distinct policy streams of human rights and human development (Martin & Owen, 2010). The term 'human rights' itself has been relegated to a subservient position within the broader human security discourse, thus further exacerbating the ambiguity and confusion.

Despite its shortcomings, human security has become mainstreamed in the Pacific security discourse through policies and activities of international aid agencies, media campaigns, international conferences attended by Pacific people, academic research, civil society campaigns and state officials visiting communities (Bryar, Bello & Corendea, 2015). Human security has been associated with the work of UN agencies, development aid, the rise in environmental consciousness in the region as a result of climate change and the general recognition of the importance of social, political and economic rights that are closely associated with human security. Coincidently, the human security concept with its interconnected dimensions seems to fit in well with the Pacific cultural world views, which conceive of society as an interrelated whole. Human security has taken root in policies, laws and institutions and has more or less become part of societal normative systems (Corendea, 2012).

Critical security paradigm: The postcolonial discourse

Framing Pacific security through the postcolonial lens is uncommon, although postcoloniality itself has been a feature in some historical, literary, educational and sociological Pacific texts (Keown, 2005; Tawake, 2000; Mishra, 2011). The postcolonial approach to security frames threat not in the form of interpretive abstraction and subjectivity, as the Copenhagen School does, nor as diffused and multiple facets of risks, as the human security approach contends, but in the context of power relations, inequality and domination arising from historically defined relationships in politically and culturally defined spaces.

Edward Said, an icon of postcolonial discourse, popularised the term 'orientalism', which was a critical deconstruction of the colonial gaze that represented the colonised in a patronisingly hegemonic manner, and helped to frame a new paradigm for postcolonial critique (Said, 1978). Said's orientalism was a critique of the way the West (which he refers to as Occidental) deployed simplistic racial stereotypes to frame colonised peoples. The distorted images, articulated in novels, paintings, films and the media, became the basis on which the colonial world was understood in the European popular imagination. This provided the basis for imperial hegemony, which posed an imminent threat to the status and survival of subaltern cultures. The same orientalist logic, as Tariq Ali argued, was used to cast Muslims and Arabs as terrorists posing a major of threat to the West, especially since 9/11 (Ali, 2003).

Said expanded a considerable part of his intellectual energy critiquing Samuel Huntington's 'clash of civilisations' thesis, which portrayed post–Cold War conflict as the inevitable struggle between the West and 'other' cultures, especially Islam. In confirmatory response to Francis Fukuyama's now moribund Hegelian narrative about the universal triumph of liberal democracy over communism (*The End of History: The Last Man*), Huntington asserted:

> It is my hypothesis that the fundamental source of conflict in this new world will not be primarily ideological or primarily economic. The great divisions among humankind and the dominating source of conflict will be cultural. Nation states will remain the most powerful actors in world affairs, but the principal conflicts of global politics will occur between nations and groups of different civilisations. The clash of civilisations will dominate global politics and the fault lines between civilisations will be the battle lines of the future. (Huntington, 1965: 22)

Said's response to Huntington was in the form of his polemically bombastic article, 'The clash of ignorance', in which he rebutted Huntington's attempt to construct static cultural boundaries in a world where cultural cross-fertilisation has been part of the dynamic human history and where politics and ideology, rather than culture, have created conditions for conflict (Said, 2001). The use of rather simplistic and generalised labels like the 'West' and 'Islam' by Huntington tended to 'mislead and confuse the mind, which is trying to make sense of a disorderly reality' (Said, 2001: 11). Said's alternative discourse in these 'tense times' was to critically examine how the dialectics of relationships shaped the world, unhindered by cultural preconceptions and ignorance:

> These are tense times, but it is better to think in terms of powerful and powerless communities, the secular politics of reason and ignorance, and universal principles of justice and injustice, than to wander off in search of vast abstractions that may give momentary satisfaction but little self-knowledge or informed analysis. 'The Clash of Civilisations' thesis is a gimmick like 'the War of the Worlds', better for reinforcing defensive self-pride than for critical understanding of the bewildering interdependence of our time. (Said, 2001: 14)

The ambiguity of the term 'West' is critically explored by Stuart Hall (1996), who saw it as an ideological construct based on a racialised discursive hierarchy where 'the West' = developed = good = desirable, while 'the non-West' = under-developed = bad = undesirable (Hall, 1996: 186). This binary of 'West and the rest' has in some ways framed the dominant contemporary security discourse, where the values of the advanced and 'civilised' West were constantly being threatened by the primordial non-West and its unrefined values.

Said's argument parallels Franz Fanon's work on the coloniser–colonised relationship. The dialectics between the powerful and the weak resonated with Franz Fanon's *Black Skin White Masks*, a study of the social psychology of racism and the dehumanisation created by colonial hegemony (Fanon, 1952). In *The Wretched of the Earth*, Fanon (1963) examined the psychological struggle between the weak and strong, coloniser and colonised, master and slave, and how the coloniser used violence to maintain dominance, thus legitimising the use of counter-violence as a means of emancipation.

The quest for answers to critical questions regarding security post 9/11, and the rise of racism and Islamophobia, provided new opportunities to revisit Said's orientalism. A core strand in this situation was the notion of power, which was explored in a phenomenological way by Michel Foucault's conception of surveillance, discipline, regulation, the biopolitics of population, and discourses of security and governmentality (Foucault, 1991). While traditionally the state was seen as the focal point of power,

Foucault recognised the diffusion, relativism and dispersal of power in society. His notion that power was universally accessible and everywhere helped to examine the way in which the media, ideas and perceptions shaped the security climate in the post-9/11 period.

Security discourse has become a dominant feature of policy thinking, military strategies, governance structures and development framing, and this, according to Foucault, contributes to the way in which power is produced and reproduced:

> Discourses are not once and for all subservient to power or raised up against it … We must make allowances for the complex and unstable process whereby a discourse can be both an instrument and an effect of power, but also a hindrance, a stumbling point of resistance and a starting point for an opposing strategy. Discourse transmits and produces power; it reinforces it, but also undermines and exposes it, renders it fragile and makes it possible to thwart. (Foucault, 1998: 100–1)

The relationship between discourse and power is also explored in Stuart Hall's work on the synergy between meaning and power, encoding and decoding, where, despite multiple meanings, the overriding meaning provides a hegemonic leverage for influence by dominant interests (Hall, 1973). In the context of applied security, this means that the meaning of security, the source of insecurity and the nature of threats are framed and reproduced by hegemonic interests. One way of understanding the contours of security is through what Cynthia Enloe (1980) referred to as 'security mapping', or the classification of relative degrees of threat and the reliability of various groups *vis-à-vis* the dominant group or state.

Today, the relationship between security, power and hegemony is manifested more markedly in the form of US global dominance. Although the United States portrays itself as a model for democracy and a global 'sheriff' for freedom, its strategic and corporate interests are largely self-serving in fulfilment of some universal truth at the cost of the 'evil' other. This prompted Noam Chomsky to refer to it as a 'failed state' operating on a 'single standard' based on the premise that '*their* terror against us and our clients is the ultimate evil, while *our* terror against them does not exist—or, if it does, is entirely appropriate' (Chomsky, 2006: 3). The propensity of the United States to demonise and eventually punish countries and groups who do not behave in accordance with its grand scheme of things is seen as part of destiny, a righteous cause and a natural American right, as Chomsky argued:

By now, the world's hegemonic power accords itself the right to wage war at will, under a doctrine of 'anticipatory self-defence' with unstated bounds. International law, treaties, and rules of world order are sternly imposed on others with much self-righteous posturing, but dismissed as irrelevant for the United States—a longstanding practice, driven to new depths by the Reagan and Bush II administrations. (Chomsky, 2006: 3)

Influenced by Antonio Gramsci's notion of hegemony and manufacturing consent (Gramsci, 2012), Herman and Chomsky make the assertion that induced adherence to the idea of US and Western moral righteousness to wage war is part of a system of ideological, intellectual and cultural control through education, media and other forms of public discourse (Herman & Chomsky, 1988). Consent is manufactured through a complex system of corporate, media and state manipulation of ideas and propaganda rather than being simply voluntary and rationalised. The 2003 invasion of Iraq was a classic case of hegemonic control of mainstream media, which acted as cheerleaders and consent-manufacturing machines for Bush's warmongering adventure.

Tariq Ali further argues that the reaction to US hegemony has been equally mischievous on the part of Islamists, who have been as 'fundamentalist' as US warmongering adventurism. Hence what we have experienced has been the return of history in a horrific form, with religious symbols playing a part on both sides, represented in politico-religious rhetoric such as 'Allah's revenge', 'God is on Our Side' and 'God Bless America'. The violence of 11 September 2001 was an Islamic fundamentalist response to the Western fundamentalist violence inflicted on the people of Palestine, Afghanistan, Iraq and Yemen and other parts of the world. The United States had been involved either directly or indirectly in almost all of these violent situations. Ali's *Clash of Fundamentalisms*, written in response to 9/11, like Said's 'Clash of ignorance', was a repudiation of Huntington's 'clash of civilisations' thesis, which portrayed non-Western cultures as deviant and threatening. Ali proposed that rival ideological fundamentalisms—Islamism on one side and Western imperialism on the other—were to be equally blamed for threatening global security and that both must be opposed (Ali, 2003). While many of the values proclaimed by the Enlightenment (from the late 17th to the early 19th centuries) have retained their relevance, portrayals of the American empire as a new emancipatory project are misguided.

The framing of postcolonial societies as a threat to the West, represented by capitalism and liberal democracy, is not merely a theoretical proposition, it is also encapsulated in policy thinking. When former British Prime Minister Tony Blair labelled Africa as a 'scar on the conscience of the world', he was reflecting New Labour's policy shift from 'development–humanitarianism' to the 'risk–fear–threat' category in the broader context of the 'war on terror'. While the securitisation of Africa helped to legitimise the 'war on terror', it, unfortunately, effectively undermined development initiatives (Abrahamsen, 2005).

There are some important conceptual lessons we can learn from the critical analysis of contemporary security. The view that dichotomises the world along the lines of the 'West' and the 'rest' creates a hierarchy whereby the non-West is seen not only as inferior but also as a source of threat. Although the militant Islamic fundamentalists responsible for 9/11 and other acts of terror constitute a small minority of Muslims, their actions have been used as 'evidence' of the primordial barbarism of non-Western peoples generally. This orientalist state of mind, as Said reminds us, is pervasive and takes various manifest and latent forms. Post–Cold War conflict is not so much a 'clash of civilisations', as Huntington suggests, but has more to do with contestation over entrenched political, economic and ideological interests, underpinned by either side's inability to understand the situation of the other, or a 'clash of ignorance', as Said put it.

One of the prominent aspects of the critical and postcolonial discourse is the feminist security discourse. As Blanchard argues, 'national security discourses are part of the elite world of masculine high politics' (Blanchard, 2003: 1289). The masculine-based realist conception of security, which puts the state and military at the centre of analysis, obscures the way the role of women has been reduced to subaltern status. Recently, feminist scholars have raised fundamental questions about the meaning of security: just who is being secured by security policies, and who is the threat? Security policies are often designed by men and security institutions such as the military, and are therefore imbued with patriarchal ideology and culture. Often the masculine personality is seen as the 'protector' just as much as it is seen as a threat, while women are the 'protected' weak and vulnerable. Yet women struggle every day against patriarchal hegemony, and this process, as Christine Sylvester states, 'is always elusive and mundane' (Sylvester, 1987: 183).

The rise of the feminist security theory has redefined the terrain of security studies as well as opened new opportunities for creating a new engendered security discourse. Part of this intellectual and political project is to privilege women's role in politics and unveil the shroud of invisibility that has rendered women hidden. The exclusion of women is linked to cultural framing and power relations and is therefore ideological in nature. Of significance here is our understanding of the power of the state in institutionalising and reproducing security discourse, and questions have been raised about whether the state actually protects women in times of war and peace. Women are often victims of violence, rape and abuse during wars and other conflicts, and sometimes these are perpetrated by soldiers themselves.

The fact that women are often victims of war has more to do with their social role as bearers of children and sources of the well-being of the family and has nothing to do with their natural inferiority. The notion of inferiority is sometimes used as the basis for constructing stereotypes that women are natural peacemakers, thereby fuelling the assumption that women are weak, docile and incapable of conspiracy, power play and war-mongering. As we have seen in the cases of Joan of Arc, Margaret Thatcher, who ordered the British invasion of the Falkland Islands, and Golda Meir, who was Prime Minister of Israel during the Yom Kippur War of 1973, circumstances can dictate realities and disprove these myths. Women are imbued with diverse qualities such as peacefulness and aggression just like men, and denying them these fundamentally human characteristics is tantamount to denying them an equal place in society.

The role of women in peace activism, peace-building and conflict resolution in the Pacific has a long history, and in many cases—whether it be Fiji, Papua New Guinea, Solomon Islands, Tonga or any other community— women have been at the forefront of political action and resistance to violence and conflict. The proliferation of gender-based organisations in the Pacific is part of the global wave of consciousness sweeping across civil society as well as states. Many of them draw inspiration from the UN Security Council Resolution 1325 on gender, peace and development as well as the Convention on the Elimination of all Forms of Discrimination Against Women (CEDAW), an international treaty adopted in 1979 by the United Nations General Assembly (United Nations, 1979).

Recent research on the Fiji military using the gender intersectionality framework has shown the deeply embedded masculine culture within the military's structure, ideology and institutional behaviour (Tagicakibau, 2018). This has been a psychological and cultural driving force behind the coups in Fiji since 1987. Militarist masculinity even pre-dates the coups and has roots in the traditional warrior culture that formed the basis of Fijian masculinity (Baledrokadroka, 2012). This will be examined in more detail in Chapter 4.

The feminist security discourse has been progressively taking hold in the Pacific, although its actual policy influence has been limited. There is now growing consciousness about gender and human security issues and their relationship, and this has provided impetus for the genderisation of security discourse and policies among regional and civil society organisations. The resistance to the feminist approach has been largely from the patriarchal establishments, such as the churches and other traditional institutions. For instance, the opposition to CEDAW in Tonga was largely from churches as well as the traditional hierarchy, who saw gender equality as a threat to their control over land and power (Ratuva, 2017b).

The feminist security discourse is part of the broader critical social theory approach of the postcolonial discourse, which we look at next.

The relevance of the postcolonial security discourse in the Pacific cannot be understated. Rather than merely providing a simple snapshot of the immediate experience of threats, such as the case with the realist and liberal security discourses that have been dominant in the study of Pacific security, postcolonial theory provides a more historicised view by looking at the origins of unequal power relations from the colonial to the postcolonial era. PICs find themselves as subaltern entities in the global power dynamics, and often they are framed by neocolonial powers and their intellectual apostles through the 'arc of instability' and 'failed states' prisms. We shall examine this in more detail in Chapter 3.

The different theories discussed above have their own strengths as well as shortcomings, and they have their own analytical value when used to study the Pacific. Table 1 summarises the narratives around these security discourses and their significance in understanding security in the Pacific. These discourses will be used selectively in discussing various aspects of Pacific security in this book.

Table 1: Security discourses and relevance to the Pacific

Security discourse	Narrative	Application to Pacific
Securitisation	Threat is embedded in the language and the circumstances of usage.	Terms like 'coup', 'arc of instability' and 'climate change' invoke connotations of threat and thus become the basis for anxiety and feelings of insecurity.
Human security	Situations, issues and factors that relate to and affect people's livelihood rather than security of the state as traditionally assumed.	Relates to a whole range of social, economic, psychological and political issues such as poverty, employment, climate change, health and education. These issues are interrelated in the Pacific.
Postcolonial	Dominant security discourses are defined in terms of the interests of the 'Western' cultural prism. The views and interests of subaltern groups, many of whom were under colonial rule, need to be considered.	Most PICs are former colonies and are at the periphery of international capitalism and global power hierarchy. In many ways this also defines their security circumstances.

Conclusion

In this chapter I have tried to demonstrate that security is not a given but a highly contested terrain and a dynamic and often arbitrary construct. Competing discourses try to define security using different ideological frames, conceptual tools, variables and contexts. For instance, securitisation theory focuses on the primacy of speech act, human security discourse is based on multiple situations of risks and threats to human well-being, the gender approach focuses on the dominance of the masculine culture, while the postcolonial approach provides an integrated narrative based on power through a dominant–subordinate relationship. The common strands in all these are two-fold: identifying the sources of threat or insecurity and ensuring peace. Again, the way these are defined is subject to conceptual and political contestation.

For the Pacific, one may be able to draw strands of thought from various security discourses to explain particular situations, not in a deductive way but in a critical and open-minded fashion in recognition of the strengths and limitations of the discourse in question. Indeed, some of the theories are fundamentally at odds with each other, and the way we use them needs to be cautiously selective and evidence-based. The use of multiple discourses can be enriching because it enables one to visualise an issue and context from different conceptual and methodological vantage points without being hindered by the limitations of singular narratives. This is important for interdisciplinary-based studies such as this one, where seemingly disparate issues are framed as interconnected horizontally (across issues) and vertically (across different levels of issues). The approach is appropriate for the Pacific because of the interrelatedness and integration of social, economic, political and cultural issues associated with kinship-based semi-subsistence communities. Additionally, the wide diversity between and within PICs requires the use of multiple lenses to illuminate the manifest and latent dimensions of security. Often, the use of singular prisms can easily lead to generalisations, which oversimplify the complex social realities on the ground.

Let it also be emphasised here that the theories discussed in this chapter should not be treated as mere superficial abstractions; rather they are applied conceptual tools to help guide our understanding of the notion of security. Theories do not exist in isolation from social reality but rather reflect the way social reality is defined, framed and understood. For PICs, the challenge is the way theories are used to make sense of the constantly changing and highly contested terrain of security. We will look at this in Chapter 3.

3

Swirling and divergent waves: Selected security dilemmas in Oceania

Just as the sea is an open and ever flowing reality, so should our oceanic identity transcend all forms of insularity, to become one that is openly searching, inventive, and welcoming.

Epeli Hau'ofa

One of the dilemmas in studying security in the Pacific is the wide diversity of cultures, political systems and states in the Pacific and the multiplicity of cultural, political, economic and cultural factors that are linked to security issues, thus making it difficult to provide a neat and generalised narrative. Attempts to create regional hard security and human security frameworks by the United Nations Development Program (UNDP) and the Pacific Islands Forum (PIF) have not met expectations due to difficulties in satisfying all the individual country conditions through unifying consensus. Like waves in a Pacific cyclone, they are often 'swirling' and 'divergent'. With this in mind, this chapter attempts to probe a number of interrelated aspects of regional security in a selected way, focusing on security perceptions and securitisation in relation to the terms 'failed state' and 'arc of instability', and the following internal political security dynamics among Pacific Island Countries (PICs): geopolitics and regional security, regional security mechanisms, human security, free trade and human security, hegemony and patronage, and climate change. Although these might appear to be disparate issues, in fact they are all connected to each other and to security at different levels and in different ways.

These selected issues are examined using some of the conceptual lenses discussed in Chapter 2, in particular the postcolonial, securitisation and human security lenses.

Because of the specific historical characteristics of the PICs and the contemporary regional and global power dynamics that confine them to a relatively subaltern position, the postcolonial prism is employed to examine political, economic and cultural dynamics of interest. As former colonies, the history, sociocultural norms, sociopolitical structures and socioeconomic systems of most Pacific states are shaped to a significant degree by colonial hegemony and the effects of that are still felt today, despite years of formal independence. However, we need to keep in mind that there is a danger in applying concepts and theories simplistically. There are complex challenges in applying concepts, especially in relation to the interpretation of knowledge (epistemology), the subjectivity of meaning and the context in which the concepts are used. These complexities are compounded by the inherent cultural, political, historical and economic diversity of PICs (referring to sovereign national entities) and Pacific communities (referring to sociocultural groupings), which are often ignored in the clamour to create a generic 'regional' narrative such as the 'arc of instability'.

In the foreword to the book *Securing a Peaceful Pacific*, which provides a collection of articles by some of the Pacific's leading experts on security, Don McKinnon, secretary general of the Commonwealth Secretariat and former foreign minister of New Zealand, proclaims:

> The first decade of the 21st century in the island communities of the southern and central Pacific Ocean is proving to be a watershed period for the region's security—change has already occurred and further change is imminent. (McKinnon, 2005: xi)

McKinnon goes on to identify three major security concerns: being 'exposed and vulnerable to wider global forces'; 'tension between traditional and … imported forms of leadership'; and 'international, trans-border issues'. McKinnon's solution lies in using collective regional approaches such as the Pacific Plan to consolidate 'regional *collaboration*' and even extending this to 'regional *integration*' (McKinnon, 2005: xi).

While some aspects of the hard security issues identified by McKinnon may still be valid, circumstances have changed in the last few years because of the increasing realisation of the importance of human security, the emergence of climate change as a dominant security concern and the reconfiguration of intraregional geopolitics as a result of Fiji's political manoeuvres since 2006. Also, the argument that regional collaboration is the panacea to national and local security problems needs closer scrutiny. While regionalism is a unifying discourse and practice, it is also potentially hegemonic and could become a political façade to hide entrenched interests and stratified power relationships. The two major Pacific hegemons, Australia and New Zealand, together with Fiji, a subhegemon, have carved out their own spheres of influence around which they define and impose their national interests over those of the other Pacific island states. Therefore when we talk of regional security we cannot sensibly talk of a unitary and shared security interest, but rather must consider a scattered, often contradictory set of ideological framings and political practices that are driven by inherent national interests, artificially framed and projected as universally applicable and consensually accepted under the euphemism of 'regionalism'.

Therefore it is important to unpack the concept of regional security in terms of different layers of interests, thinking and activities that are intertwined in a complex web of often ragged and disjointed relationships. This chapter attempts to do so by, first, critically examining the terms 'failed state' and 'arc of instability', which have been used as ideological prisms for framing Pacific security in recent years. The chapter examines the connotative and prescriptive imagery of the terms in the context of Said's notion of orientalism and how such imagery carries resonance from the scientific racism movement of the Enlightenment.

The first part of the chapter uses the postcolonial prism to unpack the 'arc of instability' assumptions regarding common primordial characteristics that run through the 'unstable' Pacific archipelagos, the so-called arc. The argument this chapter makes is that the PICs are so diverse in terms of their historical, political and cultural realities that to refer to them as an arc linked by common political and cultural experiences is an oversimplistic hypothesis. The chapter then provides a brief overview of regional geopolitics and implications on security. The following and related section looks at some regional security mechanisms and their role and implications in relation to the broader geopolitical and internal national dynamics of the region. Geopolitics is often the focus of regional security analysis in the Pacific and overrides other security considerations such as human security.

The discussion on human security that follows is based largely on the attempt to put together a regional framework, which so far has proved challenging. The chapter then provides a critical examination of free trade in the form of the Pacific Agreement on Closer Economic Relations (PACER Plus), together with its human security implications. This is followed by a discussion of the power dynamics of security, in particular the issue of patronage and hegemony and how they play out in the relationship between the small PICs countries and the bigger states, Australia and New Zealand. The last security factor to be discussed is climate change, which is a critical human security issue in the contemporary Pacific.

While admittedly these might not constitute all the security issues in the Pacific, they are significant in shaping the social, political, economic and cultural life of the Pacific and certainly do have potential to transform Pacific societies in dynamic ways in the future. The issues are not self-contained but are interrelated and shape each other in complex ways.

The Pacific context

The diverse histories of the Pacific can be understood in the context of a chronological continuum from the earliest inhabited islands in the west to the most recently inhabited ones to the east. New Guinea (consisting of West Papua and Papua New Guinea), the largest of the Pacific Islands, was inhabited about 60,000 years ago while Aotearoa (New Zealand) to the east is estimated to have been inhabited around 700 years ago. The genesis of the Pacific people who live east of the Solomons can be traced back to Taiwan and South China. After more than 10,000 years of moving down the chain of islands in South-East Asia, they reached the Pacific Islands after admixtures with those who have already settled around Papua before continuing the journey eastwards. As shown by DNA of recently discovered skeletons in Vanuatu and Tonga, certain Asian groups might have continued to migrate eastwards without admixtures on the way and settled in Vanuatu, Fiji and the rest of the eastern Pacific. The darker-skinned Papuan groups might have migrated eastwards later, resulting in more admixtures. Genetic tests indicate significant admixtures across the Pacific with varying degrees of traces of Papuan and Asian DNA, the former being prominent in the western part of the Pacific and the latter dominant in the eastern island groups (Kayser et al., 2008).

This migratory process helped to create a transnational Austronesian cultural system, which starts in Taiwan, spans South-East Asia, crosses the Pacific and even includes Madagascar. People within the Austronesian cultural system largely share linguistic, cultural and genetic characteristics and are connected by the vast migratory routes that span tens of thousands of kilometres (Spriggs, 1997).

Despite the shared Austronesian cultural complex, different communities developed social structures, languages, norms and belief systems, which reflected their local conditions. The Pacific, where about 1,500 distinct languages are spoken by about 10 million people, is now the most culturally diverse region in the world. This is 25 per cent of the 6,000 spoken languages of the world (Lynch, Ross & Crowley, 2002).

Attempts have been made in the past to categorise Pacific peoples into various anthropological groupings (Thomas, 1989). The most enduring was one by French explorer Jules Sébastien César Dumont d'Urville, who constructed and popularised three categories, namely Melanesia (black people), Micronesia (small islands and people) and Polynesia (many islands and peoples) to cover the diversity of Pacific peoples and cultures across the entire Oceanic region (D'Arcy, 2003). Although variants of the 'Polynesian' category had been used earlier, the significance of these categorisations was that they framed Pacific peoples into racial boxes that became the basis for defining their identity. These categories were problematic because they assumed primordial and distinct differences between the different categories by drawing straight rigid lines to demarcate one racial region from the others (Hau'ofa, 1975). This fallacious narrative failed to consider the fluidity, continuity and interconnectedness of cultural systems across the Pacific from west to east. Genetic studies have also shown the complex admixtures among the Pacific peoples, thus making a mockery of these rigid racial classifications (Kayser et al., 2008; Spriggs, 1997).

European encounters

The early Europeans who visited the Pacific came in phases. The first were the explorers who arrived in the 1500s and for the next three centuries were engaged in various activities, including claiming islands for their countries (Rigby, Van Der Merwe & Williams, 2018). Whalers, sealers, traders, planters, missionaries and a whole range of beachcombers arrived in the early 1800s and their influence in transforming the cultures and social structures of the Oceanic communities were profound and long lasting (Edmond & Smith, 2003). The once autonomous subsistence societies were, because of such encounters, incorporated into the global capitalist system through the setting up of plantation economies, recruitment of cheap labour for other parts of the world such as Australia and South America, and trading of local products such as bêche-de-mer, sandalwood and other things (Campbell, 2011b).

Apart from missionaries, colonialism was probably the most transformative foreign force. Almost every major colonial power was active in the Pacific, and every PIC became either a full colony or some sort of territory of a colonial power. Different European powers entered the Pacific and claimed colonies at different times with the Spanish being the first as early as the 1600s, followed by the Portuguese, Dutch, British, French, Germans and Americans in the 1700s and 1800s (Rigby, Van Der Merwe & Williams, 2018).

The Spanish annexed Guam and Mariana Islands in 1668 while the Portuguese took over East Timor in 1702 until independence in 1975 after which the Indonesians invaded and controlled the country. The British created their first colony in Australia in 1788 and Pitcairn Island, where descendants of the *Bounty* mutineers lived, in 1790. It later expanded its empire in the Pacific to incorporate New Zealand in 1840, Fiji in 1874, Kiribati (Gilbert Islands) in 1892, Niue in 1888, Tuvalu (Ellice Islands) in 1892, Solomon Islands in 1893 and Tokelau in 1899 (Fischer, 2013). The British were in competition with the French, who had established colonies in French Polynesia around the same time that Britain annexed New Zealand: Wallis and Futuna in 1837 and New Caledonia in 1853. Vanuatu was later added to the list but as a condominium with Britain in 1886, under a 'joint naval commission' and joint rule in 1906. Except for Vanuatu, none of the French colonies has become fully independent.

The Germans also acquired territories such as Nauru in 1888 and Samoa in 1900; the latter occurred after the two Samoas (East and West) were split between the Germans and Americans in 1899 (Meleisea, 1987). It also established control of the north-east quarter of New Guinea, Federated States of Micronesia (FSM), Marshall Islands and Caroline Islands. Germany lost all its colonies to the Allies during World War I with Nauru being taken over by Australia and Samoa by New Zealand. Japan assumed control of FSM, Palau and the Marshall Islands after World War I but lost them again during World War II. Although Dutch explorers were in the Pacific from the 1600s, most of their colonial activities were focused on the western part of the Pacific. Apart from Indonesia, their territories were limited to West Papua, which was initially under the Dutch East Indies from 1828 to 1949, when it became an overseas territory of the Netherlands (Matsuda, 2012).

New Zealand and Australia, which were themselves British colonies, became proxy mini colonial powers for Britain. New Zealand became the administering power for Western Samoa (1920–62), Cook Islands, Niue and Tokelau, while Australia took over administration of Papua from Britain in 1906 and German New Guinea in 1914. The United States was mostly involved in the northern Pacific. It annexed Hawaii in 1893, took control of Guam and Philippines from Spain in 1898, gained control of American Samoa in 1899, and, in 1945, took over Marshall Islands, Palau and Northern Marianas from Japan (Fischer, 2013).

The colonial encounter transformed the Pacific communities in deep and complex ways. Some of the typical reconfigurations included the centralisation of power under a single authority using both legal and coersive means to pacify the local population; imposition of a new political system that mirrored the colonial political values and structures; the establishment of a capitalist economy and development strategy to serve the interests of foreign traders, planters and investors; the imposition of taxation that forced locals to generate cash by whatever means for the colonial state; the creation of a local working class through the appropriation of local cheap labour; the alienation and commodification of land by Europeans; and the creation of a local comprador class to serve as a conduit between the colonial state and the local communities (Crocombe, 2001).

These developments had different manifestations in different PICs, given their unique circumstances. They also redefined the security configurations of the PICs in significant ways. In many cases, there was outright resistance to taxation, loss of land and political power, and in some cases there was a certain degree of collaboration and willingness by locals to accept colonial rule. By the time of independence, the colonial legacies were still instrumental in defining the shape and direction of political, economic and social changes in the PICs (Crocombe, 2001).

Postcolonial developments

The independence process in the Pacific took more than two decades, starting with Samoa in 1962 and followed by Nauru in 1968. The 1970s and 1980s saw a wave of decolonisation sweep across the Pacific with Fiji and Tonga (a British protectorate) becoming independent in 1970, Papua New Guinea in 1975, Solomon Islands and Tuvalu in 1978, Kiribati in 1979 and Vanuatu in 1980 (Firth, 1989). The US territories of Marshall Islands and Federated States of Micronesia achieved self-governing status and entered into a Compact of Free Association arrangement with the United States in 1986 and 1994 for Palau (Hezel, 2013). None of the French colonies has become independent and, officially, the British still possess a territory in the form of Pitcairn Island.

Upon independence, the PICs had to respond to the new demands of statehood in a fast-changing regional and global environment. Colonialism had transformed then into subaltern entities at the margins of global power, and one of the first tasks was to claim a place at the table of nations where they could be recognised as sovereign states, a right they were denied under colonialism (Connell, 1981). One way of doing this was to join the United Nations as full voting members and forming regional organisations such as the Pacific Islands Forum (PIF) in 1971, University of the South Pacific in 1972 and Air Pacific, to name a few. These organisations were expressions of political self-actualisation and autonomy in a region contested by the two Cold War antagonists, the United States and the Soviet Union.

The PIF was established by some independent PICs as an alternative forum to the South Pacific Commission (SPC), a regional organisation set up in 1947 by the Pacific colonial powers to provide development support for the PICS as well as to keep the Pacific in Western hands and free of Soviet influence during the Cold War (Crocombe, 2001). The PIF allowed for discussions of political matters, unlike the SPC, and, after a major reorganisation of regional institutions, it became focused on issues of governance, security and trade whereas the SPC was responsible for the more technical, cultural and scientific aspects of regional development. To some degree, the end of the Cold War lifted the pressure on small Pacific island states to adhere to the Western bloc's ideological agenda, enabling them to focus on other important aspects of regional security and sovereignty (Henningham, 1995).

The political systems of the PICs differ considerably. The former US territories, Nauru and Kiribati, have presidential systems whereas the others have various localised versions of the Westminister system (Ratuva, 2011b). Tonga is the only monarchy, modelled pretty much along the lines of its British counterpart. One of the features of the political systems is the syncretic relationship between, on one hand, the indigenous social structures and norms, and the Western model of liberal democracy on the other (Ratuva, 2004). The relationship between these two systems involves a dynamic process of accommodation, contradiction and synthesis over time. While there are moments of accommodation, there are also moments of tension and contradiction, and at times aspects of the two systems may synthecise into new structures and norms. Most PICs have experienced different types of conflict that are unique to their specific circumstances (Henderson & Watson, 2005).

While attempts have been made to paint conflict in the PICs using a broad brush under such generalised labels as 'arc of instability', the reality, as this book tries to demonstrate, is that those conflicts—whether they be coups in Fiji, violence in Solomon Islands, riots in Tonga, land conflict in Samoa, civil war in Bougainville and so forth—have nothing to do with each other and result from the specific historical and sociopolitical dynamics in those respective countries. As in any other country, most of these conflicts have their genesis in colonial and postcolonial developments and need to be understood in those contexts rather than using superficially constructed stereotypic labels to avoid the difficult questions of historical causes (Henningham, 1995).

The economies of the PICs are quite diverse in terms of size, resources and productivity (Duncan, 2016). The bigger countries to the west of the Pacific are much more resourceful than those towards the east. For instance, the economies of Papua New Guinea and Fiji combined make up more than 80 per cent of the total PICs economies (AFTINET, 2018). Fiji, with its relatively advanced industrial base, constitutes more than 80 per cent of intraregional trade outside Australia and New Zealand. The western Pacific countries of Fiji, Solomon Islands, Vanuatu and Papua New Guinea are part of the Melanesian Spearhead Group trade bloc. The disparity in the trade relations among themselves, especially given Fiji's dominance, might not be healthy for regional solidarity in the long run.

The largest money-earners for some PICs are tourism, remittances, fisheries, mining and forestry. Remittances in particular have become the economic backbone of local communities because money received is non-taxable, goes straight to families and provides an important social safety net against poverty (Choong, Jayaraman & Kumar, 2011). The large diaspora Pacific community and short-term seasonal labour schemes to New Zealand and Australia sustain the remittance economy. Aid, as we shall see later in the chapter, is still a significant source of development funds, the leading donors being Australia, the United States, China, New Zealand and Japan (Dornan, 2013). There are, however, fundamental differences in aid strategies. Australia is focused more on institutional reforms with money flowing back to Australia through the use of subcontractors and consultants, most of whom are Australian-based; US aid is focused more in its former territories in the North Pacific under the compact arrangement; and Chinese aid is through 'soft' loans for largely public infrastructural purposes (Dornan & Pryke, 2017). Chinese development assistance is the fastest growing and provides more than 50 per cent of Fiji's external infrastructural funding and 30 per cent of aid to Cook Islands, Samoa, Tonga and Vanuatu. Australia and New Zealand recently increased their aid allocation to the PICs in response to the expansion in Chinese economic influence (Lyons, 2018).

Despite the commitment to economic growth and trade, most PICs still rely on the semi-subsistence sector to support families on a daily basis. More than 70 per cent of the people in Papua New Guinea, Vanuatu and Solomon Islands live in rural areas and rely primarily on subsistence living (Ratuva, 2010). Different countries have different degrees of urbanisation and subsistence dependency. At the same time, urbanisation has been increasing at a phenomenal rate with young people moving into urban areas for education, employment and other reasons. This has led to increases in crime, unemployment and associated problems. Inequality has also been exacerbated by the push towards neoliberal growth, which has led to social and economic problems as well as threatening security (Gamage, 2015).

Despite the fact that most PICs do not export any products, many have recently signed the PACER Plus, a regional free trade agreement spearheaded by Australia and New Zealand. Perhaps the most significant regional issue now, apart from regional trade, is climate change because of its potential impact on regional economies, environment, social stability and general well-being of the people.

Outsider perceptions of Pacific peoples

Sociologically, perceptions are powerful mechanisms for framing others, and often the imagery constructed can shape subconscious attitudes to a group (Jussim, 2012). The encounter between Pacific peoples and Europeans involved both conflict and accommodation as the two strange cultures cautiously engaged and monitored each other for signs of hostility or friendliness. The two encountering groups held vastly different cultural world views. The views of the early Europeans were shaped by the philosophical, religious and cultural norms and ideals of their European societies whereas for many Pacific communities, social solidarity, reciprocity, collective ownership and subsistence production were the basis of their social organisation and cosmological world (Salmond, 1991).

Many Pacific Islands were named according to how they conformed to certain European cultural and moral imaginations (Gascoigne, 2014). For instance, when Magellan crossed the Pacific and came across Guam and the Mariana Islands by accident in 1521, he named the Marianas 'Island of Thieves' after locals who helped themselves to pieces of iron from his ship (Bergreen, 2004). Captain Cook named Tonga 'Friendly Islands' (after being surprised by the welcoming and congenial attitudes shown by locals) and referred to Hawaii as 'Sandwich Islands' in honour of John Montagu, Fourth Earl of Sandwich, who as First Lord of the Admiralty was one of his sponsors (Hough, 2003). For a long time, Fiji was known as 'Cannibal Isle', a name that compelled sailors to avoid the place (Peck, 2010). Tahiti was named 'New Cythera' by Bougainville after the Greek islands where Aphrodite, goddess of love, rose from the sea (Martin, 2008).

Jean-Jacques Rousseau's notion of humanity as naturally good and noble was influential in the way Bougainville constructed the Tahitians he encountered in mid-1767 (Martin, 2008). He coined the term 'noble savage' to refer to those who still lived an idyllic and romantic life in the islands, which were abundant in food, and where people were naturally hospitable and sex was freely practised without much moral restriction (Marcelles, 2011). This played well with the European image of the innocence of savages, untouched by the vagaries of Westernisation. Two notions of the noble savage were identified, namely 'soft primitivism', such as Tahiti, because of the romantic, easy, pure and bountiful lifestyle, and 'strong primitivism', such as Australia and New Zealand, where the indigenous inhabitants had to work hard because of harsher climates, which made them tough and Spartan. The 'soft primitivism' narrative was the more durable. It was the commodified version that became part of tourism imagery in later years. Paul Gauguin memorialised these myths in his paintings of Tahitian women (Staszak, 2004).

The other side of the coin was the term 'ignoble savage' to refer to those of darker skin colour on the western side of the Pacific, who were seen as barbarous, blood-thirsty savages and cannibals (Kabutaulaka, 2015). These stereotypes were reinforced by their classification as Melanesians, a term first used by Jules Dumont d'Urville, a French explorer, to refer not only to skin colour but also their 'inferior' and 'dark' moral and social character. Missionaries later reinforced these stereotypes through their emphasis on the 'light' and 'dark' spiritual dichotomy, which was taken literally to also include God's human creations. This played into the intra-Pacific racial prejudice with Polynesians regarding Melanesians as inferior (Kabutaulaka, 2015).

The romantic imagery of the 'soft primitivism' variant has been popularised in Hollywood movies such as *South Pacific* (1958), a romantic musical based on James Michener's *Tales of the South Pacific*, and *Paradise Hawaiian Style* (1966), starring Elvis Presley. There have been other movies with the same thematic narratives over the years, including *Moana* (2016), a celebrated animation by Disney. *Moana* was a classical attempt to construct a mythological paradise using demeaning stereotypes about the child-like, innocent and supernatural-minded nature of 'noble savages' (Perry, 2016). Disney was making about US$300 million a month from the film while the Fijian indigenous owners of the knowledge argued that this was a clear case of intellectual theft and wanted compensation (Amid, 2014). This was a case of bio-piracy and intellectual property theft that enriched a large multinational at the cost of the indigenous people.

By the 1990s, new imagery began to emerge, including the 'fatal impact' theory proposed by Alan Moorehead in his book, *The Fatal Impact, 1767–1840*, in which he argued that colonialism and European contact had caused unimaginable destruction that was beyond the control of Pacific peoples (Moorehead, 1990 [1966]). It had the social Darwinian notion that diseases and cultural influences were inevitable. The fatalistic narrative failed to consider the fact that the Pacific peoples were also conscious agents of change and active participants in historical change rather than just passive driftwood floating around at the whim of the waves in a sea of transformation. By the 2000s, scholars and policy-makers began to see the Pacific through the deficit lenses of the 'vulnerability' thesis (Barnett & Waters, 2016). Predicated on the neoliberal economic narrative of scarce resources and commodification, the Pacific countries were framed as economically backward, lacking in resources, poor in skills and low in technological innovation, and therefore in need of the saving hands of Western aid donors (Rustomjee, 2016).

The Pacific has acted as a laboratory for racial categorisation and labelling and a testing ground for those trying to ensure the workability of their stereotypic ideals and Eurocentric views about humanity. In the next section, the notions of 'arc of instability' and 'failed states' will be explored in detail in the broader context of securitisation, including their implications on intergroup perception and security.

Pacific orientalism and securitisation: The 'failed state' and 'arc of instability' imagery

As the securitisation theory suggests, using politically and ideologically loaded labels to frame a group of people or a country has the capacity to shape the security environment and people's consciousness of a threat. In the context of this approach, threat is constructed via perception and articulated as 'real'. This is where the securitisation and postcolonial approaches converge, at least to some extent. The use of words that influence action (as securitisation theorists emphasised) and the use of imagery to cast a culture in stereotypic imagery (along the lines of Said's notion of orientalism) is an important convergence point to delve into the phenomenological implications of the 'failed state' and 'arc of instability' (FASAI) thesis. Such imagery has profound implications for security because of the way they cast Pacific communities as potential threats to peace and stability, not only to themselves but also to Australia and New Zealand (the two regional Western powers) and the greater region. The FASAI discourse has been unashamedly repeated over and over again by scholars and the media to provide easy answers to complex problems, to the extent that it has gained near-universal traction as well as being institutionalised (through the introduction of the Fragile State Index) as part of the mainstream political discourse. It has even been used as a basis for framing regional intervention strategies by Australia (Fry & Kabutaulaka, 2008).

I argue that the subtexts behind FASAI go beyond the positivistic level of political science typology. In fact they conjure deeper phenomenological meanings, reminiscent of the social Darwinian idea of racialised stratification that has its theoretical genesis in the Enlightenment. Perhaps the starting point here is Said's notion of orientalism, described as:

> Dealing with the Orient [Third World] by making statements about it, authorizing views of it, describing it, by teaching it, settling it, ruling over it: in short, Orientalism as a Western style for dominating, restructuring, and having authority over the Orient … politically, sociologically, scientifically, and imaginatively. (Said, 1978: 3)

Said was making reference to a host of images predicated on negative stereotypes, paternalism and prejudiced assumptions that shaped European perception of the 'orient', which by and large referred to the postcolonial world. Today, in our changing postmodern world where cyberspace communication, social media and unrestricted information consumption envelop our daily lives, constructed imagery become powerful expressions of security and power that shape our attitude, behaviour and actions.

Over the years a proliferation of negative imagery has been used to 'securitise' the Pacific. This ranges from the region as an 'arc of instability' (Ayson, 2007) consisting of 'failed states' (Wainwright, 2003) to some even making global comparisons by referring to the situation as an 'Africanisation of the Pacific' (Reilly, 2000). An Australian political commentator argued that the notion of 'failed state' might not be reflective of the situation and suggested an equally grim label of 'barbed wire' reality (Dobell, 2007). Some have tried to express 'sympathy' by substituting the term 'arc of opportunity' for the term 'arc of instability' (Wallis, 2015) to reframe the situation, but the fundamental orientalist assumptions are still latent.

While these terms might be recent constructions, the images they conjure have similar deficit and demeaning connotations to the 19th-century notions of 'noble savages', of romantic but primitive Polynesia or the 'ignoble savages' of Melanesia, consisting of morally despicable cannibals some of whom populated the 'Cannibal Isle' (Fiji). These images continue to resonate in such terms as the 'arc of instability' and 'failed states', referring to countries deemed to consist of people who are somewhat politically unstable, unreliable, unsophisticated and warlike; lack values of good governance; are unable to run their economies; and are corrupt and perpetually in a state of intertribal antagonism. Under the façade of diplomacy, racial and cultural prejudices are often concealed but remain as latent cultural variables that seek to justify patronising and often imposing and intimidating approaches by bigger powers in the form of aid and interventionist foreign policy.

FASAI has been much more associated with so-called Melanesia, which itself is a racially loaded terminological designation, which refers to 'black' people of the western Pacific. The term 'Melanesia' has become intellectually institutionalised as a racialised category. Not only does the term describe the colour of skin pigmentation of people but also over the years it conjured up connotations and images associated with savagery, cultural backwardness and intellectual inferiority (Kabutaulaka, 2015). Dumont d'Urville (2003: 164) classified 'the many varieties of the human species that live on the various islands of Oceania' who were different by virtue of 'their many peculiar moral and physical features [which] no doubt require us to regard them as two separate races'. Melanesians, he suggested, are:

> People with very dark, often sooty, skins, sometimes almost as black as that of the Kaffirs, and curly, fuzzy, fluffy but seldom woolly hair. Their features are disagreeable, their build is uneven and their limbs are often frail and deformed … Nevertheless, there is as much variety in skin colour, build and features among the black people of Oceania as among the numerous nations who live on the African continent and make up the race that most authors have referred to as Ethiopian. (Dumont d'Urville, 2003: 164)

The reference to Africa reflected the European obsession with the 'dark continent' mythologised in European travel accounts and literature over the years (as in Joseph Conrad's *Heart of Darkness*) as the antithesis of European civilisation. Similar comparisons between Africa and Melanesia were made by a number of people, including Reilly (2000) and Downer (2003a).

Dumont d'Urville's ideas reflected the growth of essentialism and scientific racism in European thought during the period of the Enlightenment, whereby societies were stratified according to their level of civilisation and progress, and black races were positioned at the lowest stratum of humanity (Fredrickson, 2000). It was not only a matter of skin colour: deeper than that was what Western observers saw as the primitive and decadent nature of their cultural life, their low level of intelligence, their moral depravity and their archaic social system. Scientific racism had roots in the works of Chevalier de Lamarck about the inheritance of inborn biological traits over generations and was given prominence by various scholars, including Charles Darwin, who popularised the theory of evolution in his book, *On the Origin of Species* (Darwin, 1859). Some social scientists used Darwin's theory as a basis for constructing hierarchies of societies according to levels of civilisation. The dominant assumption was that Western societies were the fittest and had the capacity to outlive the inferior black races. This came to be known as social Darwinism, a discourse that heavily influenced some 19th- and 20th-century writers from diverse disciplines (Hodgson, 2004). Early colonial officials such as Fiji's first governor, Sir Arthur Gordon, were not only influenced intellectually and morally by this trend of scholarship but also used it as justification for their colonial policies to control and pacify the colonised who were deemed intellectually and socially inferior.

The Darwinian idea of lineal progression and stratification was prominent in major disciplines such as sociology, anthropology, political science, psychology, philosophy, economics, literature and other areas of study in the 19th and 20th centuries. In the mid-19th century, it shaped the ideas of such social scientists as Auguste Comte, regarded as the father of sociology, Emile Durkheim, Max Weber and even Karl Marx, all of whom attempted to use the 'scientific method' to discover laws of human behaviour to promote human freedom and progress (Seidman, 2008).

By the 20th century, the idea of human progression and hierarchical development was developed further into more complex narratives of social structures, norms and behaviour. Influential American sociologist Talcott Parsons identified variables such as 'particularism', 'ascription' and 'diffusion' as characteristics of primitive societies as opposed to 'efficacy', 'achievement' and 'specificity' for advanced societies (Parsons, 1991). These differentiated societal characteristics became the 'scientific' basis for the modernisation theory, which by the 1960s had become the mainstream development discourse to justify global capitalism. Lerner, a leading American proponent of the modernisation discourse, saw Caucasian races as more advanced intellectually and technologically and boasted:

> Modernity is primarily a state of mind-expectation of progress, propensity to growth, readiness to adapt oneself to change. The nations of the North Atlantic area first developed the social process—secularisation, urbanisation, industrialisation, popular participation—by which this state of mind came to prevail. (Lerner, 1965: viii)

For non-Caucasians, their 'traditional' status, reinforced by inherited characteristics that inhibited their drive towards modernity, would soon give way to superior cosmopolitan cultures. To this end, Cyril Black, in his book, *The Dynamics of Modernisation*, said:

> Cosmopolitan criteria of personal association replace the restraints imposed by race, creed, family and caste. The former divisions between peasants, townspeople and aristocrats have given way to a more homogeneous society in which one's position depends more on individual achievement than on inherited status. (Black, 1966: 19)

The idea of progression and stratification was also prevalent in development economics. One of its proponents, Walt Rostow (1960), outlined five stages of growth, from 'traditional' to 'high mass consumption', which many used as the defining discourse for modernity and legitimation of global capitalism as the only natural system. Rostow's theoretical schema has been criticised for being ahistorical, culturally prejudiced and a justification for US global imperialism. Nevertheless, this narrowly Western-centric view was also prevalent in mainstream political science, where people like Samuel Huntington proclaimed Anglo-Saxon models of liberal democracy to be the most developed and mature form of political system, which ought to be emulated by underdeveloped non-Western societies (Huntington, 1965).

Moreover, by the end of the Cold War, the idea of the triumph of Western culture, capitalism and liberal democracy became an ideological obsession of right-wing scholars such as Huntington and Francis Fukuyama. Fukuyama's *End of History* (1995) used the Hegelian historical dialectics discourse of the contesting interaction between 'thesis' and 'anti-thesis' (representing the competition between capitalism and socialism) to argue that capitalism had finally triumphed. With the collapse of the Soviet empire, Western liberal democracy was seen as the yardstick for political stability, democracy, participation, efficiency and progress while other systems were seen as inappropriate or 'failed'. Despite its fundamentally flawed assumptions and the fact that the 'end of history' thesis quickly became redundant as a result of fast-changing global events, for a short time it had traction and some supporters:

> The rise and fall of nation-states is not new, but in a modern era when national states constitute the building blocks of legitimate world order the violent disintegration and palpable weakness

of selected African, Asian, Oceanic, and Latin American states threaten the very foundation of that system. International organisations and big powers consequently find themselves sucked disconcertingly into a maelstrom of anomic internal conflict and messy humanitarian relief. Desirable international norms such as stability and predictability thus become difficult to achieve when so many of the globe's newer nation-states waver precariously between weakness and failure, with some truly failing, or even collapsing. In a time of terror, moreover, appreciating the nature of and responding to the dynamics of nation-state failure have become central to critical policy debates. How best to strengthen weak states and prevent state failure are among the urgent questions of the twenty-first century. (Rotberg, 2003: 1)

Rotberg's quote above is representative of widespread and entrenched views among the scholarly and diplomatic communities in the West and captures the underlying sentiments of the dominant powers in relation to the so-called 'failed states'. The same sentiments are also reflected in the words of Alexander Downer, Australia's minister for foreign affairs from 1996 to 2007:

When you have a failed state, it's a state that can be exploited by people such as money launderers, drug traffickers, people traffickers, possibly even terrorists. It's an environment which can be exploited by those types of people … It has happened where states have tottered on the edge of failure or in the case of Somalia been failed states. I don't want the analogy of Somalia to be taken too far. But I think these are very real risks and it's important Australians understand that this is expensive; there are some dangers involved in this. It's not highly dangerous like the war in Iraq, but there will be islands to become a failed state and a failed state to fester off the coast of Australia, then we don't know what that failed state could be exploited for, and by whom it could be exploited. But it does constitute risks to Australia in the medium term. (Downer, 2003a)

Downer was securitising Australia's relationship with the Pacific states by directly constructing a security divide, which saw Australia as the victim to be protected from the Pacific threat. The subaltern, postcolonial states of the Pacific, as possible spaces for nurturing terrorists, posed security threats to Australia, an advanced democracy. Rhetoric was different from reality because Australia, not the Pacific Islands, became a fertile breeding ground for terrorists, as evidenced by the capture of a number of terrorists in the country over the following years (Donnelly, 2011). The association made with Somalia intensified the Africanisation imagery that Ben Reilly, an Australian scholar, advocated:

> As these facts suggest, it is hard to escape the conclusion that we are today witnessing the progressive 'Africanisation' of the South Pacific region. 'Africanisation' refers to four interrelated phenomena that have long been associated with violent conflict and the failure of democratic government in Africa: the growing tensions in the relationship between civil regimes and military forces; the intermixture between ethnic identity and the competition for control of natural resources as factors driving conflicts; the weakness of basic institutions of governance such as prime ministers, parliaments and, especially, political parties; and the increasing centrality of the state as a means of gaining wealth and of accessing and exploiting resources. (Reilly, 2000: 262–3)

It has been argued that Reilly's theory is full of inaccurate empirical observations and fallacious assumptions (Fraenkel, 2004).

It was, however, not the first time that the Pacific had been compared to Africa, as we saw earlier in the case of Dumont d'Urville. Since the Enlightenment, Africa has often been seen in the popular Western imagination as a marker of primitivism. The tendency to link the Pacific to African countries is part of the racialisation of discourse that Said was talking about in his orientalism theory. Hall (1996), as we saw in Chapter 2, also elaborated on this in his 'West and the rest' thesis. Critics have argued that the notion of the failed state is a pre-emptive ideological strike weapon that gives big powers an excuse for intervention in the affairs of smaller powers (Nay, 2012). It had been suggested that this is a salient factor in Australia's 'cooperative intervention' policy (Fry & Kabutaulaka, 2008).

The notions of 'failed' and 'fragile' states are not just academic typologies used by both liberal and conservative scholars; they are also widely used as policy and analytical tools in the areas of peace-keeping, development strategies, aid programs, diplomatic negotiations on global security, humanitarian assistance, poverty reduction strategies, international trade agreements and foreign intervention by states, international agencies and even civil society organisations (Wallis, 2015; Fry, 1997; Wainwright, 2003). However, there has been growing criticism that the terms are ideologically and politically defined to distinguish countries that do not conform to Western values and thus provide justification for intervention in these countries under the pretext that they are security threats (Nay, 2012). The invasion of Iraq and the Regional Assistance Mission to the Solomon Islands (RAMSI) were justified by means of this narrative. The terms 'failed' and 'fragile' state are Western-centric and frame the world into a 'them' (failed) versus 'us' (non-failed) binary, which Hall (1996) talked about, and in doing so demarcates the world into a security dichotomy. This is problematic because it attempts to fit all countries into a one size fits all generic security template and ignores their cultural and historical diversity (Call, 2008).

Often the term is defined in a realist way where the state is perceived as a strong and coercive entity and its ability to exert itself on the population determines its legitimacy, stability and robustness. This narrow definition denies the existence of non-state structures, social networks, indigenous world views, cultural capital and informal social systems that keep society together. In addition to this, the term 'failed' state is defined and used liberally in different ways by different people to suit their political interests. As such it often takes on very negative connotations, which are readily used to condemn, intimidate or dismiss the state as unworthy of being included in the civilised global order.

Thus, in the broader context of Pacific regional security, the terms used matter as they can shape perception, behaviour and policies. Concepts are not isolated symbols but are part of a bigger language–cultural system that frames the world in particular ways. The terms 'failed' and 'fragile' state and 'arc of instability' are securitising terms that define images of the Pacific to suit the political and ideological fashion of the beholders. They are not 'neutral' political science typologies as some scholars want to pretend but loaded concepts that reinforce the 'them' versus 'us' security dichotomy as well as transforming the nature of interstate relationships. They are among the latest classificatory concepts within the broader discourse of lineal progression and stratification of humanity and have their theoretical genesis in the Enlightenment. Inherent in this is the dichotomous idea of 'advanced' versus 'primitive' and, in this case, 'successful' versus 'failed'. Within this dominant world view, European societies belong to the positive and non-European societies belong to the negative sides of the equation. This same intellectual tradition had branded Pacific societies as 'savages' and now deems them to have 'failed'. The point to make here is that the demarcation and ranking of people and repetition of words to reinforce these judgements becomes part of the political language and reality and an integral part of the Pacific security discourse over time.

Often Pacific regional security is defined and understood only in relation to events and geopolitical relationships. While this is significant, it is also important to understand the more subjective meanings of labels and imagery used to categorise countries and people. They represent certain views, assumptions and attitudes, often hidden behind the veneer of diplomacy, yet which have the potential to shape security thinking and policies in profound ways.

Securitising the Pacific as generic region: Deconstructing the myth

The 'Pacific' is often seen in generic terms as a region consisting of people of similar cultures, thinking and social systems. In New Zealand, for instance, the term *Pasifika*, a 'localised' version of Pacific, implies people of similar identities who are stereotyped as dumb, fat, lazy and welfare parasite 'coconuts' (Salesa, 2017). A similar deficit insinuation is implicit in the term 'arc of instability', which paints the Pacific as a bunch of countries that share the same 'unstable' characteristics that make them 'vulnerable'. There is a subconscious assumption about a virus of instability spreading like wildfire across the Pacific and enveloping the region in an infectious way. In the broader security prism, the Pacific is seen as a high-risk and volatile area that needs constant supervision and oversight by big powers.

These generalisations do not take into consideration the different historical, socioeconomic and sociocultural specificities of individual countries and the fact that their security issues are unique to their particular conditions and are not a shared characteristic. A broad scan across the Pacific from west to east will show not a pattern of similarities but a range of diversity in terms of historical experiences, sociopolitical structures, cultural norms and the factors that led to conflicts. I want to emphasise this point by briefly examining the situations in a number of countries and identifying their salient differences.

Let us start with Timor Leste, the westernmost state in the arc. Perched on the Asia-Pacific 'border', Timor Leste has been going through a process of post-independence transformation after years of colonial subjugation under the Portuguese, later the Japanese and, most recently, the Indonesians. Tens of thousands of Timorese lost their lives over the years as a result of brutality by the Japanese and Indonesian invaders. Their eventual independence in 2002 provided a chance to construct a new nation from the ashes of colonial dismemberment and civil war (Jardine, 2002). When the Indonesians invaded East Timor in 1975, Australia, Britain and the United States were complicit parties by endorsing Indonesia's takeover. Australia continues to be a beneficiary of its proximity to East Timor by claiming oil reserves within East Timor's territorial waters. This has put a choke hold on Timor Leste's economic capacity and is a major cause of the rift between the two countries. While the 'arc' theory places the blame for political misfortune on the incapacity of the country's people to sort out their own domestic affairs, the contribution of external colonial actors are often ignored. Colonisation, wars and genocide have ravaged the country so badly that it has taken considerable effort by the international and local communities to rebuild it. The simplistic label of 'unstable' does not help in understanding the country's complex colonial history.

Next door to Timor Leste is West Papua, whose only link with Timor Leste is having a common colonial power in the form of Indonesia. West Papua had been a playground for resource competition by the European powers, but the Dutch eventually made their claim in the 1800s. Indonesia claimed West Papua as well as other Dutch colonies when it became independent in the 1940s (Leadbeater, 2018). West Papua was caught up in broader Cold War politics with the United States. This thwarted the West Papuan move towards independence. Negotiations led to the New York Agreement in 1962, whereby the United States and the Netherlands, with the support of other powers and the United Nations, conspired to transfer the territory to Indonesia. To legitimise the deal, the United States supervised the Act of Free Choice as a referendum to determine whether West Papuans wanted independence or integration with Indonesia. The Indonesians picked 1,025 men out of 800,000 people and coerced them into making their pro-Indonesian choice. The vote was considered 'unanimous', and West Papua became the twenty-sixth province of Indonesia under its new name of West Irian. West Papua's relentless struggle for independence, in which hundreds of thousands of people have died, continues to this day (Leadbeater, 2018).

The point to note here is that most of the problems of West Papua thus far have been due to foreign colonial interests, including big mining conglomerates like Freeport, which benefits handsomely from Indonesia's colonialism. West Papuans do not have a state of their own to run, and this distinguishes them from other Pacific states in the 'arc'.

The situation in Bougainville (Papua New Guinea) had unique features that were different from the previous two cases because it involved indigenous landowner resistance to the exploitative and environmentally destructive extraction of their resources by Rio Tinto, the Australian mining conglomerate, facilitated by the Papua national government. The violence that followed shifted from a military-style confrontation between the Papua New Guinea Defence Force and the Bougainville Revolutionary Army to intracommunity violence. The consequences for the small Bougainville community were devastating. A peace agreement and the eventual setting up of an elected autonomous government paved the way for political stability, but the task of creating a viable economy with or without mining and total independence from Papua New Guinea remains a major challenge for the future. A planned referendum will eventually determine the future of the country (Adams, 2002).

On the PNG mainland itself, issues of law and order are not necessarily linked to Bougainville but are consequences of the country's dramatic transformation from a tribal subsistence economy with community-based sociocultural structures and norms to full-blown capitalism and liberal democracy. Enthused by an abundance of cash from natural resources, the grey area between tradition and modernity has been the site for violence, crime and corruption. This is a major challenge for many resourceful postcolonial societies where the state becomes the conduit between competing modes of production and competing elites vying for power and resources (Lucker & Dinnen, 2010).

Solomon Islands, as a former British protectorate, also has a very different colonial history from Timor Leste and West Papua. It was largely governed through the British governor in Fiji, who was also high commissioner for the western Pacific. The paternalistic governance arrangements created tension between the British and the locals, and often the punitive reaction of the British was swift. This served only to worsen the relationship. The establishment of the colonial plantation economy created a system of internal labour migration, and the consequent pressures on land and resources contributed to tension between the people of Guadalcanal, who were the local landowners, and the people of Malaita, who were mostly migrant labourers (Moore, 2004). The growing inequality and power imbalance further aggravated the tension, which erupted into full-fledged intertribal violence in 1999. Regional intervention through RAMSI was an Australian-funded regional initiative to respond to the escalating security situation in Solomon Islands. RAMSI will be examined in more detail in Chapter 6.

The Vanuatu situation is quite different from the Timorese, West Papua, Bougainville and Solomon Islands situations in several respects. Vanuatu was a condominium (joint colony) of France and Britain and, while there was an attempt at secession by a group backed by French and other business interests, the country has been relatively stable, except for riots in 1989, a prison breakout, the occasional stand-off between the police and the military, and changes in government as a result of changing loyalty of politicians. The National Council of Chiefs, or Malvatu Mauri, has been a strong cultural pillar in reconciliation in times of disturbances. Competition over wealth by the elites, as seen in PNG, is not much of an issue in Vanuatu because of a lack of mineral resources. Instead, there is a major push by the government and community for preservation of the subsistence indigenous economy and a disdain for individualistic capitalism (Wirrick, 2008). However, there have also been cases of corruption involving politicians and, in a recent case, a former prime minister was imprisoned for bribing other parliamentarians, who also met the same fate.

Fiji's political and security situations are quite distinctive from those of other countries mentioned for a number of reasons. For a start, a large diaspora population consisting mainly of Indo-Fijians, together with other ethnic groups, shaped both the demographic and ethno-power politics, which largely revolved around contestation for power by the indigenous Taukei and the Indo-Fijians. Although ethnicity has often been seen as 'the' major driver of conflict in Fiji, the situation is much more complex and needs to be understood in terms of the dynamic interplay between ethnicity, elite competition for political power, socioeconomic inequality, intracommunal loyalty, racialised perception, religious affiliation, role of the military, cultural identity and the politics of land and resources. On top of these is the role of ethnic entrepreneurs in whipping up ethnic sentiments to serve political ends. The coups in Fiji between 1987 and 2006 were associated with various combinations of some of these, and in any particular case some factors would be more dominant than others (Ratuva, 2011a).

While some of the variables associated with Fiji politics might be similar to those present in other PICs, the nexus between them, including the historical and the sociopolitical circumstances under which they occur, are quite different from interactions elsewhere, and the results and consequences are also different.

Although, in terms of history, genealogy and culture, Tonga and Fiji share a lot in common, the factors that shape their internal security situations are very different indeed. Tonga's political conflict emanates primarily from its rigid class system, whereby the monarchy and its loyal band of nobles rule over an increasingly disgruntled commoner class (Campbell, 2011a).

The differences between the hereditary ruling class's desire to maintain its power and privileges and the commoner's desire for emancipation from the clutches of the constitutional monarch through greater democratisation of the political system led to tension, culminating in the 2006 riots. The constitutional reforms in 2010 saw the relinquishing of some power by the monarch and the establishment of provisions to enable the first commoner prime minister to be elected.

In Samoa, conflict tends to be confined to villages, where social fractures caused by disputes over land and titles are pervasive and are among the major causes of tension and instability (Tiffany, 1980). Although Samoa does not have a military, unlike Fiji, Tonga, Vanuatu (which has a paramilitary force) and PNG, it does have a well-equipped riot police unit armed with semi-automatic high-powered rifles, which is deployed when there is a serious security situation. The widespread use of firearms in village conflicts in Samoa is a threat to future stability in a country where strict adherence to tradition and admiration for modernity are simultaneously celebrated in a paradoxical way.

Conflict in the French territories of New Caledonia and French Polynesia has been influenced largely by socio-economic inequality and resistance to colonial rule, although there are also existing intercommunal tensions between non-French groups (Fisher, 2013). In New Caledonia, violence in the form of killings, hostage crises, riots and assassinations have been common. The referendum on independence on 4 November 2018 was won by anti-independence voters (56.4 per cent to 43.6 per cent), a victory that was followed by unrest triggered by dissatisfied indigenous Kanaks. Under the Noumea Accord agreed between the political leaders, there is a possibility of further referendums in 2020 and 2022 (Fisher, 2018).

However, as yet, there is no timetable for independence for French Polynesia, although it has been reinscribed on the UN decolonisation list despite protests by France. The push for independence is still strong, and how it plays out in the future remains to be seen.

These brief examples show that conflicts among the Pacific countries have little relationship with each other in terms of one directly influencing the other. While it is undeniable that national conflicts have some degree of influence on regional politics and security in terms of regional responses, they are generally self-contained and, apart from RAMSI in Solomon Islands, solutions to conflicts are often found within the affected countries themselves. The growing consciousness about peace-building at the regional level has led to the growth of civil society organisations, regional organisations such as the Pacific Islands Forum Secretariat (PIFS) and international organisations such as UNDP, participating actively in conflict resolution and security projects. Regional solutions to national conflict problems might work up to a point, but, for sustainability, local citizens must be at the helm in providing direction and the appropriate mechanisms.

The point here is that securitising an entire region using generalised narratives such as 'arc of instability', 'Pacific identity', 'Pacific way', 'Pacific security' and so forth does little to eliminate complex local realities. While there are of course shared security issues relating to inequality, gender, climate change, poverty and other human security factors, these are universal conditions, happening elsewhere in the world, which emanate from similar circumstances taking place simultaneously but are not transmitted from one country to another. Addressing specific historical conditions and their local consequences is important in understanding the security situation more clearly, rather than framing generalised securitising narratives and labels that neither illuminate the historical and security reality nor help in formulating viable strategies for addressing them. This is the reason for using the detailed comparative case studies approach in this book.

Geopolitical security narratives and responses

Because it is sandwiched between the major powers in the form of the United States to the east and Russia and China to the west, the Pacific Ocean has inevitably become a common space for strategic, political and economic interaction (Ratuva, 2014). While the economic and strategic focus has been on Asia, the PICs, despite their small size, also play a vital role in the bigger strategic picture. The geopolitical significance of the Pacific to global politics was first realised during World War II when it became the battleground against Japanese invasion. Almost all countries in the northern and western Pacific were invaded by Japanese forces, and other PICs contributed to the war effort by sending soldiers to fight the invading Japanese military (Van der Vat, 1992).

The end of World War II and the start of the Cold War heralded a new era of Pacific regional security. The two contending nuclear powers, the US and the USSR, and their respective allies, used the Pacific for naval and other military bases, and as a testing ground and deployment arena for their forces (Firth, 1987). Meanwhile, PICs—many of which were colonies of Western powers like Britain, Australia, New Zealand, France and the Netherlands—were shepherded into a Western sphere of influence to prevent their being influenced by communism.

One of the first attempts to do so was the setting up of the South Pacific Commission (SPC) under the Canberra Agreement of 1947. The work and policy prescriptions of the SPC, consisting of the colonial powers and their colonies, were based on technical and developmental issues and deliberately ignored political and security matters that were of concern to most PICs. The need to openly address political and security issues such as independence and nuclear testing, which the colonial powers were not willing to discuss, was a decisive factor that led to the formation of the Pacific Islands Forum in 1971 by the independent PICs (Crocombe, 2001).

Regional security in the Pacific from the 1940s to the 1980s was very much shaped by Cold War geopolitics. Under the policy of 'strategic denial', the ANZUS (Australia, New Zealand and United States) treaty provided a broad security umbrella to keep Soviet influence at bay and to maintain the Pacific as an 'American lake' (Hayes, Zarsky & Bellow, 1987). Aid was an important source of leverage to ensure that PICs remained within the

ANZUS political and ideological orbit at a time when PICs were eager to express their independent identities in a dramatically changing world. To cement their nuclear and strategic capabilities, the major colonial powers—the United States, France and Britain—tested nuclear bombs in their respective territories (Firth, 1987). The United States tested their bombs in the Marshall Islands from 1946 to 1958, France on Moruroa Atoll in French Polynesia from 1966 to 1996 and Britain on Christmas Island in Kiribati from 1956 to 1958. Within the half-century from 1946 to 1996, the three nuclear powers conducted more than 315 nuclear tests in the Pacific (Maclellan, 2015).

These tests had environmental, health, economic and political consequences for the islands. Many islanders, like servicemen who were involved, were exposed to large doses of deadly radioactive materials, which continued to linger over the years. In the broader geopolitical context, the tests incorporated the Pacific peoples as reluctant participants in the realities of Cold War contestation and the arms race and made them pawns in the swirling politics of global power. While it is easy to dismiss nuclear tests as merely matters of military and strategic interest, we must not forget that they had a profound influence in providing coercive legitimacy to colonialism at a time when anti-colonial 'winds of change' were blowing around the world. The nuclear bombs were a symbolic representation of the big powers' hegemonic territorial claims, although, unlike the local population, citizens of the big powers did not have to live with the environmental and health consequences. Having said this, it is important to also emphasise that many servicemen involved in the tests suffered both short-term and long-term health consequences as a result of the tests (Maclellan, 2018).

The tests were just part of the broader trend of militarisation in the Pacific in the form of military bases and alliances. Although the United States was, at least in terms of Roosevelt's rhetoric, not predisposed towards classical British-type colonialism, it nonetheless had formal control of a number of PCIs in the north, which it used to serve its strategic interests. As part of its strategic containment thrust against the Soviet Union, the United States had numerous military bases and other military facilities around the Asia-Pacific region. There were 343 of these in 1947, 235 in 1949, 291 in 1953, 256 in 1957, 271 in 1967, 183 in 1975 and 121 in 1988 (Blaker, 1990). The number of bases decreased further over the years, especially after the Cold War.

Sandwiched between the two major contesting adversarial powers, the Pacific people found themselves reluctant players in a game of domination by foreign powers, and this inspired the establishment in 1975 of people-led resistance movements against nuclear imperialism in the form of the Nuclear Free and Independent Pacific (NFIP) movement (Robie, 1992). This testified to the growing discontent of Pacific peoples about the activities of the major powers in their part of the world, as well as concern about the future security and livelihood of the region (Maclellan, 2015). The multiple campaign issues of the NFIP movement recognised the interconnected nature of different aspects of colonial hegemony, including nuclear tests, land rights, militarisation, unequal and exploitative development, human rights, colonialism, environmental degradation and other related concerns. For a long time it was the major critical voice against colonialism and the major advocacy network for both hard and human security in the Pacific.

It must be remembered that the NFIP movement was part of the wave of anti-nuclear sentiment that swept the world. In the Pacific this led to the declaration in 1984 of a Nuclear Free New Zealand by the ruling New Zealand Labour Party under Prime Minister David Lange, who, in an Oxford Union debate against Jerry Falwell, leader of the American Moral Majority, declared nuclear weapons to be 'morally indefensible' (Lange, 2004). This was followed by the signing of the South Pacific Nuclear Free Zone Treaty (SPNFZ) by 13 member countries of the Pacific Islands Forum on 6 August 1985 in Rarotonga, Cook Islands. As we will see later, the SPNFZ was the first regional security agreement, and it set the tone for more regional security agreements in the future.

By the end of the Cold War there was a dramatic shift in the regional security configuration as a result of both internal and external dynamics. The United States started to reduce its economic assistance to PICs, except for its northern Pacific territories. It closed the USAID office in Suva and reduced its military presence around the Asia-Pacific region, including closing the Subic Bay naval base and Clark air force base in the Philippines and reducing the numbers of military personnel in Japan. This withdrawal meant that Guam, in the North Pacific, became the major fall-back position.

The resulting strategic vacuum in the Pacific was quickly filled by China, a growing world power whose economic and political influence in the Pacific increased greatly as a result of its soft power approach in the form of aid and other non-military means (Wilkins, 2010). This has been a major challenge to Australia and New Zealand, two close allies of the United States, whose sense of territorial hegemony as major regional players was often based on the rather paternalistic ideological assumption that the Pacific was their 'backyard' (Fry & Kabutaulaka, 2008).

The involvement of external powers in the Pacific had a competitive dimension, with countries trying to win support and loyalty. Obama's pivot to Asia and the Pacific saw the intensification of US economic, political and strategic engagement in the Asia-Pacific region at a time when China had established itself as a major Pacific power. Over the years, China had outdone the United States in providing aid to the Pacific and in gaining diplomatic leverage (Ratuva, 2014). Concerns about losing control of the Pacific (Hayes, Zarsky & Bello, 1987) inspired a reversal of the immediate post–Cold War strategy of rolling back from engagement with the region towards re-engagement, culminating in the visits to the Pacific by presidents Bush and Obama, as well as senior US officials such as Hillary Clinton, who attended the Pacific Island Forum leaders meeting in Rarotonga in 2012. The PICs have always voted with the United States and the Western allies in the UN general assembly, and this was an asset the Western bloc did not want to lose to China or any other potential adversary.

On the other hand, the Chinese, who have become the largest aid donor for many Pacific states, had to deal not only with the United States but also with Taiwan in a long-running battle for global recognition (Atkinson, 2010). Since the 1980s, both have been involved in cheque book diplomacy as a way of gaining recognition as the legitimate representative of the Chinese people among the PICs. Taiwan actually needs recognition by other states as a way of fulfilling the UN definition of a 'state'. Six countries in the Pacific (Marshall Islands, Solomon Islands, Tuvalu, Nauru, Palau and Kiribati) recognise Taiwan as a result of economic inducements. The competition between China and Taiwan has influenced the behaviour of political elites and internal political instability in various ways in Solomon Islands, Vanuatu (which changed allegiance) and Kiribati over the years (Ratuva, 2014).

Apart from the Chinese, other powers like Russia and Georgia began to show interest in the Pacific Islands because of their voting potential in the United Nations. Russia has been campaigning for recognition by the United Nations of the Georgian breakaway provinces of South Ossetia and Abkhasia, whereas Georgia has been adamant that this is not going to happen. Both countries therefore splashed money to win hearts, minds and, of course, votes (Ratuva, 2014). The Arab League also actively campaigned in the Pacific before the UN vote to accord Palestine a 'non-member observer state' status in 2012. Four Pacific states (Nauru, Palau, Marshall Islands and Federated States of Micronesia) voted against Palestine, and the rest abstained. Indonesia has also been actively campaigning diplomatically to counter the region-wide support for West Papuan independence (Firth, 2013).

Among the Pacific island states themselves, the existence of subregional groupings in the form of the Melanesian Spearhead Group and the separate leaders' meetings of the Polynesian and Micronesian groups has created a certain degree of political division in the region, although they have not really led to any deep fragmentation in the region. Perhaps the most divisive issue revolved around Fiji. After Fiji's suspension from the PIF, it proceeded to set up its own alternative regional body called the Pacific Islands Development Forum (PIDF) (Dornan, 2013).

The tension between Fiji and the two big Pacific powers, Australia and New Zealand (whom Fiji consistently accused of spearheading its suspension from the PIF), had repercussions for regional stability and security. Fiji used the opportunity to engage proactively with its 'look north policy', which saw China being embraced as a saviour in Fiji's hour of need. The close political, economic and military links between Fiji and China raised concerns among the Western powers, which felt threatened by what they saw as China's expansionist agenda in the central Pacific, close to Australia and New Zealand. Relationships between Fiji, Australia and New Zealand began to thaw, and full diplomatic relations were restored after the Fiji general elections in 2014. Despite that, tension still lurks beneath the surface.

The brief regional security narrative above is really meant to provide a broad overview of some of the salient geopolitical issues that have shaped the geopolitical security environment in the Pacific. There are a number of important points to remember here. First, while the individual countries have unique historical experiences and internal sociopolitical dynamics, as discussed earlier, at another level, they are linked by strands of security policies, thinking and practices, emanating from external powers or from among the PICs. Regional security therefore becomes the site for negotiation between national sovereign security interests and collective regional and global security interests. Second, when we talk about regional security, we are referring to a changing and dynamic phenomenon. Changes in the geopolitical balance of power, as witnessed at the end of the Cold War and with the rise of China, often result in changing security dynamics and responses of individual PICs or groups of PICs (as a regional bloc). Third, the PICs often find themselves subsumed into a vortex of security contestation of the big powers, as we saw during the Cold War and the period after. In some cases, PICs saw themselves as pawns in the power game between the contending external powers (Ratuva, 2017a). Fourth, PICs can no longer ignore the fact that they are now part of the bigger global security agenda, and the challenge they face is how they redefine their identity in a way that comfortably facilitates both the local and global narratives. Fifth, as we saw in the case of Fiji, emerging fault lines caused by political differences may see more intraregional tension, more so at a time when subregional groups are beginning to exert their identity and significance. The last point here is that, in the long term, regional security problems will need to be sorted out internally using local mechanisms for conflict resolution. This should be built into the regional architecture as part of the political process rather than something to be activated only when problems arise.

Regional security mechanisms

Members of the PIF countries share a growing consciousness about their role in determining the future trajectory of regional security as a result of emerging issues relating to transnational crime, development, environmental concerns and political stability (Anderson & Watson, 2005). The response by the PIF was to put in place a number of declarations that were meant to be guidelines for dealing with emerging security situations. The first of these was the Declaration on Law Enforcement (Honiara Declaration) signed in Honiara, the capital of Solomon Islands, in 1992 (PIF, 1992). Although this declaration focused largely on regional cooperation regarding law enforcement relating to crime, it had the latent function of regionalising the security concerns of individual PIF countries. The rationale was that an adverse law enforcement environment posed a major threat to the sovereignty, security and stability of the region. The Forum Regional Security Committee (FRSC), consisting of security-related government personnel and departments, was tasked with coordinating security-related activities and met just before the leaders' meeting in order to provide advice for the leaders on matters pertaining to security.

Five years later, in 1997, the PIF leaders crafted the Aitutaki Declaration during their retreat on the island of Aitutaki in the Cook Islands. This agreement was more comprehensive than the Honiara Declaration and was far more specific about issues of regional security. It outlined a number of principles relating to: promoting a comprehensive, integrated and collaborative approach to security; good governance, sustainable development and international cooperation, including preventive diplomacy; overcoming vulnerability, building mutual confidence and strengthening the overall security of states in the region; and recognition of the need to resolve conflict by peaceful means, including by customary practices. An interesting aspect of the Aitutaki Declaration was the recognition of the need for preventive diplomacy using the FRSC, the offices of the Forum Secretary General, eminent persons, fact-finding missions and third-party mediation (PIF, 1997).

These principles reflected the shifting realities on the ground, anxiety about unpredictable political conflict and the need for collective responses with an emphasis on preventive measures. However, it just fell short of prescribing intervention—this was to be provided for by the Biketawa Declaration. Signed in Kiribati in November 2000, the Biketawa Declaration was a direct response to the Fiji coup in May 2000 and the Solomon Islands political crisis of the same year. It reiterated and also tightened up key aspects of the Aitutaki Declaration, but perhaps the most significant provision dealt with the possibility of intervention. While it respected 'the principle of non-interference in the domestic affairs of another member state', the Biketawa Declaration proclaimed:

> Forum Leaders recognised the need in time of crisis or in response to members' request for assistance, for action to be taken on the basis of all members of the Forum being part of the Pacific Islands' extended family. The Forum must constructively address difficult and sensitive issues including underlying causes of tensions and conflict (ethnic tensions, socioeconomic disparities, lack of good governance, land disputes and erosion of cultural values). (PIF, 2000: 1)

One of the significant aspects of this provision was that possible intervention was to be requested by a member country. A formal request by the Solomon Islands Government led eventually to the signing of the agreement for RAMSI deployment in 2003. However, the situation was much more complex than it appeared to be. Two Solomon Islands prime ministers had earlier made requests to Australia in 2000 and 2001, at the height of the conflict, but these were turned down. In fact the Australian Foreign Minister, Alexander Downer, was adamant that:

> Sending in Australian troops to occupy the Solomon Islands would be folly in the extreme. It would be widely resented in the Pacific region. It would be difficult to justify to Australian taxpayers. And for how many years would such an occupation have to continue? And what would be the exit strategy? The real show-stopper, however, is that it would not work … foreigners do not have answers for the deep-seated problems afflicting Solomon Islands. (Downer, 2003a)

As a result of 9/11 and the changing global security climate, Australia made a U-turn and agreed to the Solomon Islands' request. Underpinning this change in view was the assumption that Solomon Islands was a 'failed state' and a potential breeding ground for terrorists, from where they could attack Australia. Thus, on 24 July 2003, Solomon Islands signed an agreement with six member states of the Pacific Islands Forum, namely Australia, New Zealand, Papua New Guinea, Fiji, Tonga and Samoa, to allow the security forces from those countries to enter Solomon Islands under the umbrella of RAMSI. We will look at the details of the conflict in Solomon Islands, as well as some of the shortcomings of RAMSI, in Chapter 6.

On the other hand, the PIF response to the Fiji crisis in 2006 was an exercise in futility because Fiji's coup leader, Commodore Frank Bainimarama, did not take the eminent persons delegation of the forum seriously and ignored the PIF's appeal for an early election. This was one of the reasons for Fiji's suspension from the PIF, a decision that still has repercussions today. Fiji's suspension provided it with an opportunity to create an alternative geopolitical configuration to suit its regional ambitions. We look at the Fiji situation in more detail in Chapter 4.

While the Biketawa Declaration has attracted considerable attention, little is known of the Nasonini Declaration, another regional agreement signed in the wake of 9/11 following the UN Security Council Resolution 1373 on counter-terrorism. Signed in Suva in 2002, this was an anti-terrorism declaration framed within the broader rubric of global and regional security. Governments and regions around the world were required to put in place anti-terrorism mechanisms in support of Resolution 1373 and, for the PIF states, the Nasonini Declaration, named after the Suva suburb where the PIFS office is located and where the signing took place, was part of their contribution to the war on terror.

While the various security declarations above unified the Pacific under formal security rubrics, the reality on the ground in terms of internal political dynamics is more complex than any universal regional agreement can fully grasp. Even the Pacific Plan, which was created in 2005 as a blueprint for regional governance, growth, sustainable development and security, failed to address the multiplicity and complexity of security issues. The new Regional Framework established in 2015, and meant to be the substitute for the Pacific Plan, has been facing difficulties in terms of implementation because of the challenges in addressing the diversity and complexity of security issues.

Regional human security: Integrating diversity

We saw in Chapter 2 how the notion of human security has taken global policy thinking by storm since the 1990s. Although human security is a relatively new concept in the Pacific, its influence on regional and national policies has grown exponentially over the years. This growth is due to the combined efforts of international agencies and aid donors in instilling the virtues of human security in Pacific island states and civil society organisations through multilateral and bilateral relations, aid, policy engagement and civic education. Although hard security has been the dominant regional narrative (see for instance Henderson & Watson, 2005), the affirmative reception to the concept of human security is due to its all-encompassing nature, which blended well into Pacific indigenous cultural world views where political, social, economic, psychological and cultural components of life are inseparably linked.

The regional human security framework is a result of a series of consultations between the UNDP, PIFS, civil society organisations and governments over a period of a few months in 2007. The consultations arrived at some degree of broad understanding about some of the shared human security issues in the Pacific relating to development, land, ethnic relations, climate change, environment, resources distribution, inequality, gender, education, human rights and other issues (UNDP, 2007). Nevertheless, there is still a divergence of opinions over what human security should specifically entail, especially given the diversity of Pacific cultures and national interests. For instance, there is debate as to whether human security should be framed in terms of threat to individuals, as the UNDP argued, or threat to the community, as many Pacific civil society organisations suggested during the consultation. The compromise reached was that both are important. One of the lessons learnt by UNDP during a regional consultation in Nadi, Fiji, was that the cultural context is important and, for many Pacific communities whose ethos revolves around communal-based and semi-subsistence life, well-being is fundamentally defined by the shared culture of the group.

The 2007 consultations, which were attended by the author, also reached a consensus that gender equality was a critical issue in understanding the security of the group, especially in times of transition and conflict in predominantly patriarchal Pacific communities. Gender issues, it must be noted, permeate social categories and communities, although how they are conceptualised differs considerably across the social spectrum; at one end of the continuum are the more conservative cultural traditionalists and fundamentalist Christians, who believe in the natural inferiority of women, while on the other side of the scale are the more educated and progressive thinkers who believe in gender equality (UNDP, 2007). And there are, of course, those who oscillate in between. Participants in the consultation saw the progressive position as providing the necessary ideological fulcrum for the future trajectory of gender relations and social transformation in the Pacific. The tension between the two ends of the social continuum will continue, and arriving at a consensus, especially at the national and community levels, is a major challenge.

One of the major challenges with the operationalisation of the concept of human security in the Pacific is the difficulty in incorporating it into public policies in a genuinely serious way. The political pressure by donors and international partners might open up possibilities of countries manufacturing data that could get them a higher ranking in the UNDP Human Development Index (HDI), where human security variables are used extensively. Annual reports of human security projects are also written in an exaggerated way to please donors. The lack of expertise in appropriate interdisciplinary field methodologies is a major drawback, more so because most professionals in the Pacific are trained in a mono-disciplinary fashion. Another major drawback is the lack of consciousness of what human security is and its importance in national development.

In response to these concerns, PIFS devised a common template for a human security framework for the small island states. The framework resulted from a region-wide consultation in collaboration with UNDP, other regional organisations, civil society organisations and government agencies. The framework aims to 'provide a clear common foundation and strategic guidance to Forum Island Countries, the Secretariat and other stakeholders for improving the understanding, planning and implementation of human security approaches in stand-alone and broader peace, security and development initiatives in the unique Pacific context' (PIF, 2009). Apart from the consultations held between 2006 and 2008, the framework also draws from the major regional security declarations including the Aitutaki Declaration (PIF, 1997), Biketawa Declaration (2000), Leaders' Vision (2004), Pacific Plan (revised 2007) and directives from the FRSC in Outcome Statements (2006–11).

One of the problems with the framework is that it is too rigid in its definition and, at the same time, too abstract; it lacks clarity about the way it is to be actualised in unique real-life Pacific situations. One of the PIF's dilemmas is to ensure that policy-makers in member governments understand the policy utility and beneficial outcomes of human security in relation to development, governance, well-being and security generally. Even the FRSC, whose task is to provide regional security policy direction for the Forum leaders, has been unable to fathom the significance of the term. At its Auckland meeting in 2008, attended by the author, it was clear that 'hard' security was still paramount and should remain a primary factor in the regional human security framework. This position was not surprising because of the way in which traditional hard security psychology was firmly implanted in the perception and ideology of state institutions. It will take time to ensure that human security becomes an integral component of contemporary strategic and policy thinking.

Although the regional human security framework is based on the five principles of being preventive, localised, inclusive, collaborative and people-centred, there is no clear direction as to how these are to be applied in practice. Not only does the framework lack internal conceptual coherence, it also lacks analytical depth and strategic direction for effective implementation. It is largely an isolated document created by regional bureaucrats who have minimal links to communities outside the PIFS headquarters in Suva, Fiji.

Free trade and human security

In recent years, the impact of free trade on Pacific communities, especially its impact on human security, has been vigorously debated. Central to the debate is whether free trade is necessary to enhance the development of Pacific societies or is destructive to their lives and undermines their well-being. The discussions have revolved around the possible impact of PACER Plus, the region's most recent free trade agreement, which was signed on 14 June 2017 by Australia, New Zealand, Tonga, Niue, Nauru, Samoa, Solomon Islands, Kiribati, Tuvalu and Cook Islands.[1] Fiji, Papua New Guinea and Vanuatu refused to sign, although Vanuatu has since changed its mind and will probably sign soon. Other countries that did not sign were Marshall Islands, Palau and Federated States of Micronesia, and the excuse given was transportation difficulties.

Proponents of PACER Plus are of the view that regional free trade is a panacea for the future growth challenges of PICs' economies. Trade liberalisation and alignment with World Trade Organization (WTO) trade rules, it is argued, will allow for greater competition and a wider variety of choices in terms of goods and services for Pacific customers, thus driving down prices. Although import tariffs, an important source of revenue for governments, will be lifted, based on a formula implemented progressively over time, advocates of neoliberal policies firmly contend that other forms of taxation such as Value Added Tax (VAT) will make up for the deficit. For instance, Ronald Duncan, a well-known Australian scholar and advocate of neoliberal economics argued:

> Trade liberalisation with the rest of the world is likely to be the most beneficial policy for Pacific countries to follow, whether done unilaterally or by joining the WTO … Once trade liberalisation is identified as an important policy reform, the most important issue

---

1   Apart from PACER Plus, other regional trade agreements include the South Pacific Regional Trade and Economic Cooperation Agreement (SPARTECA), a non-reciprocal preferential agreement between the PICs and including Australia and New Zealand, which started in the 1980s; Pacific Island Countries Trade Agreement (PICTA) between the PICs and excluding Australia and New Zealand; and the Economic Partnership Agreement (EPA), a trade agreement with the European Union.

would be the identification and removal of the binding constraints to its adoption. These may be institutional, economic, policy-related, or cultural, among others—including the opposition of vested interests. Within the Pacific, opposition to open markets is very strong and supported by vested interests, ideology, and cultural beliefs. Economic issues also constrain the response to changes in the terms of trade through trade liberalisation, such as insecurity of land tenure and poor access to credit. (Duncan, 2008: x)

The reference to social and cultural issues as 'binding constraints' that need 'removal' represents a typical neoliberal narrative, which sees unrestrained hard economics as undisputedly paramount over other aspects of human security. The reference by Duncan to 'vested interests' is contentious because it assumes that critics of free trade in the Pacific, who largely consist of academics, activists and civil society organisations, somehow stand to gain financially from the absence of free trade.

In 2009, Australia's Minister for Trade, Simon Crean, vaunted the virtues of PACER Plus as both a free trade and development-based agreement that goes a long way to integrating the Pacific economies as well as opening up their borders to a greater flow of goods, labour and services:

> PACER Plus is not just a trade agreement: it is fundamentally concerned with developing the capacity of the Pacific region. It is clear that PACER Plus could address a number of issues common to the whole region. For example, how to comply with the quarantine requirements into Australia and New Zealand; developing consistent rules of origin within the region; the importance of improving aviation links to encourage greater tourism; and liberalisation of the telecommunications industry are just a few areas that have been raised with me. It is also clear that there is great potential to develop a region-wide labour mobility and skills development program for the Pacific. Of course, each country will have individual concerns specific to their nation and people—and we envisage that this too will be part of the structure of future discussions as we move forward. (Crean, 2009)

Although in the same speech Crean denied that Australia pressured the PIF to start negotiation on PACER Plus, the chief trade adviser for the PICs, Dr Chris Noonan (a University of Auckland academic), thought otherwise: 'The pressure to negotiate a WTO-compatible agreement is coming from Australia and New Zealand rather than the Forum Island Countries. That's been the whole history of the PACER-Plus process' (Maclellan, 2011).

Australia and New Zealand committed themselves to providing funds of up to A$1 million initially for three years for the Office of Chief Trade Adviser (OCTA) to provide advice for the PICs in response to their plea for more advice and capacity-building towards future negotiations. This financial offer complicated matters because it was perceived as compromising the independence of the OCTA. Australia even suggested that, as chief bankroller, it should have a say in the governance of the OCTA. Shifting the OCTA to Port Vila was seen as a much better idea than having it housed in the PIFS in Suva because of direct influence by Australia through the economic governance director, an Australian (Pacnews, 2010).

Strong sentiments were expressed about the need to make OCTA independent from the PIF because of possible interference by Australia and New Zealand. Noonan resigned as director of OCTA due to what he saw as the bullying tactics by Australia and New Zealand in leveraging their powerful position to force negotiations on small island states. He was replaced by Dr Edwini Kessie, a WTO employee and passionate believer in trade liberalisation, who oversaw the negotiations until the end.

The major pro–free trade narratives revolve around a number of selling points, including creating a more open and predictable trading environment; consistency and transparency of rules throughout the region on sanitary and phytosanitary measures, technical barriers to trade and customs procedures; greater liberal and product-specific rules of origin; growth of investment in the region, particularly by New Zealand and Australian investors; greater certainty around tariffs for exporters; more opportunities for trade-related development assistance for PICs; and a more mobile labour force in the region (NZMFAT, 2017).

When PACER Plus was finally endorsed on 20 April 2017, the event was hailed as a great success by the New Zealand Minister for Trade, Todd McClay, who said:

> This is a significant achievement. After 8 years of negotiations, we can now focus on implementing an agreement which future-proofs our access whilst helping develop their export economies … PACER Plus is a unique trade and development agreement. It includes a development package of more than $55 million

that will help raise standards of living, create employment opportunities and increase export capacity in Pacific Island countries … The agreement will also create a common set of trading rules covering goods, services and investment in support of economic growth. These rules will help reduce tariffs and red tape for exporters and investors, which will increase the attractiveness of the region for trade and investment. (NZMFAT, 2017)

Is agreement on free trade to be considered a 'success' or, as opponents would argue, a threat to the well-being of the Pacific people? The argument that PACER Plus is a threat to vulnerable PICs is based on broader human security concerns. The removal of tariffs means a significant reduction in revenue for import-reliant PICs. PICs will need to make up this financial loss through other means such as VAT and other forms of taxation, which will burden local consumers further. In addition, local industries, especially in manufacturing, processing and agriculture, can be overwhelmed by the unrestricted flood of foreign goods entering the local market. Local industries do not have the resilience and ability to compete with global producers on a level playing field. The reality is that there is no level playing field because foreign companies have the advantage of greater capital outlay, technology and resources and are backed by more powerful economies. Although goods might be cheaper, the resulting unemployment can lead to poverty, social marginalisation and crime. Economic grievances built up over time have the potential to fuel political agitation and violence. We have seen this in Fiji, Solomon Islands and Tonga, the three case studies in this book, where feelings of socioeconomic marginalisation have readily translated into explosive political grievances and violent action.

The unrestricted availability of cheap unhealthy food such as New Zealand mutton flaps is a major concern for Pacific peoples at a time when the rate of diabetes and obesity among them is one of the highest in the world. Already the propensity to consume cheaper manufactured food such as noodles and fizzy drinks is high in many Pacific communities, and this can be exacerbated by the availability of more varieties of cheap high-sugar and high-carbohydrate foreign food products. In addition, the waste from the manufactured food products adds more pressure on already fragile atoll environments, where waste disposal and the impacts of climate change have been major challenges. Climate change has damaged and transformed the coastal configuration of many islands and limits their capacity for waste storage.

Another major concern is the hegemonic power leveraging and imposition of dominant interests associated with the agreement. Behind the veneer of diplomacy, it has been observed that discussions on PACER Plus were fraught with subtle bullying tactics. The trade justice campaigner for the Pacific Network on Globalisation (PANG), Adam Wolfenden, said:

> Australia and New Zealand are again using PACER Plus to get what they want out of the Pacific, this despite the constant rhetoric from the region's biggest neighbours that this is a development agreement for the Pacific. The Pacific Island Countries have long argued that Labour Mobility and Development Assistance are the two areas of possible benefit to them under PACER Plus and yet those are the areas that Australia and New Zealand are showing practically no flexibility on. That some of the smallest nations in the world are the ones who are shouldering the flexibility in these negotiations is typical of what we have come to expect in relationships with our biggest neighbours in the region. The power dynamics in the PACER Plus negotiations mean that Pacific Island Countries development gets sacrificed to demonstrate our good faith. It is the Island Countries who continue to negotiate in good faith. (Fonua, 2014: 1)

Other PIC officials expressed their displeasure with the PACER Plus negotiations. The chair of the Negotiating Group on Labour Mobility for Solomon Islands expressed regret that:

> We are nowhere near achieving an agreement on the core demands of the PICs … While we acknowledge the efforts of New Zealand to bridge the gaps in the negotiating positions of the Parties, we believe that the proposed Arrangement falls far short of our expectations in many respects. (Fonua, 2014: 1)

As expected, a number of compromises had to be made as the Tongan chair of the Negotiating Group on Development Assistance asserted:

> We have managed to demonstrate considerable flexibility to overcome some of the initial divergences we held at the inception of these negotiations … In the spirit of compromise, we have been able to overcome that fundamental difference, without which we would not be seeking to elaborate on the structure of the 'Development Assistance' component. (Fonua, 2014: 1)

Despite these reservations, the chief trade advisor for the PICs, Edwini Kessie, remained optimistic and suggested that:

> We are making good progress in the negotiations, especially on the sticky issues of labour and development assistance and other issues such as sanitary and phytosanitary measures, technical barriers to trade and customs procedures as well as negotiations on trade in services and investment. (Fonua, 2014: 1)

Kessie criticised the PANG opposition to PACER Plus by saying:

> A PACER Plus Agreement will help the PICs to put in place a coherent trade and investment policy framework that should create the necessary conditions for trade and investment to flourish and for the long-term economic development of their countries. The Agreement should enable them to push through reforms that would provide a pathway for the sustainable growth and development of their economies. (Pareti, 2014)

Dr Roman Grynberg, a former senior economist with the PIF, disagreed with this optimistic assessment:

> It is very likely that the two principle bargaining objectives of the Pacific Islands, to get a trade agreement that gives them security of labour market access for Pacific islanders to Australia and New Zealand (ANZ) and security of development assistance, will not be met. ANZ have made it perfectly clear that they will never make bound commitments in either area because of the precedent this will establish for FTA negotiations with India and other large countries. What ANZ are expecting is a profoundly unequal treaty, i.e. the islands agree to bind their tariffs at zero or at low levels and in return ANZ promise to be nice and, if they are in the mood, will grant labour market access and development assistance but certainly no legal commitments on either issue. This outcome is all the more absurd and unjust given that the island states already have duty free access for their exports under the unilateral SPARTECA treaty and so will stand to gain almost nothing from Pacer Plus. (Grynberg, 2014: 2)

Despite the fact that PACER Plus is now signed, debates about its impact will continue. The disagreement over PACER Plus's conditions is reflective of the bigger power dynamics of inequality and hegemonic relations. The fact that Australia and New Zealand provide most of the funds for regional organisations such as PIF and SPC is seen as justification for influence and control of these regional organisations.

The long-term economic security of the small PICs depends very much on a number of critical factors, including the conditions of trade and aid they have to engage with. Often, trade imbalance and poorly implemented development aid can undermine their capacity for growth and sustainability. The only PIC with a sizeable manufacturing, processing and export base is Fiji, which also controls about 80 per cent of intraregional trade, and its absence from PACER Plus means that the power balance is extremely skewed, with Australia and New Zealand providing approximately 90 per cent of the goods for trade. The trade-off in the form of labour mobility will depend very much on changes in the immigration and labour policies of New Zealand and Australia in the future. The current seasonal workers schemes have been working satisfactorily in terms of providing employment for unskilled workers, while the recent attempt to hire skilled workers will affect the progressively depleted skilled labour force in the PICs. How the increasingly strict rules that restrict skilled immigration to New Zealand and Australia will affect labour mobility in the future is a cause for concern.

For countries that have largely subsistence economies, the prospect of benefiting from a free trade deal might not be the best way forward because of their inability to participate equally and meaningfully. Free trade is sensible and workable as a two-way process only where there is reciprocal trade and power is shared relatively equally. This is far from being the case with PACER Plus, where trade flow is one-directional and the distribution of benefits skewed. This raises a range of concerns in relation to equity, food security and other forms of human security.

Patronage, economic disparity and security

One of the significant factors in security is the imposition of power, as Foucault (1991) reminds us. In a situation of patronage, the imposition of power and power imbalance can create conditions for oppression and marginalisation of smaller or weaker groups, which could exacerbate differences. Economic power differentials in the Pacific revolve around the patronage-type dominance of Australia and New Zealand in the economic as well as political affairs of the region (Ratuva, 2008). A classic example of this is in regard to PACER Plus, which is, as we saw earlier, an agreement between countries with extremely unequal power. For instance, the combined population of Australia and New Zealand is about 30 million with a combined GDP of about US$1,560.231 trillion and an average GDP per capita of US$54,506. This compares rather unfavourably with the combined economic capacity and performance of 10 PICs that are members of the World Bank (Fiji, Kiribati, Marshall Islands, Federated States of Micronesia, Palau, Samoa, Solomon Islands, Tonga, Tuvalu and Vanuatu) with a total population of 2.28 million, a total GDP of US$8.009 billion and average GDP per capita of $US3,460 (World Bank, 2013).

This large disparity is also reflected in the trade figures, which favour Australia and New Zealand disproportionately. For instance, in the calendar year ending 31 December 2011, New Zealand's exports to the Pacific were worth more than NZ$1.5 billion, reflecting a 12 per cent growth from 2010. This was in contrast to a mere NZ$98 million worth of exports from the PICs to New Zealand, representing a deficit of NZ$1.4 billion (NZMFAT, 2012). The lack of domestic production and export, as well as New Zealand's strict biosecurity rules, have contributed to the disparity.

Australia and New Zealand's patronage is further strengthened through aid. Aid for building up trade capacity, together with the prospect of more labour mobility, were used as leverage to buy the consent of PICs to sign PACER Plus. Both countries have been prolific dispensers of aid in the region, with New Zealand disbursing more than half of its total aid in the islands, justified on the basis that the Pacific includes 'some of the world's smallest and most isolated states' and 'the region faces a range of economic and social development challenges, and much of the region is vulnerable to natural disasters' (NZMFAT, 2014). New Zealand's total estimated aid to the Pacific in the 2014–15 period was NZ$121.5 million for bilateral aid and $NZ19.5 million for Pacific regional agencies. At the same time, Australia's aid to the Pacific (excluding PNG) was A$174 million in 2013–14 and A$196.9 million in 2014–15. Apart from bilateral aid, its multilateral aid program for the period 2014–17 included A$21.6 million for the PIF, A$51.5 million for the Secretariat of the Pacific Community and A$14.9 million for the Pacific Leadership Program (PLP). Australia's view is that bilateral and regional aid complement each other:

> Australia's regional program complements our bilateral program investments to support economic growth and poverty reduction in the Pacific. Many of the Pacific's challenges cannot be addressed solely on a country-by-country basis. The regional program adds value where it is more efficient and effective to work through regional approaches. (DFAT, 2014)

Australia's justifications for its aid to the Pacific are based on:

> Isolation, both in terms of geography and communications; small, often dispersed, populations and markets that limit economies of scale and domestic revenue opportunities; limited natural resources; rapid population growth that outstrips job creation, income earning opportunities and social services; a shortage of critical infrastructure with poor maintenance; high vulnerability to the impacts of climate change and natural disasters, and economic shocks such as fluctuating international fuel and food prices. (DFAT, 2014)

These challenges, it is argued, are 'exacerbated by the limited capacity in Pacific island public sectors', difficulty in 'managing the requirements of modern business and government' and their inability to 'deliver essential functions including providing services such as health, education and policing' (DFAT, 2014). In 2012, Australia's bilateral aid to the PICs consisted of the following: Fiji (A$46 million), Kiribati (A$35 million), Papua New Guinea (A$494 million), Samoa (A$41 million), Solomon Islands (A$235 million), Tonga (A$33 million) and Vanuatu (A$66 million). In per capita terms, aid to some of the PICs is among the highest in the world. While aid flows were justified using manifest deficit narratives, the more politically latent role of aid to maintain a sense of patronage and manufacture consent among the PICs cannot be discounted easily. Australia, together with New Zealand, largely funds the PIF, and this makes the regional agency susceptible to ANZ control and influence (Grynberg, 2014).

Interference in the Economic Partnership Agreement

This power imbalance and patron–client psychology was also reflected in the Economic Partnership Agreement (EPA) negotiations between the Pacific-based African Caribbean and Pacific (ACP) countries and the European Union, in which Australia and New Zealand insisted on provisions for their involvement, although the agreement had nothing whatsoever to do with them. In doing this, the two countries hoped to keep their regional patronage undisturbed by the influence of other outside powers.

Roman Grynberg described this thus:

> This [EPA negotiation] was deeply resented by Australia simply because the Forum works on consensus and the fact that the islands would provide a consensus on trade issues and prior to the ACP group, Australia could effectively veto anything they did not like. But what the ACP negotiations provided to the islands for the first time in their history was a relatively well-funded mechanism by which they could come to decisions in their own interests without having to appease Canberra and Wellington. This sort of independence by Canberra's vassal states in the Pacific islands, i.e. what it sees as 'its lake', was unacceptable to their policy-makers. (Grynberg, 2010: 1)

The use of the term 'Canberra's vassal states' is interesting here and connotes a feudatory relationship, in which the economic and political survival of Pacific communities is predicated on their loyalty to the two countries and, in turn, on the two countries' patronage of Pacific countries.

Australia and New Zealand are always wary of the influence of the European Union in the region through the EU-funded Pacific ACP group, which included only the 14 Pacific Islands and excluded the two larger powers. Australia, in particular, felt uneasy about the fact that its power to veto any PIF decision and its capacity to induce a consensus were going to be undermined by another competing hegemon. The ACP negotiations provided the opportunity for the small island states to make 'decisions in their own interests without having to appease Canberra and Wellington' for the first time in their history (Grynberg, 2010: 1).

Attempts to initiate trade agreements through PICTA, which did not involve Australia and New Zealand, with China, Taiwan and also Australia and New Zealand did not succeed. In 2009, Roman Grynberg, the PIF director of trade who had been sympathetic to the small island states' cause and was a thorn in the side of the Australians, was removed and was replaced by an Australian. That Australia exercises direct influence on some PICs, such as Papua New Guinea, through Australian businessmen in PNG who influence trade policy 'has long been the talk of the Forum', as they have 'sabotaged the EPA negotiations by negotiating behind the backs of other Pacific islanders and completely undermined Pacific solidarity' (Grynberg, 2010: 1). The concern raised here is that, by signing a separate EPA deal with the EU for fish market access, PNG would be in a position to solicit fish supplies from other PICs, a move that would benefit these Australian commercial interests. Agreeing to an EPA that was devoid of important provisions such as labour mobility and aid, crucial for PICs, would have provided a very bad precedent for the PACER Plus negotiations.

The EPA negotiations have been temporarily suspended due to the inability of the EU and the PICs to achieve consensus on some issues, such as EU access to fishing resources in the Pacific as payoff for some concessions. PACER Plus has been endorsed and signed, although some countries, including Fiji and Papua New Guinea, have refrained from committing themselves. The refusal of those two countries to sign is based on the recognition that the agreement has the potential to undermine their productive capacity by killing off local industries that cannot compete against bigger Australian and New Zealand importers and investors. For the small PICs, who have been led to believe that the agreement is the panacea for their economic woes, the full impact of free trade is still to set in and, because they are bound by the agreement, it will not be easy to extricate themselves in the short term.

The point to emphasise here is that, while Pacific regionalism is often hailed as a consensual and harmonious configuration of consenting sovereign states, the reality is very different. The two dominant powers, Australia and New Zealand, wield much greater power than any other state, which enables them to keep the small states under their hegemonic control. Their ability to influence and buy loyalty through aid creates a regional patronage relationship that is hidden beneath the façade of regionalism. The security implications of these arrangements are latent rather than manifest. The loss of sovereignty and autonomy of small island states to determine their own foreign policy direction and economic development choices is a great concern in an era of globalisation, where states are expected to be more assertive and independent minded. External manipulation and patronage can be disempowering and create a sense of insecurity. Expressing one's political sovereignty, independence and determining one's policy trajectory for the future provides a sense of self-empowerment and security. This is an important psychological prerequisite for both national and regional stability.

Climate change and human security

There is a growing consensus that climate change is probably the single most important future threat to human security in the Pacific. Many low-lying, small island countries such as Tuvalu, Kiribati and Marshall Islands are not in a position to mitigate the persistent increase in sea level and erosion in the foreseeable future. In addition, the increase in the number of climate-induced disasters such cyclones, coral bleaching due to high sea temperatures, floods and droughts are socially and economically disruptive and, in many cases, very costly. While these trends have been part of the Pacific people's daily challenges for years, it is only in the last 20 years or so that, as a result of greater consciousness-raising through international and regional campaigns, the issue of climate change has become prominent.

The discourse on climate change is highly political, as much as it is environmental and scientific. Although about 97 per cent of the world's scientists now acknowledge the climate change phenomenon to be 'real', there are climate change 'agnostics' (who are not sure about aspects of the matter) and even outright deniers, some of whom are linked to the energy industry and conservative political camp and who see climate change as a left-wing fear-mongering scam. The deniers' position has been given an ideological boost by US President Donald Trump's stance that climate change is a 'Chinese hoax' and by his anti-climate change policies, which include potential US withdrawal from the Paris Agreement (COP21) on climate change, expected withdrawal from the Green Climate Fund (GCF) and the undoing of Obama's climate change strategies. Any US withdrawal from the estimated US$100 billion GCF will affect the small Pacific island states. The United States had committed itself to giving US$3 billion to the fund, with US$1 billion being paid so far. The discontinuation of the US contribution means that funds for climate adaptation and rehabilitation will be reduced considerably, thus affecting the small Pacific states' mitigation and resilience capability. So far, six Pacific island states have acquired funding from the GCF: Fiji (US$31 million for an urban water supply and wastewater management project), Tuvalu (US$36 million for a coastal adaptation project), Vanuatu (US$23 million for climate information services for resilient development), Samoa (US$57.7 million for integrated flood management to enhance the climate resilience of the Vaisigano River catchment), Cook Islands (US$17 million for the Pacific Islands renewable energy investment program) and Solomon Islands (US$2.5 million for the Tina River hydro power development project) (GCF, 2017). Other island countries are still processing their applications through various accredited institutions.

Increasingly, various other forms of bilateral and multilateral aid to the Pacific are related, either directly or indirectly, to steps to mitigate the short-term or long-term effects of climate change. However, a main concern is whether aid related to climate change actually reaches those who really need it. Although conventional assumptions perceive climate change aid as humanitarian, the reality is that it is latently political. Climate change has now become a commodified political issue, and many donors use the opportunity to be seen as generous, hoping that this will help promote their status as good global citizens. This competition for glory and tight control over the GCF have overshadowed its humanitarian aspects. The challenge is how to connect the global political discourse to realities on the ground. The influx of aid and climate change experts into the Pacific, funded by the GCF and other donors, can be disempowering for local communities whose innovation and indigenous knowledge of adaptation and resilience have been undermined and considered irrelevant amid the newly introduced and externally funded technologies and skills.

A major challenge is how to create space for conversation between the externally driven global discourse on climate change and local indigenous innovations and knowledge in the Pacific. The state, as a conduit for global and regional policies, can play a critical role in engaging and integrating the two levels. This requires changes in thinking and in approaches to engender more inclusive and diversified policies in response to climate change. One way forward is to frame climate change as a human security issue that affects the livelihood of the local communities and to seek ways in which local communities can be empowered to directly participate in climate change mitigation. This could promote the importance of community-based innovations and knowledge for adaptation and resilience.

While climate change is a creeping disaster that has the potential to affect all aspects of security in profound ways—economic, social, cultural, environmental or political—the way Pacific communities respond to it depends very much on, first, their understanding of the problems; second, the will to address the problems; and third, the availability of the means to address these problems. The first issue is critical because it affects the second and third issues. In some countries such as Tuvalu and Kiribati, many still believe that climate change is the 'will of God' and that there is nothing we can do about it, while some even argue that climate change mitigation is against God's will. At the same time, the more progressive members of the churches have been actively trying to confront this view through greater consciousness-raising with the help of governments and civil society organisations. The challenges associated with changing people's thinking are immense and one of the greatest barriers to climate change campaigns.

For some island countries such as Tuvalu and Kiribati, the option of relocation is now a real possibility. Kiribati has purchased 6,000 acres of land in Fiji as a possible site for relocation if the situation demands it. Climate change migration poses even bigger challenges in relation to logistics, integration and political status. For instance, for argument's sake, if the 116,000 people of Kiribati decide to migrate to Fiji, there are a number of challenges that need careful consideration. Will they migrate as individuals, to be absorbed and integrated into Fijian society? Will they relocate as a 'state', in which case Kiribati would become a mini 'state' within the Fijian state? Or will Fiji give them a semi-autonomous status to run their own affairs as part of the Fijian state, similar to the Banaban people, who were relocated from Ocean Island in Kiribati to Rabi Island in Fiji by the British in 1954, after their island was mined for phosphate? Another critical question is what will happen to the submerged atolls, reefs and so on after the relocation of the state? Do they still remain part of the sovereignty of the relocated Kiribati state or would Kiribati make a deal with Fiji to make Kiribati's exclusive economic zone a part of Fiji's territory in exchange for setting up an autonomous Kiribati political entity in Fiji?

The issue is more complex than it seems, especially if one considers the issue of land politics, resource distribution, ethnic relations and population expansion in Fiji, a country already beset by a multitude of security issues. What we might see in this situation are layers of security issues feeding on one another. This is why it is important to have very clear guidelines in the beginning, based on dialogue for a win-win end result between Fiji and Kiribati. Nevertheless, Fiji has declared its willingness to take in people from Tuvalu and other Pacific Islands as climate change migrants, although, in the broader scheme of things, the region should be involved proactively through the PIF. Unfortunately, Australia and New Zealand's ungenerous refugee and immigration policies might not be conducive to a comprehensive and humane regional approach.

Moreover, climate change is an issue that has deepened the wedge between Australia and New Zealand on the one hand and Pacific island states on the other, especially in relation to what is perceived as Australia and New Zealand's lack of commitment to reduction of carbon emissions under the Kyoto Protocol. A former Australian prime minister, Tony Abbott, suggested that like-minded centre-right governments around the world should form an alliance to resist global moves towards carbon pricing and in favour of more 'direct action' measures. Representing the voice of desperation of small island states, Kiribati's president lamented:

> We're not talking about the growth GDP, we're not talking about what it means in terms of profit and losses of the large corporations, we're talking about our survival. What will happen in terms of greenhouse gas emissions levels agreed to internationally will not affect us, because our future is already here … we will be under water. (ABC, 2014)

The same sentiment was expressed by Christopher Loeak, president of the Marshall Islands, a country that still suffers from the effects of US nuclear tests in the 1950s:

> I'm very concerned that the Prime Minister [of Australia] is setting the wrong tone in what needs to be a very determined effort to tackle climate change. Prime Minister Abbott's comments on Monday with Canadian Prime Minister Stephen Harper are a further indication that Australia is isolating itself on this issue. We see all the time the problem is getting worse, but we don't want to lose hope. We believe that there are still opportunities to curb this problem and we look forward to working with the world community to talk about it, and to do anything we can to help them to do something about climate change. (ABC, 2014)

The PICs have also been critical of the fact that many developed countries have not fully committed themselves to the Green Climate Fund (GCF). Even the UN Kyoto Protocol Adaptation Fund established in 2001 has been largely shunned by prospective donors. Furthermore, access to the GCF has been bureaucratically cumbersome. This involves applying for assistance through accredited organisations, which will help put together a proposal for the government concerned.

In July 2014 representatives of four of the world's most vulnerable atoll countries—Kiribati, Maldives, Marshall Islands and Tuvalu—met in Kiribati to discuss some of their shared challenges in relation to global warming. To make their voice stronger they formed the Coalition of Atoll Nations on Climate Change (CANCC). Such international solidarity by small states plays a crucial role in providing psychological security and hope in a world where parochial national interests supersede global moral responsibility.

The issue of climate change has raised the global profile of PICs in international forums, and Pacific leaders have assumed prominence in the global campaign. By chairing the Conference of the Parties (COP25) on climate change by global leaders, Fiji has demonstrated the deeper sense of global responsibility that Pacific island states have in saving their islands and planet Earth. Despite the turnabout by the United States, the momentum of the global campaign will continue and, in the Pacific, the people will have to respond to climate change challenges by consolidating their efforts, both locally and globally.

The empire strikes back: The new Pacific diplomacy

The response of the PICs to the need to engage with the big power more effectively was to pull their political and moral resources together using more creative diplomatic approaches. This required some independent and strategic thinking because of the need to overcome some of what they see as patronising and exploitative tendencies by the bigger powers such as Australia and New Zealand (Fry & Tarte, 2015).

This 'new Pacific diplomacy', as Fry and Tarte (2015) call it, seems to have been galvanised in part by Fiji's suspension from the Pacific Islands Forum and the rise of climate change as a major security threat. Following its suspension in 2009 and sanctions by Australia and New Zealand, Fiji proceeded to unravel the regional governance and security architecture as part of its 'revenge'. One such move was the setting up of the Pacific Islands Development Forum (PIDF) as a counter to the PIF, which has been dominated by Australia and New Zealand through funding and direct political influence. Although PIDF has faced funding challenges over the years, its diplomatic and geopolitical symbolism and statement of resistance was unmistakable. This geopolitical manoeuvre was aimed at weakening the hegemonic foothold of Australia and New Zealand in the region as well as softening the dominance of traditional regional organisations such as the PIF (Dornan, 2013). Some countries showed support for the PIDF while still members of the PIF but some did not.

In addition to the PIDF was the invigoration of the Pacific Small Island Developing States (PSIDS) as the main lobbying group for small Pacific states at the United Nations. This was in recognition of their much sought-after UN votes as well as the desire to be independent of the PIF, which had been the major negotiating mechanism for the PICs (Manoa, 2015). The PSIDS started in the early 1990s as a collective negotiation group for the PICs, but it took on a new political energy and trajectory after 2009 through Fiji's influence. Also associated with this is Fiji's attempt to breath energy into the Melanesian Spearhead Group (MSG), again as a way of weakening the 'core' of regionalism in the form of the PIF. However, internal tensions within the MSG probably overshadowed any hope of a strong subregional bloc. Fiji's opposition to the PIF might have also been influenced by its opposition to Australia and New Zealand, which it wanted expelled from the PIF because of their sanctions on Fiji after the 2006 coup, among other reasons. Fiji's headship of the UN G77 countries (which included China), as well as presidency of the UN General Assembly, gave it the international status to leverage its influence within as well as beyond the Pacific.

Protecting Pacific resources from foreign resource predators in the form of fishing fleets has always been a major challenge for Pacific states, and this was one of the reasons behind the formation of the Parties to the Nauru Agreement (PNA) by the Federated States of Micronesia, Kiribati, Marshall Islands, Nauru, Palau, Papua New Guinea, Solomon Islands and Tuvalu, which control about 60 per cent of the western and central Pacific's tuna supply. The role of the PNA was to empower the PICs to protect their quickly depleting tuna stock as well as protect the environment from overexploitation and destructive fishing methods (Tamate, 2013). Only certain PICs are members of PNA. There have been other cases of the way the new Pacific diplomacy scenario has unfolded, including the new policy directions by Meg Taylor, secretary general of the PIF, and the push to separate the PACER advisory office from the PIF (Fry & Tarte, 2015).

The issue of climate change has heightened the status and significance of PICs considerably. With Kiribati's and Tuvalu's voices being echoed internationally and Fiji's leadership of the COP25, PICs have now found themselves at the forefront of the global fight against climate change (Williams & McDuie-Ra, 2018). The question of how this translates into states committing themselves to the Paris Agreement is still to be seen.

My criticism of the new Pacific diplomacy concept is that some of the manoeuvrings involved, such as Fiji's attempt to outflank New Zealand and Australia, are actually beyond the realm of diplomacy and involve geopolitical contestation of power and influence. This regional power contestation (rather than 'diplomacy') caused fractures within the regional diplomatic regime, and it took not so much diplomacy but unfolding of political developments, such as the Fiji election, for relations to normalise. Also, the term 'new' can be misleading because, while the actual events described were somewhat new developments, some of the underlying principles and dynamics, including intra-Pacific consensus and solidarity *vis-à-vis* contestation, are not new at all (Ratuva, 2005). Even the formation of the PIF itself was based on resistance to political domination by the colonial powers that controlled the South Pacific Commission. The cycle of consensus and contestation has been part of the normal process of diplomacy and geopolitics in the Pacific, and new variations of these have emerged when circumstances demanded. Some of the hype of a decade or so ago has fizzled out, and what was seen as 'new' then has now become 'old'; consequently, resurrection of 'old' ideas and practices can now become 'new'.

Conclusion

The notion of a speech act, as the securitisation theorists remind us, is a powerful mental and political tool to influence and transform our thoughts. The power of words and texts associated with security shape our beliefs and attitudes and contribute to securitising the social climate. Indeed terms like 'failed' and 'fragile' states as well as 'arc of instability' play a decisive speech act role in the securitisation and orientalisation of the Pacific. As this chapter has tried to demonstrate, the implications in terms of policies and regional power relations places PICs in a neocolonial subaltern position. The need to deconstruct these ideologically, culturally and politically prejudiced terms is required from critical scholars as a way of demystifying regional politics.

Furthermore, cultural, socioeconomic, political and historical diversity in the Pacific makes it rather naive to attempt to make generalisations about security in the Pacific. Even using a particular conceptual framework might not capture the multifaceted and diverse manifestations of security dynamics in a region so wide and scattered yet so globalised and constantly in a state of transformation. The Pacific peoples are scattered around the globe; for some countries, there are more citizens living outside than inside the country, and therefore the changes they exert in their respective communities are wide-ranging and profound. Security in the Pacific must be understood in the context of multiple forces, circumstances and lenses. This includes a combination of external factors such as the impact of global neoliberal capitalism, international cultural imperialism and climate change, and of internal factors such as geopolitical contestation, disputes over resources, competition over political power and issues relating to well-being.

The concept of human security can be useful in linking aspects of political, economic, social and cultural life that threaten the Pacific people's well-being. However, at another level it becomes too nebulous in the way it securitises almost every aspect of life, to the extent that it becomes quite challenging for policy-makers to frame relevant policies to address security issues. Because the human security framework is top down in its conceptualisation and implementation, there is a large disconnect between international and regional discourses and policies at the national level. Even within a country, there is a gap between the state policy bureaucracy and the local community, because, for many Pacific island communities, daily security priorities are often determined by daily needs, which are often different from those of pre-designed official templates.

Security issues such as resource disputes and contestation of power at the local level have the potential to expand and create much bigger conflict issues and dynamics at the national level, and also have the potential to oscillate downwards, as we will see in the case studies of Fiji, Tonga and Solomon Islands in Chapters 4, 5 and 6. While there are unique issues that are locally induced, there are some, such as climate change, that are more global than local, although there are locally devised innovations designed to mitigate their effects. Climate change is probably the most high-profile and most devastating and costly security threat to Pacific communities, largely because it is associated with climate forces beyond human control.

Pacific leaders have been at the forefront of campaigns to mitigate climate change in an effort to persuade industrialised countries to reduce their carbon emissions.

There are other security issues that are created by human activity and ordinarily are too overwhelming or even impossible for small Pacific island states to change. These include issues relating to global economic crises and free trade, which have the potential to harm local communities. Debates about the desirability of free trade, such as PACER Plus, continue, and the fact that most PICs have signed up to PACER Plus means that voluntary risk-taking is part of the way we deal with security. Thus, rather than being passive players in a world of global economic competition, small states still have access to windows of opportunity, albeit in a limited way, to affect policies that could affect their long-term economic security.

The gap between regional and local security discourses poses a challenge in terms of legitimacy and the practicality of security policies, especially when regional security thinking is defined by global security templates. Rather than a top-down approach, there should be more emphasis on grounded and localised discourses as the basis for building up a national and regional security framework. In addition, the specific circumstances of the individual countries should be taken into consideration and, rather than just providing a regional solution, there should be innovative responses based on local dynamics and realities. The three case studies in Chapters 4, 5 and 6 show that, rather than manifesting similarities, there are wide differences between PICs—differences that are often overlooked in favour of quick fixes and easy explanations based on negative stereotypes that cast the Pacific as consisting of 'failed' or 'fragile' states in an 'arc of instability'.

4

End of coups?: Fiji's changing security environment

Power does not corrupt men; fools, however, if they get into a position of power, corrupt power.

George Bernard Shaw

Fiji was chosen as a case study because of some unique features that make it different from other PICs. These include the nature of contestation for political power between a diaspora group and the indigenous community (referred to as Taukei, a term used throughout the chapter) and how this interplays with socioeconomic factors and land and identity issues. In addition, Fiji is the only PIC that has undergone regime change through military coups; hence the role of the military and the associated culture of politico-masculinity has been a major factor in shaping the country's security context. In a broad and exploratory way, this chapter examines the interplay between some of the factors that have shaped Fiji's security environment over the years and their impact on the country's evolution.

When the chief of staff of the Republic of Fiji Military Forces (RFMF) declared on 16 July 2017 that the military had 'moved out of the coup culture and was no longer a threat to the country' and was going to accept the 2018 election results (Swami, 2017), the national mood was one of both jubilation and anxiety. Jubilation because of the feeling of comforting reassurance this announcement provided and anxiety because similar guarantees had been heard before. The future will tell whether Fiji is now entering the 'no coup' phase of its history or whether history is, given the right circumstances, likely to repeat itself (Fraenkel, Firth and Lal, 2009). This very much depends on a number of interrelated security dynamics, which this chapter will examine.

For a country that has had six coups,[1] the security situation has to be understood in the context of a number of cross-cutting issues relating to, first, what Stewart (2008) refers to as 'horizontal inequality' or ethnocultural disparities or perception of them; second, ethnopolitical contestation for power between the two major ethnic groups (Taukei and Indo-Fijian); third, politicisation of identity, religion and culture; and finally, socioeconomic inequality and competition over resources. While some of these issues might be more prominent than others in different historical or contextual spaces, they all contribute in their own ways to shaping the security configuration in the country.

However, contrary to conventional stereotyping of Fiji in predominantly ethnic terms, the situation is much more complex and syncretic. For instance, while there is ethnic tension, there is also trans-ethnic mutual engagement and convergence of ethnic interests, and while there are distinct cultures, there is also space for transcultural interaction and integration.

By using selected aspects of the postcolonial, securitisation and human security approaches, this chapter explores in an overarching way the dynamic interplay between various political, economic and social forces that have shaped Fiji's security climate in phases of historical change from the precolonial and colonial to the postcolonial era. It starts by looking at the notion of warrior chiefs and their role in providing security for the community. The chapter then looks at the imposition of colonial security designs and the way these transformed Taukei society. This invoked resistance to colonial hegemony, as we will see next. The resistance movement led to a more intensive and brutal pacification drive by the British to keep the Taukei within the ambit of their security boundary.

---

1   The generally accepted view is that Fiji has had four coups (two in 1987, one in 2000 and one in 2006). I have argued that, technically, Fiji has had six coups (two in 1987, two in 2000, one in 2006 and one in 2009). The first coup in 2000 occurred when George Speight and his group stormed Parliament on 19 May 2000 and took members of the government hostage, and the second coup (or countercoup) occurred when the military dismissed the president, abrogated the constitution and declared martial law on 29 May. The first coup by Speight was against the government and the second coup by the military was against the state, although it was carried out under the pretext of saving Fiji from the rampaging ethnonationalist group that had overthrown the government and caused havoc in other parts of Fiji. See Ratuva (2011a).

The chapter then focuses on the institutional, coercive and hegemonic strategies of the colonial state to maintain its security agenda. Divide and rule system of governance (i.e. native policies that locked the Taukei into a regressive semi-subsistence way of life) and legal mechanisms were deployed as means of control. Following this, we will examine the process of securitisation after independence and how political, constitutional and legal means were used to maintain security. We will also discuss the issue of economic security and how this fed into the changing political dynamics.

The chapter then examines the role of state security institutions such as the military and police in the bigger security framework before looking at the issues of perceptions and ethnic framing as security factors. Finally, the chapter explores the importance of community peace-building and conflict resolution in addressing long-term security issues in Fiji.

Warrior chiefs, power and security in precolonial Fiji

To fully grasp the genesis of some of the factors that have shaped Fiji's current security environment, we need to retrace the evolution of some salient cultural strands back to the precolonial era when politics, culture, resource distribution and identity formed an integrated system in a communal subsistence habitat and where contestation for power between chiefdoms defined the security terrain of the land. How these were framed by early missionaries were far from positive and some descriptions were reminiscent of the social Darwinian European mindset of the time, as we examined in Chapter 2. This mindset is reflected in the words of the Revd Thomas Williams:

> But the savagism of the Fijian has a more terrible badge, and one whereby he is principally distinguished by all the world; his cruelty is relentless and bloody. That innate depravity which he shares in common with other men, has in this case been fostered into peculiar brutality by the character of his religion, and all his early training and associations. Shedding of blood to him is no crime, but a glory. Whoever maybe the victim—whether noble or vulgar, old or young, man, woman or child—whether slain in war or butchered by treachery, to be somehow an acknowledged murderer is the object of the Fijian's restless ambition. (Williams, 1858: 112)

The imagery of the 'savage' and 'cannibal' Fijian survived over the ages and found its way into folklore and orientalised racial stereotypes. Today, these racial perceptions still pervade in latent forms. These orientalised narratives obscure the dynamic sociopolitical realities in Fiji, which need to be discussed as a starting point to frame our analysis of security. A more sober analysis of this power struggle is provided by Joseph Waterhouse, an Australian-English missionary who was in Fiji in the mid-1800s:

> The occasions of war are very numerous. The possessions of land and women, and the commission of murder, are the principal causes. To these may be added personal affronts to chiefs; the refusal to give up a particular club, bird or shell; the unlawful eating of the turtle, the lust of conquest; the wish to murder, amidst the din of battle, a chief of their own, who is suspected of ambition, a violation of the tabu, love-affairs, and last, not least, a determination, on the part of the country at large, to check despotism. (Waterhouse, 1866: 315–16)

Causes of war varied according to the situation. Over the years, as Mary Wallis, wife of an American bêche-de-mer trader noted, competition over access to European trading goods became a major cause of war between the dominant powers such as Bau, Macuata, Bua, Lakeba and Cakaudrove as the desire for wealth took root (Routledge, 1985). As missionary Joseph Waterhouse noted, Cakobau, a powerful chief from the island of Bau whose power and influence covered a significant portion of Fiji, accumulated both traditional goods through serfdom of his vassals in conquered territories and European goods through the use of forced labour to provide bêche-de-mer for European traders (Waterhouse, 1997).

In times of disputes, clans and communities were often at risk of being attacked by hostile neighbours, so they had to be at the ready with men, women and children engaged in a well-rehearsed division of labour in a siege situation. While men would be directly responsible for front-line fighting, women and children would play roles such as lookouts, messengers and providers of food through planting, harvesting and fishing (Clunie, 1977). Villages were located strategically, on the basis of a number of factors including the availability of water and food, and defensibility. Many villages were on fortified hills or circular mounds, surrounded by ditches as a form of defence (Field, 1998; Best, 1993).

Chiefs formed alliances through intermarriage and reciprocal friendship agreements as a way of maintaining good relations and stability. This was the case with the major polities of Lakeba, Bau, Somosomo and Rewa where the chiefs were closely related by blood. Sometimes, intermarriage also led to conflict because of the divergent loyalties of children of the chief's competing spouses (Waterhouse, 1997). In times of war, intertribal alliances were activated as chiefs requested the help of neighbouring chiefs to fight a common enemy. Often *tabua* (whale's tooth), a highly valued cultural artefact, was used by A to request B to fight C, and C would try to reverse the process by presenting a *tabua* to B to help defeat A. Strategic alliances were fluid and volatile, and *liumuri* (back-stabbing) was a clever tactical manoeuvre to outwit the enemy. The complex cycle of treachery helped to maintain a sense of political equilibrium because it ensured that chiefs kept a close check on each other's power. Being alert to both internal and external threat was a major social asset to ensure security. Some chiefs, such as Tui Lakeba, Tui Cakau and Vunivalu of Bau, even sought assistance from the Tongans, who had a long association with Fiji (Reid, 1990). For some time, Fiji had been a 'refugee' centre for exiled or runaway Tongan chiefs, as we shall see in Chapter 5.

Power struggles between sons of chiefs, who were often children of different mothers, were common, and in some cases brothers would kill each other as they competed for the right of succession. A central plank of this power struggle was competition over who would be the undisputed *qaqa* (warrior). The most successful contender had to prove his prowess in war and leadership skills at an early age. Clunie (1977) makes the point that socialisation into warriorhood started quite early in life through exposure to cannibalism, war role-play and warlike sports.

The construction of the warrior personality permeated almost every aspect of social life, including community security, sports, division of labour, religion, cannibalism and even sexuality. The warrior personified protection, power, authority and wisdom. Chiefs had to be the strongest warriors in the community, and a warrior's status was legitimised by the use of coercion, treachery and tactical wisdom (Calvert, 2003). Successful warriors were defined in terms of the number of people they killed in war, accorded high status in society, hero-worshipped and given special names; their clubs were provided with sacred names, reified and mythologised (Clunie, 1977). Warriors could take any woman of their choice and, after death, they became part of the eternal cosmology as protective ancestral spirits. As protectors, warriors provided the major security system, which kept social disruption in check, ensured social cohesion and provided continuity and survival of the group. This reified imagery of the warrior continues to be part of a Fijian boy's socialisation process through the inculcation of notions of *yalo qaqa* (bravery), *tagane* (manliness) and *dau vala* (fighter) among others. These personality traits helped to nurture a natural fit into the *yalo ni mataivalu* (military spirit), which was glorified through *meke* (traditional dances), *vucu* (chants), *sere* (songs) and *tukuni* (mythology). A corollary of this is the entrenched self-perception that indigenous Fijians are individually natural soldiers and collectively a martial race (Ravuvu, 1991b; Nawadra, 1995). We shall return to this point when we discuss the role of the military in contemporary Fijian politics.

Large areas of Fiji came under the authority and protection of powerful chiefs who extracted tribute from their subjects (Routledge, 1985). In fact, protection by conquering chiefs was predicated upon payment of tribute, provision of slave labour and subservient loyalty. The relationship between chiefs and commoners played out in the context of the internal hegemonic rule and influence of chiefs at different levels of social relationships. The security of chiefs was seen as the security of the rest of society. It was common for chiefs to collect tribute from people within their own communities as well as from conquered tribes under their control as a way of consolidating their power (Roth, 1953).

Threats to the warrior chief's position were both internal—from competing brothers or cousins—and external, often in the form of chiefs from other tribes, some of whom were their own relatives. War captives were classified as *bokola* (human flesh to be eaten) and were ceremonially consumed in feasts that symbolised internalisation of the enemy's power as well as psychological and spiritual dominance over enemies (Williams, 1982). At a time when polygamy was a marital norm, chiefs were at liberty to appropriate commoner wives from their own communities or neighbouring tribes. The chief's main wife was usually another chief's daughter, and intermarriage between tribes was a way of maintaining peace and forging long-term alliances, although this did not work all the time, as evidenced in the wars between the two powerful polities of Rewa and Bau, where the chiefs were close cousins (Routledge, 1985). One of the fundamental roles of the social structure and its division of labour was to provide social, economic and political security for chiefs, rather than for ordinary members of the community. Glorification of chiefly status and *mana* was central to the language of diplomacy and ceremonial discourse (Hocart, 1913).

Social transformation as a result of external influence started with the early beachcombers. Shipwrecked sailors, runaway convicts from Australia, whalers and adventurous sailors settled among the locals, became Fijianised and introduced guns and diseases (Maude, 1964). The missionaries were probably most influential in terms of transforming belief systems, cultures and the way security was redefined and articulated in everyday life. Instead of relying on the fearsome warrior and traditional gods for protection, the new security paradigm was based on protection by the Christian God, European technology and muskets (Waterhouse, 1866). To some extent this new paradigm undermined the legitimacy of the warrior personality, and altered the relationship between chiefs and the ordinary people.

The new sense of security introduced by missionaries was predicated on belief in European superiority and the denigration of everything 'heathen' (Ryle, 2010). Even before turning Christian, Cakobau was an avid collector of European goods, including a schooner and countless treasure boxes of European goods, which he saw as enhancing his wealth, prestige and power (Waterhouse, 1997). By the mid-1850s, competing chiefs possessed European firearms and cannons, which were used in wars. European artefacts and clothes were seen as symbolic of a new and higher culture, a belief planted and nurtured by early Europeans, including missionaries (Campbell, 1980). Missionaries saw themselves not only as saviours of souls but also as agents of Western civilisation and progress. To them, the future spiritual, social and political security of Fijians lay in Christianity, and the easiest way to achieve this was to convert chiefs and transform the warrior personalities (Williams, 1982; Calvert, 2003). It was expected that the rest of the community would automatically follow their chief's conversion. The conversion process became part of the political competition between chiefdoms and even led to wars in Bua, Tailevu, Lau and other parts of Fiji between chiefs and *vanua* that had accepted *lotu* (Christianity) and those opposed to it (Routledge, 1985). Opposition to *lotu* was based on the fear that the new religion would take away their identity, *mana*, power and authority and terminate the highly cherished continuity with the ancestral world, which had been cast as 'evil' and 'demonic' by the new religion (Thornley, 2002; Ryle, 2010).

Much of the early to mid-1800s saw the clash between two security systems: the Fijian and the European. By the 1850s, most chiefs in the eastern part of Fiji, through Tongan and missionary influence, had succumbed to the new religion (Scarr, 1984). Ma'afu, a Tongan chief who was leader of the Tongans in Fiji, extended his influence and became a threat to Cakobau, who set up his own government with the support of some Europeans (Spurway, 2015). These new governments provided a new form of security framework, which integrated both the Taukei and European systems. European-type laws were enacted that overruled local norms, and taxes were imposed in a similar manner as the old tributary system. On the island of Vanuabalavu, given to Ma'afu by Tui Cakau (paramount chief of Somosomo), Ma'afu set up a land tenure system whereby young men were given lots on which they farmed in order to pay their tribute to the Ma'afu government (Spurway, 2015). The same system found resonance in Tonga and is still in use now. Cakobau basically converted his conquered territories into a new 'modern' state using new European symbolism such as a flag (with a peace dove on it), an army reinvented from his *bati* (warrior clan), European advisers, taxes and new laws. Security was now imposed not through the whims of warrior chiefs and threats of war clubs but through European-styled laws endorsed by a council of chiefs and European advisers (Scarr, 1984).

Anti-colonial resistance and the security contours

By 10 October 1874, when Fiji was ceded to Britain by the local chiefs, security in Fiji was influenced by a number of perceived threats, including growing fear of the all-powerful Ma'afu, the prevalent lawlessness of European settlers and the continuing alienation of land by Europeans, some of whom were assisted by some chiefs (Maude, 1964; France, 1969). This deed of cession marked a significant turning point in Fiji's history as a new centralised state system was brought to bear in a country that hitherto consisted of competing chiefdoms (France, 1969). The deed of cession, which was signed by 12 Taukei chiefs together with British representatives, saw the establishment of a politically powerful and legally coercive system, which subjected the indigenous Fijians to British law, political institutions and norms (Newbury, 2011). Supported by various acts, it redefined the security discourse by shifting the emphasis away from the chiefs and community to the state and Crown.

The real intent among the indigenous Fijians of the deed of cession has been the subject of debate over the years. As Newbury observes:

> Time changes the perspectives. Later interpretations of the sovereign basis for concessions in the dialogue resulting in the transfer of political power between two cultures express the tension implicit in the use of historical documents lifted out of their historical context by a later generation of protagonists to serve very different political agendas. (Newbury, 2011: 28)

Some believe that the deed of cession was based on a contract between Queen Victoria and the Taukei chiefs, and therefore the instrument of independence should have been returned to the Taukei community and not to Fiji as a state (Baledrokadroka, 2003). This has thrown into question the legitimacy of Fiji as a state, which might be a laughable proposition but at the same time a serious one by some ethnonationalist lawyers and political activists in recent years.

Meanwhile, the establishment of the British colonial state was far from being a peaceful affair. In fact it was to be the beginning of a long, bitter and complex struggle, which saw interconnected moments of resistance by many indigenous Fijians, particularly those from the western side of Fiji, who saw British colonial rule together with their comprador Fijian chiefs, who were largely from the eastern side of Fiji, as posing a direct threat to their sovereignty and well-being (Durutalo, 1986). A series of resistance movements emerged that took different forms, from the direct use of force to more subtle modes of mobilisation and rebellion using religion and the withdrawal of labour and support for the colonial regime (Ravuvu, 1991a).

One of the very first and also possibly one of the most violent acts of dissent was a major rebellion in western and central Viti Levu in 1876, which came to be known as the Colo Wars, a mere two years after Fiji became a British colony (Nicole, 2006); Routledge, 1985). The term *colo* (pronounced *tholo*), which literally means inland or interior, was a derogatory label (which connotes being uncivilised, savage and wild) used by those along the coast and by colonial officials to refer to those in the interior of Viti Levu who had not embraced Christianity and were opposed to British colonial rule. The *Kai Colo* (people of Colo) were independent-minded and sought to protect their culture, land and social autonomy from encroaching external domination in the form of Christianity, colonialism and the hegemonic power of Bau, a chiefdom that was in alliance with the colonial state (Nicole, 2006).

Bau had been a powerful kingdom in precolonial times and had extended its empire through conquest to various parts of Fiji, except on the western side and in the interior of Viti Levu, which were not readily accessible and were well defended by local chiefs and their warriors. The anti-Bau, anti-Christian, anti-European planter and anti-colonial resistance spanned miles of territory linking villages across the borders of Nadroga, Serua, Namosi, Naitasiri and Ba provinces in a broad resistance alliance (Nicole, 2010; Thornley, 2002). The local grievances included tension with missionaries who had embarked on an aggressive program of conversion using local missionaries; European planters alienating arable land, often using dubious means; and the role of eastern chiefs in expanding their influence and power using the colonial state. The rebellion by the *Kai Colo* was brutally suppressed by the colonial state using the Armed Native Constabulary (ANC), which consisted largely of Taukei young men, recruited from 'friendly' villages, under the command of European officers (Brown, 1998).

The same grievances that provoked the Colo Wars also motivated the Tuka Movement of 1879–91, a broad-based rebellion opposed to the exploitative and oppressive attitudes and practices of Bauans, settlers, labour recruiters, missionaries and the colonial state and its institutions. Led by a charismatic leader, Navosavakadua ('he who speaks only once'), from the province of Ra, the Tuka Movement assumed a religious–cultural approach, a strategy that had a deep influence in mobilising the powerless and subaltern communities around Fiji (Kaplan, 1995). Ra had been subjugated by Bau for years. Many of its young men had been recruited for work as labourers, and some of its best land had been alienated through deceitful means. In the interior of the province lie the sacred Nakauvadra Ranges, believed to be the home of Fiji's supreme deity, Degei, the snake god (France, 1966). This sense of spirituality gave the Tuka movement a cosmological character that connected well with the religious-minded locals. The response by the colonial state was harsh, leading to the obliteration of some villages and the exiling of Navosavakadua to Rotuma, an isolated island in the north of Fiji.

In Vanua Levu, the second largest island in Fiji, there was also rebellion by the Seaqaqa people against the decision to bring the district of Sasa, which had close ties with the southern district of Wailevu, under the direct rule of Naduri, the seat of power of the high chief of Macuata, Tui Macuata. This resistance attracted the wrath of the ANC, which crushed the rebellion and whose leaders were either hanged or banished (Ali, 2008).

Opposition to the heavy-handed and oppressive style of colonial leadership through selected chiefs, who were designated high positions within the colonial regime, was rife, and many saw that the solution lay with forming a federation with New Zealand, a movement that was at its height from 1901 to 1903. In the first three decades of the 20th century, a charismatic leader, Apolosi Ranawai, was a major centre of attention because of his alternative socioeconomic scheme for indigenous Fijians. He set up the Viti Kabani (Fijian Company) for the purpose of empowering Taukei growers and businesses by undercutting European intermediaries who controlled the banana and copra market (Sutherland, 1992). This was tantamount to a revolt against the colonial capitalist economy, colonial state and chiefly order and therefore called for drastic response. Again, the reaction of the colonial state was to supress the movement by exiling Ranawai to Rotuma and later to New Zealand (Nicole, 2006).

Continued resistance to colonial rule also employed more subtle means in the form of semi-religious and political groups such as the Luveniwai Movement. This resistance was in response to taxation (*vakacavacava*), continued alienation of land by some chiefs, paternalistic colonial rule and exploitation of labour. Although there were strict rules under the native policy for movement of people, Fijians devised means of absenteeism from villages to avoid burdensome state-sponsored responsibilities such as taxation and the practice of *lala* or provision of goods and services to chiefs upon demand (Chappelle, 1970).

These forms of resistance were in direct response to the excesses of colonial rule, which threatened to undermine and usurp the autonomy and power of tribes as well as transform them into subservient entities of the Crown through the imposition of the Christian ethos, taxation, the reorganisation of land tenure systems and governance structures to reflect the interests of colonial capital in alliance with comprador chiefs (Nicole, 2010; Sutherland, 1992).

Crafting colonial security: Coercion, hegemony and divide and rule

The British response to colonial resistance took various forms, including the direct use of military force using the ANC, imprisonment, execution, village relocation, banishment from villages and exile of leaders (Ravuvu, 1991a; Nicole, 2006). More subtle means, such as surveillance, use of chiefly authority through the native administration and 'traditional' appeal, use of church influence and even the use of sports such as cricket, were deployed, sometimes cautiously and sometimes more enthusiastically, to keep indigenous Fijians under the tutelage of colonial hegemony.

Perhaps the most potent force for colonial pacification was the ANC, a paramilitary force that acted as police and army at the same time, set up through the *Royal Gazette* of 10 October 1874. The founding commander was Lieutenant Henry Olive of the Royal Marine Light Infantry, and senior officers were mostly Europeans. As in other colonial armies, the ordinary rank and file were local indigenous people, who were often pitted against other indigenous Fijians in the name of law and order. The ANC evolved from Cakobau's Royal Army, which was set up in 1871 and was used extensively to subdue tribes in central Viti Levu and Lovoni on Ovalua Island. At first, Europeans saw Cakobau's army as a threat to their security, but they changed their mind as the threats from the *Kai Colo* increased and Cakobau's army was the only available means of providing security (Brown, 1998).

The ANC brutally put down anti-government and anti-Christian insurrection against the *Kai Colo* around the Nadroga–Navosa area in what came to be known as the Little Wars (Brewster, 1922). The British used chiefs who were coopted into the colonial bureaucracy at the district level (*buli*) and provincial level (*roko*) to recruit villagers by leveraging traditional and kin-based loyalty. This was to be the pattern of recruitment into the Fijian armed forces for much of the 20th century (during World War I, World War II and the Malayan Emergency of the 1950s). In the service of the Crown, chiefs used their *mana* to invoke the masculine values of *yalo qaqa* (warrior spirit and bravery) and *dau vakarorogo* (loyalty and obedience) as a way of extricating young men from their daily communal responsibilities to become coercive agents of the colonisers. This created a situation of colonial paradox whereby the colonised were used as instruments of oppression against other colonised. The native soldiers were institutionalised, imbued with a new identity and ideological outlook and let loose among their own relatives, described thus:

> The ANC had performed well. Reports on the affair [Little Wars] stress that the indigenous troops of the government did not hesitate to kill men of the same race when ordered to do so by their officers. Nor did they hesitate to punish their own men. (Brown, 1998: ii)

4. END OF COUPS?

Gordon's idea was that wrongdoers were not to go through the mainstream British justice system all the time and were also to be judged by district commissioners with advice from Fijian assessors. The idea was to make use of the Fijian Administration mechanism as a way of maintaining and sustaining colonial hegemony without having to resort to force (all the time) to ensure submission. Despite this, the use of direct force continued unabated. The ANC was deployed to quell the rebellion in Seaqaqa in 1894, mentioned earlier. The governor declared a state of emergency, and 39 *sotia* (soldiers), commanded by Epeli Nailatikau, son of Seru Cakobau, were deployed on this operation. The rebellion was broken, and some survivors were arrested and sentenced to death, but this sentence was later commuted to imprisonment (Nicole, 2010; Brown, 1998).

The very first laws to set up Fiji's security forces were Ordinance No. XXX of 19 December 1876, which provided regulation of the police force, and Ordinance No. XXXI of 29 December, which provided regulation of the ANC (Colony of Fiji, 1876). There were four different classes in the disciplined forces: the ANC, whose members were called *sotia* (soldiers); the regular police (*ovisa*) in Suva and Levuka, at that time the only two urban centres; the rural police (*ovisa ni yasana*), who reported to the district commissioners; and the village police (*ovida ni koro*), who reported to the village headman (*turagani koro*).

Despite the existence of the ANC, local Europeans, consisting of merchants and plantation owners who modelled themselves along the lines of European landed gentry, were still uncertain of the capacity of Taukei soldiers to protect them. They persuaded Governor George O'Brien to enact an ordinance to establish a volunteer force in 1897. One of the primary reasons for this measure was to quell local disturbances against plantation owners. Another reason was to respond to rumours about a possible New Zealand invasion. This ordinance was repealed in March 1906 and was replaced by the Fiji Rifle Association Ordinance, which allowed the mobilisation of rifle clubs in case of a New Zealand 'invasion' (Colony of Fiji, 1906). These clubs formed a private army of sorts, which operated outside the ambit of state control. The real intention of the 1906 Ordinance was not so much defence against possible invasion as protection of European economic and political interests in Fiji at a time when the colonial policies on land, under Gordon's orthodoxy, were seen by many Europeans as being too pro-native (Brown, 1998).

The security dynamics in the colony gained an extra ethnic dimension after 1879 with the arrival of Indian labourers in that year to work on the sugar plantations (Lal, 2004). European–Taukei relations, based on vertical political patronage and paternalism, gave way to a more horizontal intercultural relationship predicated on suspicion and hostility. The influx of Indians meant the indigenous Fijians were no longer seen as the only subaltern group that posed a major threat to Europeans but were viewed instead as a convenient strategic leverage against the Indians, who were seen as troublesome and in need of coercive control.

Fiji's new ethnically demarcated society was characterised by ethnicised division of economic, social and political spaces, which provided the security environment conducive to the protection of European capital and political interests at the cost of the other two subaltern groups: the Taukei, who lived a subsistence village life under the tutelage of chiefs, and Indo-Fijians, who lived a regimented and oppressive plantation life within the cane belt (Sutherland, 1992). The security apparatus of the colonial state ensured that the social lines which demarcated ethnic spaces were clear. A manifest consequence of this was the way in which the subaltern groups (in this case the indigenous Fijians and Indo-Fijians) were pitted against one another through separate representation in the legislature, ethnic economic division of labour and separate political governance system for indigenous Fijians (Fijian Administration). This institutionalised system of demarcated governance provided the security pillar for what was known as the 'divide and rule' policy (Macnaught, 2016).

The use of hegemony, in the Gramscian sense, as a security strategy was evident and worked very well for British colonial control, in fact more effectively than the deployment of coercion through the ANC. Hegemony was articulated through a complex system of administration, political representation and cultural control and reproduction. These included a syncretic mixture of British state bureaucracy to legally frame the process of decision-making (Macnaught, 2016) as well as the use of Taukei chiefs to preside over the various levels of Taukei administration at the national, provincial, district and village levels, and rigid rules under the Native Act to keep indigenous Fijians within the social rubric of communalism, a form of social organisation that the British deliberately imposed to keep ordinary Taukei subservient to chiefs who acted as compradors for the colonial state (Ratuva, 2013; Sutherland, 1992).

A separate Fijian Administration (*Tabacakacaka ni Taukei*) structure was created in 1876, with the Great Council of Chiefs (*Bose Levu Vakaturaga*) as the apex deliberative body. This system defined the boundaries of cultural identity and political rights of the indigenous Fijians in a paternalistic way, often by arbitrarily imposing decisions and declaring them sacrosanct and beyond questioning. Submission to the officially sanctioned Taukei code of cultural dispositions and behaviour was legitimised through appeal to the belief in an immemorial and divinely ordained chiefly culture (*i tovo vaka-turaga*) and the indispensability of kinship ties (*veiwekani*). The native policy defined the ethno-administrative boundaries of Taukei identity as well as the 'security' parameters that demarcated the Taukei from other ethnic groups, principally the Indo-Fijians, who were made out to be a threat to Taukei land, culture, rights and political interests (Nayacakalou, 1975). This system of social insulation acted as a political security buffer as well as a system of control by the colonial state, whose policies not only reinforced the separation of the different ethnic groups but also pitted one against the other.

The changing global security climate in the British Empire and the world generally had some influence on security at home. Soldiers from Fiji (most of European origin) participated in the Boer War in the late 1800s and early 1900s as well as World War I (1914–18), as both were expressions of loyalty to the empire. Indigenous Fijians, like other coloured colonised people under the British Crown, were not allowed to bear arms and fight at the front during World War I and instead were confined to membership of the labour corps. This changed during World War II when a Fijian battalion was sent to fight in Solomon Islands against Japanese forces under New Zealand and US officers. The wars were opportunities by the British to tighten their security grip on the colonies using emergency powers and enlistment of able-bodied men to fight their wars (Nawadra, 1995; Ravuvu, 1991b).

Meanwhile, rebellion in the plantations by Indo-Fijian labourers was common in the late 1800s and early 1900s and in the 1920s. In some cases policemen were sent to quell the disturbances (Gillion, 1962). Intervention in sugar plantation tension served three major purposes. First, it was a way of keeping industrial peace, which served the interest of colonial capital; second, it helped to keep Indian workers and their grievances isolated from Taukei Fijian workers, who also expressed opposition to exploitation; and third, it presented an opportunity for the colonial state to affirm its authority and legitimacy in the new colony (Sutherland, 1992). This had resonance with the broader security framework of the 'divide and rule' policy to maintain ethnic separation as a way to ensure that aggrieved Indo-Fijian and Taukei workers did not join forces and pose a direct threat to colonial capital.

Chiefs were readily deployed to isolate Taukei workers and persuade them to refrain from participation in industrial strikes and other forms of dispute because they undermined the Taukei sense of community and cultural respect. An example of this occurred during the oil workers' strike of 1959, when workers of different ethnic groups took part in an oil workers' strike, which spread to other industries and culminated in a major anti-colonial riot in central Suva. Chiefs used their traditional authority to call indigenous Fijian workers together and ask them to refrain from any activity that would bring disrepute to the chiefly system and Taukei culture (Sutherland, 1992). The appeal to tradition and loyalty to chiefs was a powerful psychological tool to deter anti-state resistance among indigenous Fijians. This was a technique used throughout the colonial period to break up trans-ethnic proletariat solidarity and reinforce the power of the chieftocracy, a close ally of the colonial state (Durutalo, 1986).

Responses to the use of security strategies such as direct coercion, institutional control, ideological and cultural domination and political manipulation were diverse. While such strategies ensured submission to the whims of colonial hegemony, they also generated multiple responses in the form of cynicism, evasive tactics and direct opposition. The multiple nodes and expressions of power (in the Foucauldian sense) attempted to institutionalise control at one level, but at another level it was not easy to contain, control and transform the multiple and diffused manifestations of power in the community. Security in the colonial contest therefore became highly contested in a way that saw the hegemonic and subaltern discourses engaging in both mutual and contradictory ways. Upon independence in 1970, the security environment changed, although some of the underlying ethnic, economic, cultural and political factors remained and continued to influence postcolonial relations.

Postcolonial transformation: The politics of securitisation

Some of the more salient features of security in the postcolonial era were, in the main, defined in ethnopolitical terms, articulated in three ways. The first was the sense of self-preservation and parochialism about a group's own security and how this was contained within a well-defined cultural boundary (Norton, 1977). The second was how this boundary would impinge on and even intersect with other cultural boundaries. The third was how the area of convergence of these boundaries could be negotiated to create a balance and an overriding national identity. In other words, how was communal identity to be reconciled with national identity in a way that ensured political equilibrium and stability (Ratuva, 2005)?

This was a classic case of communal nationalism versus civic nationalism, as articulated by Stavenhagen (1996), where the desire to protect and promote group interest often collides with the collective interest, represented by the state. However, Stavenhagen tends to dichotomise the relationship between the two forms of nationalism and fails to take into consideration the syncretic relationship between them, which often involves the simultaneous coexistence and interaction between contestation, accommodation and synthesis (Ratuva, 2004). Rather than assuming a stereotyped binary configuration, ethnic relations in Fiji articulated themselves in multiple forms: while there was tension, there was also accommodation; while there was racialisation, there was also multicultural engagement; while there was communalism, there were also individual rights; while there was authoritarian rule through coups, there was also popular democracy (Ratuva, 2004). This complex syncretic configuration shaped the trajectory and character of Fijian political and social discourse and security in the postcolonial period.

The perception of security in Fiji needs to be understood in the broad context of this complex syncretic interplay of diverse forces, rather than the narrow emphasis on ethnicity. The racialised discourse should not be seen in isolation but must be linked to issues such as group rights and identity, resources including land, power, inequality and socioeconomic status. The simplistic ethnic lens has the potential to construct premeditated threats in the form of the other, and this manifested itself in a Taukei sense of anxiety whipped up during the colonial days regarding a possible takeover of their land by Indo-Fijians, and the Indo-Fijian fear of loss of citizenship and rights. Communal anxieties fed into each other, creating a vortex of distrust, which was exacerbated in times of crisis.

Racialised constitutional engineering and insecuritisation

Since independence in 1970, Fiji has had four constitutions (1970, 1990, 1997 and 2013), and all have either been victims of or results of coups, political conflict and anxiety about group security, and rights. Constitutional engineering was often seen as a mechanism for conflict resolution through provision of ethnic representation, but in the 2013 constitution, the emphasis on ethnic representation was curtailed in favour of common trans-ethnic representation through a single national constituency under a proportional representation system.

The 1970 constitution, the first after independence, provided for a whole series of mechanisms to respond to perceptions of group insecurity by both Taukei and Indo-Fijians. The first of these was political representation. Of the 52 parliamentary seats allocated, 22 were reserved for indigenous Fijians, 22 for Indo-Fijians and 8 for other minorities (European, part-Europeans, Chinese, Pacific Islanders and so on) usually categorised as 'general electors'. The 22 seats for each of the two major ethnic groups were further divided into 12 communal (elected by members of the same community) and 10 national roll seats to be elected cross-ethnically. For general electors, the division was three communal and five national roll seats (Fiji Government, 1970). This communal system of seat reservation was meant to provide a sense of balance and national confidence to respond to fears by indigenous Fijians of possible domination by the numerically superior Indo-Fijians, who over the years have been persistent not only about independence but also about exerting their political rights through a one-person one-vote system of election. In 1966, four years before independence, Indo-Fijians comprised 51 per cent of the population, as opposed to 42 per cent for the indigenous Fijians, a demographic balance that indigenous Fijians feared would give Indo-Fijians electoral advantage. Fear of loss of political rights through elections and loss of land rights through foreign and Indo-Fijian speculation and entrepreneurship were powerful factors in the minds of many indigenous Fijians (Ali, 1972).

During the 1969 constitutional talks in London, the agreement between the leaders of the Alliance Party, representing Taukei and minority interests, and the National Federation Party, representing Indo-Fijian interests, revolved around a discursive process of ethnic bargaining. The result was a constitution that represented two competing interests synthesised into a common national trajectory. This consensus of sorts was re-elected in the post-independence 'multiracialism' philosophy of the ruling Alliance Party, which won the pre-independence election in 1966 and the first post-independence election in 1972 (Ali, 1972). The multiracial experiment consisted of two competing discursive philosophies: coexistence and distinctiveness. The former referred to different ethnocultural and religious groups living side by side, observing each other's holidays (such as Christmas and Easter for Christians, Diwali for Hindus and Mohammed's birthday for Muslims), sharing common national symbols such as flag and anthem, sharing daily cultural artefacts, food, music and values and promoting ideological consciousness about a unified national identity. The second aspect, paradoxically, appeared to be a counteracting ideological force and referred to the idea of ethnocultural distinctiveness, whereby individual communities maintained and expressed their distinctive identities and interests. This formula was predicated on the assumption that multiculturalism was workable only in a situation where diversity and distinctiveness existed side by side and was articulated simultaneously as part of a unifying national identity (Ratuva, 2004).

In the broader security schema, this was probably a workable arrangement then, given the prevailing circumstances, because the opposing forces converged in a middle space where they negotiated and appeased each other, at least at the level of parliamentary politics and everyday ethnic relations, although this did not fully address the deeper schisms that were to manifest themselves later in times of crisis (Robertson & Sutherland, 2002). The interaction between coexistence and distinctiveness was part of a syncretic dynamics—meaning that there was a simultaneous occurrence of cultural accommodation as well as contradiction, which maintained a certain degree of harmony in the first 13 years after independence. It was not an overwhelmingly tense and racialised situation, but a situation where relationships oscillated between tension and consensus in a dynamic way within the broader rubric of the Alliance Party's multiracial philosophy. However, the paradox was that this synergy also helped to deepen and consolidate the Alliance Party's hegemonic strategy to maintain political and ideological dominance of a trans-ethnic alliance between chiefly and business elites. Multiculturalism was a Trojan Horse of sorts to maintain this alliance. The chiefly elites had strong political leverage over the Taukei Fijian population, and multiracialism was seen as workable only if the interests of these elites were left unchallenged (Robertson & Sutherland, 2002). The communal distribution of seats and ethnopolitical culture, or what has been termed 'communal democracy' (Ratuva, 2005), reinforced this sociopolitical arrangement and at the same time rendered it fragile.

Sociologically, this situation created a syncretic condition that pitted communal and civic nationalism against each other, as Stavenhagen (1996) talked about, where tension and accommodation between the exertion of ethnocommunal difference and reconciliation of diversity for national unity take place simultaneously, with one overcoming the other in particular instances. The contestation between the two modes of nationalism becomes acute in times of crisis, particularly when ethnonationalism becomes an unrestrained force that seeks to transform and overtake civic nationalism as the dominant political and ideological force (Horowitz, 1985). The situation often becomes critical when contestation over state power, threat to cultural group rights, protection of identity, competition over resources and perception of exploitation and marginalisation become part of the political equation and are exploited by ethnic entrepreneurs for political advantage (Jenkins, 2008). The use of aggressive institutional leveraging and ultimately force by the dominant ethnocultural group can result from this contested synergy and thus create a situation of insecurity for the state and other ethnic groups, and can undermine civic nationalism as the unifying force for the state.

That is exactly what happened in 1987 when the cloak of civic nationalism, buttressed by the multiracialist ideology, was overcome by the power of Taukei ethnonationalism. The crisis was provoked by the defeat of the Alliance Party, which had total control of the state apparatus, including the military and other powerful neocolonial indigenous institutions, such as the Great Council of Chiefs (GCC), the Fijian Affairs Board, the Native Land Trust Board and Provincial Councils, with the backing of the European and Indo-Fijian business community and most of members of the indigenous population. As mentioned earlier, despite its multiracial philosophy, the Alliance Party's real power was anchored on the power and privilege of the Taukei chieftocracy, which provided the primordial *mana* and cultural legitimacy for ethnonationalist agitation after the Alliance's electoral loss during the April 1987 general elections (Robertson & Tamanisau, 1988).

The victorious coalition, consisting of the newly formed Fiji Labour Party (FLP) and the Indo-Fijian–dominated National Federation Party (NFP), posed a direct threat to the Alliance's political hegemony as well as to the Taukei institutions that were part of its broader alliance. The national destabilisation activities of the Taukei Movement, an extremist ethnonationalist vigilante group consisting of Alliance supporters, were targeted at the Indo-Fijian political 'take-over', which was perceived as posing a threat to Taukei political rights, land security, economic interests and religious beliefs. The harmonious balance between communal and civic nationalism was broken as a result of the shift in political gravity away from Taukei political control. The underlying contradictions between the notions of coexistence and distinctiveness, which encapsulated the philosophy of multiracialism, were thrust to the surface, with the latter overshadowing the former as it asserted itself in an aggressive and violent way (Prasad, 1989).

The military, which was closely aligned with the chieftocratic system—culturally, politically and historically—intervened on behalf of the Alliance historical bloc, despite its constitutional role as the 'neutral' vanguard of national security. The role of the military, as we will later consider in detail, was largely shaped by a rather uncomfortable mixture of institutional praetorian norms learnt in military colleges and Taukei sociocultural values of warrior masculinity, inculcated through close association with the chieftocracy and indigenous cultural ethos (Sanday, 1991).

To the Taukei ethnonationalists, the capture of state power by the military provided considerable relief. Many felt that, with the help of the military, Taukei communal rights and political ascendancy were now secure, and this was constitutionalised in 1990 (Reeves, Vakatora & Lal , 1996). A pertinent aspect of the 1990 constitution was the way it conceptually connected national security and Taukei security as being symbiotic; that is, national security was possible only through protection of Taukei security:

> The events of 1987 were occasioned by a widespread belief that the 1970 constitution was inadequate to give protection to the interests of the indigenous Fijian people, their values, traditions, customs, way of life and economic well-being … the indigenous people of Fiji are endowed with their lands and other resources and the right to govern themselves for their advancement and welfare. (Fiji Government, 1990: 12)

Taukei political ascendancy was further bolstered by the communal representation system, which provided 37 seats for Taukei, 27 for Indo-Fijians, one for Rotumans and five for other ethnic minorities in a 70-member parliament (Fiji Government, 1990: 49). To secure Taukei political control further, the 1990 constitution ensured Taukei dominance in the 34-member senate, in which 24 seats were allocated through nomination by the Taukei-dominated Great Council of Chiefs (GCC), one seat was for the Rotuman community and nine for Indo-Fijians and others. The GCC was constitutionally required to appoint the president, and this effectively meant that the position of head of state was to remain perpetually in Taukei hands (Lal, 1998).

The process of state capture and the attempt at political ascendancy by the Taukei to entrench their group security merely institutionalised and increased the political insecurity of Indo-Fijians. This security zero-sum game was to be the dominant pattern of ethnopolitics for a number of years even after the 1997 constitution, which provided for 25 open seats and 46 communal seats, was promulgated (Fiji Government, 1997). Despite the attempt in the 1997 constitution to provide a sense of shared security for all citizens through the new Alternative Vote (AV) electoral system, a Bill of Rights and social justice provision, the perception of insecurity among the more marginal members of the Taukei community persisted, and ethnic entrepreneurs took advantage of this to whip up ethnonationalist fervour. Thus, when Mahendra Chaudhry was elected as the first Indo-Fijian prime minister in 1999, ethnonationalism reared its ugly head again and agitation increased in tempo, culminating in yet another coup in May 2000 (Robertson & Sutherland, 2002).

This time the role of the military was more ambivalent than in the two coups in 1987. The reason for this was that there was confusion due to the number of players with different motives involved. For instance, the elite Counter Revolutionary Warfare Unit (CRW) of the military was involved, together with ethnonationalist politicians and activists, and senior military officers were divided as to whether the military should support the coup. The military eventually decided to 'officially' oppose the coup; it imposed emergency powers, removed the president and the constitution (in another coup), arrested the coup-makers and set the country on a path towards re-democratisation. This series of events raised fundamental questions about the dramatically oscillating security dynamics in Fiji, especially the changing position of the military in relation to framing security, the unreliability of constitutional engineering in protecting group security and, as we saw in 1987, the power of ethnonationalism to spawn dramatic political change in the name of Taukei security.

The 2000 coup was paradigm shifting in the sense that it marked the reconfiguration of the military's relationship with Taukei chieftocracy and ethnonationalism. Instead of being seen as allies, as in the 1987 coups, these powerful political forces were now seen as sources of insecurity. Although the military had appointed Laisenia Qarase, a fervent ethnonationalist, interim prime minister in 2000, he was later vilified by the military, even after he won the 2001 and 2006 elections, as posing a threat to national security because of his political beliefs. The continuing differences between Qarase's party, the Soqosoqo Duavata ni Lewe ni Vanua (SDL) and the military, led by Commodore Frank Bainimarama, created a national security crisis that was soon to plunge Fiji into another period of turmoil (Ratuva, 2011a).

Central to this security crisis was the way the military, the most powerful security institution of the state, was at loggerheads with the elected government on a number of issues, including the dispute over the extension of the commander's contract and differences over two controversial Bills that the SDL had planned to put through Parliament. The first was the Reconciliation, Truth and Unity Bill, which called for the release of George Speight, leader of the 2000 coup, and his fellow coup-makers as a condition for national reconciliation, among other things. The second was the Qoliqoli Bill (Fishing Rights Bill), which was aimed at transferring ownership of the foreshore area from the state to Taukei landowners. Opposition to these Bills by the military was framed around their potential to inflame inter-ethnic tension and heighten insecurity. Threats by Bainimarama against the overthrow of the Qarase government attracted charges of treason, which the police had started investigating (Fraenkel & Firth, 2007).

The tension escalated, resulting in the overthrow of the Qarase government by the military in December 2006. Later, in March 2009, the Supreme Court ruled that the coup was illegal. Less than 24 hours later, the president abrogated the constitution and reappointed Bainimarama as prime minister in what was technically another coup. The abrogation of the constitution was significant, because it meant that all constitutionally prescribed state institutions, positions and power were completely annulled and state control shifted entirely to the military.

The military regime accelerated the pace of social, economic and political transformation in line with the People's Charter, a document put together earlier in 2007–08 as a blueprint for post-coup reform (Fiji Government, 2008). Among the changes were the abolition of the GCC, which the military regarded as a threat to national security, reform of the Taukei neocolonial institutions, deployment of military officers in key government positions, prosecution of perpetrators of corruption by the newly formed Fiji Commission Against Corruption, aggressive national development strategies and the use of the term 'Fijian' for all Fiji citizens of different ethnic groups (Ratuva, 2013).

The abolition of the GCC in particular was controversial, and people reacted to it differently. For more conservative Taukei, the abolition of the GCC and reform of the neocolonial institutions posed a threat to their sense of cultural security. The more progressive Taukei saw the GCC as an archaic institution whose role in sustaining chiefly privilege had to end. From the viewpoint of some Indo-Fijians, the abolition of the GCC provided a sense of relief that a major legitimising tool of ethnonationalism, which had in the past posed a threat to their political security, was now history. However, some Indo-Fijians had close links with some chiefs who were members of the GCC and who acted as a restraining force on extreme ethnonationalism. There were those who feared that the abolition of the GCC would resurrect and regalvanise ethnonationalism in an ugly manner. The prediction by some that FijiFirst, the coup supporters' party, would lose the 2014 election under the new 2013 constitution because of the abolition of the GCC did not eventuate. In fact, FijiFirst won a landslide victory and also secured more than 50 per cent of Taukei votes (Ratuva & Lawson, 2016).

The coups, as we have seen briefly above, have shown that even constitutional safeguards were not sufficient to avoid ethnopolitical conflict and state capture. While constitutional engineering helped to reconfigure state structure, provided norms for representation and legitimised the operation of the state, it failed to contain ethnonationalism and ethnic contestation. The successive constitutions dealt only with structural and normative issues and did not address the deeper ideological and cultural issues. The constitutionally prescribed communal representation system in the 1970, 1990 and 1997 constitutions helped to institutionally entrench and socially legitimise ethnopolitical contestation and antagonism, although in different degrees. Despite its attempts at providing ethnic balance and multiracial security, the 1970 constitution merely created conditions for the potential unravelling of multiracialism in crisis situations. The 1990 constitution mainstreamed ethnonationalism, provided security for the Taukei and reigned in insecurity for Indo-Fijians and other ethnic minorities. The thawing of ethnic relations and the establishment of the 1997 constitution, considered to be one of the most progressive in the world, failed to curb the excesses of ethnonationalism leading up to the 2000 coup and the tension that precipitated the 2006 coup.

The promulgation of the 2013 constitution is based on the assumption that the 2006 coups and the subsequent transformation of Fijian society has removed once and for all the scourge of ethnonationalism, and has replaced it with a multiracial society predicated on trans-ethnic equality and supported by the open proportional representation system. Its promulgation and legitimacy have been widely criticised and questioned because of the politics associated with the constitutional process. The draft constitution put together by the Constitution Commission led by Professor Yash Ghai was rejected, and the government created its own version by cannibalising aspects of the Ghai draft. The 2013 constitution attempts to guarantee security in different ways such as the removal of ethnic representation, strengthening the role of the military as a security 'watchdog' and, ironically, giving more power to the executive in appointments as well as giving amnesty to perpetrators of past coups, among others.

The cumulative effect, as we see today, is the greater centralisation of power in the hands of the attorney general and prime pinister, unwanted intervention in parliamentary political debate by the military and use of fear as a means of manufacturing consent among the civil service and population. It is fair to say that the 2013 constitution was founded on the premise of security to facilitate the interests of a range of players, including coup perpetrators, executive, ruling party and a state system that has a much deeper and authoritarian control over the civil service and population. Any action that militates against the dominant order, such as strike action by unions or attempts at political extremism and dissention, is often met with efficient response through the use of a range of legalistic mechanisms meant to inhibit rather than encourage democracy. The election in 2014, won through a 60 per cent majority by the military-backed FijiFirst, was the first under the 2013 constitution, and in a way it institutionalised the security narratives mentioned above.

However, the result of the November 2018 election saw the ruling FijiFirst winning by only 50.02 per cent of the total vote. While this majority is sufficient to sustain a stable government in the next four years, the real question is, if this trend continues, what might happen if the Taukei-based Social Democratic Liberal Party (SODELPA) wins the next election in 2022? Will the military maintain its constitutional role as an independent security institution, or will it maintain its loyalty to the FijiFirst and intervene extralegally on its behalf as it has done in the past?

Politics of economic security

Perhaps one of the most salient security factors closely associated with ethnic politics over the years has been perceived and experienced inequality. Associated with this was mutual self-victimhood whereby both Taukei and Indo-Fijians saw the other as privileged while considering themselves to be marginalised and exploited. The Taukei saw Indo-Fijian dominance in the retail, commercial and professional sector as 'evidence' of economic domination, self-enhancement and even exploitative tendencies. On the reverse side of the coin, Indo-Fijians saw ownership of about 90 per cent of the land by Taukei landowning groups as symptomatic of unequal rights and wastage of resources.

The Taukei sense of economic disadvantage had deeper roots in the colonial epoch when a series of laws and policies under the native administration locked Taukei into a rigid communal life revolving around the village subsistence sector under the tutelage of chieftocrats, who also acted as comprador functionaries for the colonial state (Fisk, 1978). This system drew inspiration from the protectionist ideology of the first British Governor, Sir Arthur Gordon, whose social Darwinian belief was that the best way for the Taukei to survive the vagaries of Western influence was through preservation of their culture and the inalienability of their land:

> To have preserved the actual institutions of native society might have stemmed the rapid decrease in the Fijian population; to have encouraged the adoption of European institutions might have enabled the survivors to adjust themselves to the changing world introduced by the white man. (France, 1969: 31)

The policy cocooned the Taukei in a communal system characterised by feudalistic subservience and greater institutional control over their lives, and this had a profound and long-lasting effect on the socioeconomic situation and political psyche of the Taukei.

While the Taukei were locked into the communal subsistence village life, other ethnic groups had a head start in education and commerce, thus creating and solidifying inequality, which saw the Taukei at the bottom of the commercial, educational and professional ladder. This intersection between ethnicity and class shaped perception and attitudes between communities and, for the Taukei, it was a latent source of their grievances. When the native policies were relaxed towards the mid-1960s as Fiji moved towards independence, these grievances were articulated more readily and became a source of ethnonationalist sentiment (Nayacakalou, 1975).

Socioeconomic grievances and envy were readily translated into political grievances against Indo-Fijians because of their preponderance in retail and commerce. The relationship between economic insecurity and political grievance is noteworthy here because in the colonial and even postcolonial economy the two were closely related. Part of the Taukei sense of resentment emanated from their awe of the capitalist economy and all its technological aspects and commercial institutions that they had been made to believe were superior to, and more progressive than, the subsistence economy under which they lived. The Taukei came to see themselves as 'inferior' to the Europeans and Indo-Fijians who controlled the capitalist economy. This sense of marginalisation and disempowerment became a psychological breeding ground that nurtured ethnonationalism in later years.

Attempts to address the economic security of the Taukei through piecemeal introduction of the cash economy in the 1950s, 1960s and 1970s failed to make any substantive transformation (Spate, 1959; Belshaw, 1964; Ratuva, 2013; Bain, 1986). Among numerous reasons was the control of these development projects by chieftocrats selected by the colonial state, whose interests were largely focused on accumulation of wealth and power for themselves. This was a case of 'inherent obstacles to economic advance imposed by the traditional system' (Spate, 1959: 55). By the time of independence, the Alliance government, aware of the growing disparity, integrated the notion of Taukei special development into a series of five-year development plans. This, too, failed to have any significant impact on the socioeconomic situation of the Taukei because it was treated almost like a mere footnote to the development plans (Ratuva, 2013).

Underneath the euphoria of independence and hope of a new national identity and destiny was the problem of socioeconomic inequality (Fisk, 1970). The private sector was controlled largely by European and Indo-Fijian capital, while the professional and educated Taukei were mostly concentrated in the civil service, which also had a preponderance of Indo-Fijians. These economic grievances were used as agenda for political mobilisation in 1975 when the Fijian Nationalist Party was formed by a group of urban Taukei entrepreneurs who found their business endeavours constantly thwarted as they competed against the monopoly of the Indo-Fijian commercial class, which controlled retail, real estate and other commercial enterprises. When the Taukei-supported Alliance Party lost the election to the Indo Fijian dominated National Federation Party – Labour coalition in April 1987, there was a major shift in the balance of power away from the Taukei. As a consequence, the grievances came to the surface and precipitated ethnic tension and created a major schism. In the ensuing riots, Indo-Fijian shops and properties were indiscriminately targeted.

The affirmative action policies put in place by the Soqosoqo ni Vakavulewa ni Taukei party, led by coup leader Sitiveni Rabuka after the 1987 coup were predicated on the belief that the best way to avoid future coups was to bridge the economic gap between the Taukei and Indo- Fijians. One of the aims of this affirmative action program was to create a Taukei business class to balance the Indo-Fijian commercial dominance. Concerted energy to create equality through the shortest possible time was seen as an imperative to achieve economic parity, social justice and intercommunal harmony. The state, now under Taukei control, provided preferential policies in the form of special Taukei loans, scholarships, business licences, taxi licences, fishing licences and other forms of grants. Unfortunately, the patronage system within the Taukei political and commercial hierarchy got in the way of what was theoretically a socially progressive program. This led to widespread corruption, whereby some leading Taukei bureaucrats were able to manipulate their links and power within the state system to divert state funds to their investments. Perhaps the worst consequence of the patronage system and corruption was the collapse of the National Bank of Fiji, which dished out a flood of cash to elite Taukei under the justification of economic empowerment. As a result the bank became insolvent and had to close after losing more than FJ$300 million (Ratuva, 2013).

After the 2000 coup, a more systematic affirmative action framework, called the 20-Year Development Plan (2001–20) for the Enhancement of Participation of Indigenous Fijians and Rotumans in the Socioeconomic Development of Fiji, was put in place by the SDL, under Prime Minister Laisenia Qarase. The document made the optimistic assertion that:

> In conflict resolution, affirmative action helps address the grievances of particular groups who have been historically disadvantaged, and have used extremist political means to articulate these grievances. In this way, affirmative action directly targets the grievances by removing the existing inequalities, and thus assists in minimising political tension and conflict. (Fiji Government, 2002: 24)

Unfortunately, these noble goals were not achieved because of the corruption and scandals associated with the program, which led to the prosecution and imprisonment of a number of civil servants and a prominent businessman.

After the 2006 coup, the strategy for addressing Taukei economic security changed from affirmative action, which was abolished, to an integrated development strategy for national development. The military regime, which in September 2014 returned to power through a landslide victory under the banner of the FijiFirst party, also introduced social protection polices in the form of free education, free buses for students and elderly citizens, and an increase in social welfare allocations, among other things.

Although economic affirmative action as a measure to address security did not work as well as hoped, the consolation was that educational affirmative action was perhaps the most successful initiative because it helped many Taukei achieve higher levels of education and at the same time contributed to the expansion of a sizeable Taukei middle class. Although affirmative action was a state-driven program to uplift the economic security of the Taukei, it was seen by other ethnic groups, especially the Indo-Fijians, as a form of discrimination against them.

The military and security

The Fiji military has come under serious scrutiny in recent years because its behaviour since 1987 in relation to staging coups, and its responsibility for human rights abuses, has raised questions about its reliability as the last bastion of security. Despite changes in the justifications for coups (in 1987 it was in support of Taukei ethnonationalism, and in 2006 it was purportedly to thwart ethnonationalism) and institutional transformation from 1987 to the present, its interventionist tendencies continue and have been further strengthened by the 2013 constitution, which prescribed a more proactive security watchdog role for the military. Studies of the Fiji military have largely revolved around its praetorian character and contemporary interventionist role in politics, staging coups and imposing authoritarian rule (Sanday, 1991). Sometimes we overlook some of the deeper cultural dynamics associated with the notion of warrior psychology, as we discussed earlier, and its role in providing cultural framing of both Taukei masculinity and Fiji military. A better understanding of the military could be gleaned from analysing it at two levels: the sociocultural and the institutional.

Sociocultural norms and psychology of the military

It is interesting to note that one of the legacies of the precolonial era is the notion of warrior culture psychology. The warriors in precolonial days were not part of a specialised institution but were individuals bound by sociocultural norms and expectations to *taqomaka* (protect) the community from other tribes (Waterhouse, 1866). During times of conflict, warriors were drawn from the ranks of ordinary young men in the community or friendly tribes; otherwise the role of protecting the chief was the responsibility of the warrior class or *bati*.

The warrior psychology was premised on two interrelated discourses. The first was the notion of *tagane* (masculinity) and how this was stratified in relation to one's level of *qaqa* (physical prowess) and *yalo kaukauwa* (bravery). The second was the bestowing of honour through community praise and the construction of a mythology to differentiate the hero-warrior from ordinary men. The elevation of the warrior to the level of cosmological stardom brought honour, respect and glory to the entire community. In the early days, successful warriors were given special names to signify their social status. While Taukei society has changed dramatically over the years, the cultural reification of masculinity and warrior psychology continued to be passed down through the ages via gender socialisation. As young boys grow up, they are initiated into martial ways to become a *tagane* (tough man), which in many ways prepares them for a future soldering life. Many Taukei young men see themselves as 'natural' soldiers. The community-wide impact of this belief is pervasive. Almost every Taukei has a close relative in the military (Baledrokadroka, 2016).

The idealised construction of the past remains a potent social force that influences male identity and sense of being. Failing to live up to honourable warrior virtues is considered demeaning and unworthy of a Fijian warrior. This collective martial consciousness found expression on active duty during international military operations. In peacetime, it is embodied in situations requiring the articulation of masculinity, such as rugby and street-fighting; other manifestations include patriarchal hegemony and the domestic abuse of wives.

The notion of warrior psychology becomes a security threat when framed and articulated in an ethnicised way. Often Indo-Fijians are considered *lamulamu* (cowards) and *malumalumu* (physically weak) and therefore have no place in the military, considered the natural enclave for Taukei (Durutalo, 1986). The overt military expression of masculinity became prominent during the series of coups since 1987, in which the military's coercive might was used to usurp constitutional and state authority. The interplay between the traditional notion of the warrior and the modern notion of the professional soldier defines the identity of a Taukei soldier, and in some ways the military frames the Fiji security environment. However, despite this, the military can still play a syncretic role: first, as leverage for ethnonationalism, authoritarianism or for human rights abuse; second, to promote stability, security and peace. The Fiji military and the deeply embedded warrior ideology have played a major role in shaping the security discourse and climate in Fiji, and they will continue to do so in the future.

Institutional role of the military

Views about the Fiji military, a 3,000-strong institution, have been framed in two opposing ways. First, it is seen as a coup-making institution whose very existence poses a threat to the security of democracy (Baledrokadroka, 2016). The second view is that the role of the military (as defined by Chapter 81 of the Army Act) is for 'defence and state security of Fiji in the maintenance of Law and Order in land and sea' (Fiji Government, 1955). The reality is much more complex and involves a syncretic mixture of both of these positions. The image of the military is constructed from various political and ideological viewpoints that attempt to frame security in different ways. Whether the military is seen as a security threat or as a provider of security depends very much on the historical and sociopolitical context and the ideological lenses used to frame the manifest and more latent behaviour and activities of the military.

Even the official role of the military has been redefined over the years to reflect changing security circumstances. For instance, Section 3 of the RFMF Act 1961 (revised 1985) states that:

> The Forces shall be charged with the defence of Fiji, with the maintenance of order and with such other duties as may from time to time be defined by the Minister. (Fiji Government, 1961: 1)

This provision recognised the salience of both 'defence' of Fiji from undefined external forces and internal threats, as suggested by reference to the 'maintenance of order'. Although there was no identifiable external threat, the military's role in internal control, especially in supressing anti-colonial rebellion and quelling activities deemed subversive, were common features of the colonial legacy.

Upon independence, the RFMF Act provided the functional and operational framework for the military, and its role was not even mentioned in the 1970 constitution, which was the main blueprint for Fiji's post-independence political development. Only the position and appointment of the commissioner of police were mentioned (in Sections 84 and 107, respectively), and it was probably assumed that the military, whose role was seen either to be ceremonial or to fight external wars, was considered relatively autonomous of the mainstream state governance system and therefore did not require constitutional mention. After 96 years of British rule, it was assumed that the military would continue to express the same commitment to patriotism and respect for state authority. This assumption evaporated in May 1987 after the first coup.

After state capture in 1987 by the military in support of ethnonationalist concerns, the country awoke to the idea of the military as an institution capable of sudden political intervention and transformation. This reshaped the perception of the military in mainstream national consciousness from being a subservient tool of state security to an institution capable of usurping state authority and power. This shift in the military's political role shaped its own self-perception as well as the broader dynamics of civil–military relations in Fiji, as it now sees itself as the ultimate arbiter and protector of security. This was reflected in Section 94 of the 1990 constitution, which redefined the role of the Fiji military thus: 'It shall be the overall responsibility of the Republic of Fiji Military Forces to ensure at all times the security, defence and well-being of Fiji and its people' (Fiji Government, 1990: 106). In addition, the constitution officially changed the name from Royal Fiji Military Forces to Republic of Fiji Military Forces, in line with the declaration of the country as a republic.

The term 'overall responsibility' represents a sense of overarching control as undisputed overlord of national security, which overshadows any other form of collective participation by non-military sectors of the community. The emphasis on 'well-being' shows the expansion of the boundaries of responsibility away from simply defence to people's everyday life. On experiencing the sumptuousness of civilian political power and its associated trappings after taking over the government through coups, the military-backed regime decided to constitutionalise the role of the military not only in the context of its defence role but also as a political and social watchdog of people's well-being. This raises fundamental questions about the line of demarcation between the military sphere of operations and the civil sphere of engagement. In a latent way, this watchdog role provides justificatory leverage for the military to intervene in civilian politics and affairs under the guise of protecting the nation's well-being. Ironically, it could provide a licence for future coups.

The 1997 constitution (Section 112 [1]) simply endorsed the 1990 provision by reiterating that 'the military force called the Republic of Fiji Military Forces established by the Constitution of 1990 continues in existence'. In addition, the appointment process of the commander as stipulated in the two constitutions were similar; that is, the president, acting on the advice of the minister, must appoint a commander of the Republic of Fiji Military Forces to exercise military executive command of the forces, subject to the control of the minister (Fiji Government, 1997).

Perhaps the most far-reaching proposals in redefining the role of the military were provided in the 2012 constitutional draft by the Constitution Commission led by Professor Yash Ghai. The draft, which was eventually rejected by the government, expanded and elaborated the role of the military and proposed that it: first, be 'responsible for the defence and protection of the sovereignty and territorial integrity of the Republic'; second, 'assist and cooperate with other authorities in situations of emergency or disaster when so directed in writing by the National

Security Council'; third, 'be deployed to restore peace in any part of Fiji affected by unrest or instability, only if requested in writing by, and under the control of, the Commissioner of Police, and with the prior approval of the Minister responsible for defence'; and, fourth, 'may be deployed outside Fiji' only with the prior approval of Parliament or Cabinet (Fiji Constitution Commission, 2012: 142). The draft constitution also recommended a National Security Council to which the military would be accountable.

In some ways, these provisions made the military more accountable to civilian authorities. Clearly, with the lessons of the six coups in mind, the commission saw the need to bring the military under civilian oversight for the long-term civilianisation and democratic reform of security institutions. This did not go down well with the military hierarchy, which had enjoyed its stint in power and who were determined to steer the country towards a particular path of political and economic development. Hence the rejection of the 2012 constitutional draft by the military-backed government did not come as a surprise, especially when, in its submission to the Constitution Commission, the military stated in no uncertain terms that it was the 'last bastion' of law and order in Fiji and would continue to provide guidance for the governance of the country, ensuring that peace, prosperity and good governance was practised and adhered to (RFMF, 2012). This statement was seen to 'indicate that the RFMF sees itself as supervising the civilian government, rather than responsible to it' (CCF, 2013: 36–7).

The role of the military under the 2013 constitution, which was put together by the government itself, ironically reverted to the 1990 provision for the role of the military, stating that: 'It shall be the overall responsibility of the Republic of Fiji Military Forces to ensure at all times the security, defence and well-being of Fiji and all Fijians' (Fiji Government, 2013: 83). The image that the military had been trying to propagate after the 2006 coup had been that of an ideologically inclusive and multiculturalist stance, in opposition to divisive ethnonationalism. Replicating the role prescription from the 1990 ethnonationalist constitution seems paradoxical indeed.

Although the military sees this constitutional provision as a safeguard against forces of instability such as unregulated ethnonationalism, others see it as a constitutional licence to intervene in national politics at any time under the excuse of ensuring security, defence or well-being.

The legal security institutions

The roles of the police, the courts and prisons are important in maintaining a certain degree of social order in a society scarred by ethnopolitical conflict. The capacity of these institutions to carry out their constitutional role ultimately depends on a number of factors, including their responsive capacity, operational philosophy and available resources as well as the nature of the conflict. The series of coups had the direct effect of relegating these institutions to roles that saw them as subservient to the military, which saw itself as the last bastion of security (RFMF, 2013). In a political environment where coups have blurred the line and redefined the relationship between constitutional state authority and extralegal military coercion, the powers and roles of the police, courts and prisons are often subsumed into the extraconstitutional demands of the coup-makers.

During the first coup in 1987, the police force was directly under the control of the military. The police commissioner and his deputy were removed by force, military-appointed 'loyal' police officers were given top positions, including a military colonel as commissioner, and police stations were literally taken over by soldiers (Robertson & Tamanisau, 1988). Many policemen became collaborators with the military by helping in the arrest and imprisonment of anti-coup activists. The professionalism and political independence of the police was compromised, and the institution lost its credibility as it came under the political and ideological control and manipulation of the post-coup regime.

The police force also went through the post-coup 'Fijianisation' program in the civil service, as part of the broader pro-Taukei affirmative action program (Ratuva, 2013). The 2000 coup put further pressure on the police, this time not as coup collaborators (as in 1987) but as a largely ineffective security buffer between the coup perpetrators and the public. The real test for the police was during the riots, burning and looting in Suva's central business district following the overthrow of the government by some ethnonationalist politicians with the support of the CRW. The commissioner, Isikia Savua, an army colonel who was alleged to have been a coup conspirator himself, did not issue any definite order; nor was any security plan in place against possible violence by ethnonationalist marchers on the fateful Friday, 17 May. The marchers, protesting against what they saw as Prime Minister Mahendra Chaudhry's meddling in

Taukei issues such as land, ended up running amok in Suva City after they heard of the takeover in Parliament (Robertson & Sutherland, 2002). A TV shot of the commissioner inspecting the result of the mayhem a day later with a golf club in hand was not only a pitiful sight but also symbolic of the utter failure of the police to prevent or respond to the civilian riot.

Many in the police rank and file questioned the suitability and credibility of the commissioner of police. These grievances were vindicated in the few days after the coup when armed civilian supporters of the coup roamed at will around Suva and other places around Fiji, intimidating citizens, looting cattle and crops to feed the coup supporters camping at the parliamentary complex, and forcefully taking over control of some towns. In the process, police stations were taken over and policemen were forced to 'surrender'.

The balance of force was rather unequal because the police were not armed while the coup supporters were, and, around the city of Suva, policemen on duty were sworn at and humiliated by coup enthusiasts. This led to considerable loss of morale, and many police personnel experienced depression and had to seek counselling (Fiji Police counsellor, personal communication, 2009). For days, fear and anxiety gripped the population of Suva as waves of rumours of civil unrest, instigated by the rebels, spread like wildfire around the capital, causing unprecedented panic, which forced people to go home early or leave the capital altogether. The thought that the police were utterly powerless in the face of armed thugs roaming the city with impunity worsened mass hysteria and caused near-chaos.

The fluid security situation after the 2000 coup caught people by surprise. After the arrest of members of the government, the president used his constitutional prerogative to declare a state of emergency and, in the process, 'sacked' the government, now in captivity, on the grounds that it was 'unable to act'. This left a serious power vacuum and, without the support of the military, President Ratu Sir Kamisese Mara could not exercise authority as effectively as he would have wanted. The military stepped in, asked the president to *vakatikitiki* (move aside) and took over executive authority on 29 May, technically staging another coup.

The takeover by the military shifted the balance of power away from the coup-makers (although they still possessed guns acquired from the military). To the relief of the people of Suva, the military took control and peace of mind returned for many. The new security environment enabled the police to operate more confidently, and they were able to rearticulate their security role, although under the protective shield of armed soldiers.

The 2000 coup provided a critical lesson for the police in terms of its role in the broader national security paradigm. The instability wrought by the 1987 and 2000 coups rendered the police ineffective as a security institution with a national mandate for maintenance of law and order. There had to be serious thinking about its fundamental strategies. The task of reforming police structure, rebuilding police morale and reprofessionalising its operations was given to Andrew Hughes, a senior Australian police officer.

The relationship between Hughes and the military commander, Bainimarama, was cordial at first, but deteriorated as a result of the police's investigation into a possible charge of treason against Bainimarama. This followed Bainimarama's threat to remove Qarase's government by force over the renewal of the commander's contract. Qarase's attempt to pass the Reconciliation, Truth and Unity Bill, mentioned earlier in the chapter, inflamed the situation. To complicate matters, the police set up its own special unit and tried to import new automatic rifles for its armoury as a way of responding to any future coup attempts. The military felt threatened by this and intercepted the weapons at the Suva wharf and also raided the headquarters of the special police unit in Nasinu, outside Suva.

The final straw was when Hughes and two other senior police officers went to New Zealand to arrest Bainimarama, who was having talks with Qarase through an invitation by the New Zealand Government. When this failed, Hughes, fearing for his life, did not return to Fiji (Hunter & Lal, 2018). The two senior police officers who accompanied him lost their jobs. The significant point here is that Fiji was facing a situation in which the two main institutions of national security were pitted against each other as they contested for legitimacy and control while the country was going through a crisis spawned by the 2000 coup and that, in turn, spawned the 2006 coup. The contestation was not based on any noble agenda such as how best they could strategise about national security, but rather on a complex hodgepodge of divergent personal interests between the heads of the two institutions, competing versions of their functions and legitimacy, and irreconcilable framings of security. To legitimise its stance, the police relied on the 1997 constitution (Part 4, Section 111), which established the position of commissioner of police. The police force was also guided by the Police Act of 1966, which formalised the role of the police as such:

> The Force shall be employed in and throughout Fiji for the maintenance of law and order, the preservation of the peace, the protection of life and property, the prevention and detection of crime and the enforcement of all laws and regulations with which it is directly charged; and shall be entitled for the performance of any such duties to carry arms. (Fiji Government, 1966, Part 2, No. 5)

On the other hand, the military's claim to legitimacy was based on two instruments—one legal, the other coercive. The legal mandate was based on the 1997 and 1990 constitutional provisions about the 'overall responsibility' of the military 'to ensure at all times the security, defence and well-being of Fiji and its people', as we have already discussed. This legal discourse was the fulcrum on which the more aggressive and threatening behaviour of the military was launched. The military also gained self-bestowed political and moral authority as a result of taking over state power after the 2000 coup and after determining the future political trajectory of the country by appointing an interim prime minister.

The collision between the two security institutions paradoxically became a security threat in itself because each one was trying to nullify the other's legitimacy. In the end, the power of coercion won the day, as the military, with its greater firepower and training for combat, overshadowed the largely unarmed and less pugnacious police. There were a couple of incidents when a shootout between the two forces almost happened; if it had, it would have been disastrous, as it would have threatened the safety and security of citizens.

After the military took over political control following the 2006 coup, the police force literally became a part of the military command system. Esala Teleni, a senior naval officer, was appointed commissioner, although officially and operationally the police remained 'autonomous'. Teleni's term as police commissioner was full of controversy as a result of a combination of factors, including the abruptness of his military-style leadership, which contradicted routine policing norms; his constant suspicion that police officers were secretly pursuing an anti-coup investigation against him and were attempting to sabotage his leadership; and the role of the commissioner's brother, a Pentecostal preacher who tried to use the police force to gain leverage for spreading his religious message and gaining converts to his New Methodist group, which had broken away from the mainstream Methodist Church.

The increasingly acute crisis within the police led to the appointment of Major General Ioane Naivalurua, another senior military officer and former commissioner of prisons, as commissioner of police. His task was to reform the governance structure and strategic direction of the institution and to arrest and resuscitate the plummeting morale of the police officers. Naivalu's reform of the prison system as commissioner of prisons won him accolades as a dynamic and imaginative visionary. Those reforms introduced innovative initiatives such as the Singaporean-styled Yellow Ribbon project aimed at rehabilitation and community involvement, as well as commercial projects and skills development for prisoners. Naivalu was later posted to a diplomatic position and was replaced by a South African, Major General Ben Groenewald, who was tasked by Nelson Mandela to reform the South African police in the post-apartheid era. Groenewald resigned and left Fiji in November 2015 and was replaced by yet another military officer in the form of Brigadier Sitiveni Qiliho.

The militarisation of the police was not total but nevertheless provoked various levels and pockets of resistance among senior police officers who felt threatened professionally by the intrusion of military officers into their domain, and by the coercive and often illegal tactics of the military officers when dealing with public 'threat'. This created a cycle of resistance and counter-resistance within the police force, which threatened its sense of institutional cohesion and operational effectiveness.

The challenge for the police in the future will be how it redefines its role in the bigger security picture, especially how it draws the boundaries of its operation and modes of engagement in ways that are distinguishable from those of the military. The demilitarisation and reprofessionalisation of the police must work hand in hand to transform the institution for a sustainable and stable police force. More importantly, the reform must create citizens' trust in an organisation that has in the past engaged in arbitrary acts of violence on captured prisoners and other members of the public. A number of initiatives, like Neighbourhood Watch and community policing, have been deployed in the past to integrate the police into the community and nurture cooperation with civilians in the battle against crime. Although these might have been successful in solving some incidents of crime, they have not really addressed the deeper causes of insecurity.

Perceptions, ethnic framing and threats

Human behaviour, especially its predisposition towards violence, is shaped by an array of cultural, psychological, ideological, economic, religious and political forces acting in either direct or subtle ways (Jenkins, 2008). Our behaviour is intrinsically linked to our perceptions and attitudes, and often threats are constructed in response to what might be perceived to be hostile behaviour by the other.

In multi-ethnic societies such as Fiji, the construction of others, definition of social group boundaries and creation of common spaces for interaction take place in symbolic and dynamic ways. Contrary to mainstream perception about a dichotomous tense relationship between ethnic groups, principally Taukei and Indo-Fijians, the relationships are much more complex and involve both tension and accommodation taking place at the same time. Intergroup perception expressed in the form of prejudiced imagery and stereotypes or affirmative perception could range from being superficial and temporal to being extreme and deep-seated, and there is often a dynamic oscillation of perception between the two poles, depending on the circumstances. While there have been cases of expressions of extreme ethnonationalism by Taukei in the past, these largely took place in the context of political crisis fuelled by the active role of ethnic entrepreneurs who take advantage of the situation to instil fear and agitate for ethnic and religious hatred, thereby making it easier to mobilise and control people to serve their political interests and ideological agenda.

Mobilisation and politicisation of ethnically based framing has the potential to inflame group passion and communal tension. Fiji's postcolonial history shows how this phenomenon can shape political culture and the political landscape significantly in dynamic ways. In Fiji, ethnically based framing of others has been nurtured by a number of manifest and latent factors with roots in the colonial epoch, as we have seen.

The demarcated social worlds in which Taukei and Indo-Fijians lived during the colonial days were reinforced by the British policy of divide and rule (Narayan, 1984). Separate political representation and the socioeconomic division of labour, which saw Indo-Fijians concentrated in the cane belts as workers and farmers while the Taukei were largely locked into village subsistence life controlled by rigid communal laws under the tutelage of chiefs, ensured that the separate and rarely linked spaces inhabited by the two communities shaped antagonistic consciousness of each other. The construction of otherness was a response to the demarcated and contested political space. This was institutionalised in the constitutions, which prescribed ethnic representation, separate schools, separate trade unions and separation in general social life such as sports and residential areas.

The stereotypes and negative perceptions emanating from these conditions can pose security threats on their own. This is because feeling and attitudes of the people have the capacity to inspire political action, despite the security roles of the state, military and police. Indeed people do change and influence society generally. One way of changing people's ethnic consciousness at the informal level is community-based peace-building, which we look at next.

Community-based peace-building as response to security

When we talk of community-based peace-building systems, we refer to a whole range of approaches, some 'traditional', some more contemporary and some spontaneously and contextually constructed, which are often used to respond to local conflicts in the rural, urban and peri-urban areas. Often those involved are familiar with each other, either culturally, professionally or socially, and have a common understanding of the significance of resolving conflict, although their versions of the conflict may differ. Different cultural groups have different approaches to peace-building. The Taukei, for instance, tend to rely on a mixture of culturally based practices of reconciliation, Christian notions of love, forgiveness and conflict resolution, and more contemporary forms of mediation. These are used either individually to respond to specific contexts or together in a hybrid way, depending on the complexity of the conflict. Hindus and Muslims also use aspects of their religious philosophies as well as more contemporary forms of mediation practices to respond to conflict situations.

Perhaps one of the most pertinent questions is how local and culture-based means of conflict resolution can be used transculturally. This was attempted by Qarase's government in a national reconciliation ceremony in Fiji in 2005 through the use of the *veisorosorovi* (intergroup reconciliation) model earlier proposed by Ratuva (2003). While the initiative brought some of the perpetrators and the victims of the 2000 coup together in a symbolic and widely publicised solemn ceremony, the impact on the broader ethnopolitical situation in the country was minimal. In fact the whole process failed because the military and the Fiji Labour Party, two key players during the 2000 coup, refused to participate. The *veisorosorovi* model was workable only if all parties consensually agreed on a common aim and vision using the Taukei protocol.

Use and abuse of the *veisorosorovi* model in national reconciliation

The failure of the *veisorosorovi* model in the national reconciliation initiative in 2005 was not due to the weakness of the approach but to the blatantly political intent of the organisers and to the tense political conditions that prevailed in Fiji at the time.

The term *veisorosorovi* comes from the word *soro*, which refers to a number of social and behavioural values, including to submit oneself, to surrender, to humble oneself or to give in. In the Fijian cosmology, this could be framed in relation to submission to supernatural or divine authority and, in sociopolitical and cultural terms, it means humbling oneself as a means of appeasement. The term *veisorosorovi* refers to different modes of peace-building such as *bulubulu* (literally meaning to 'bury') or *matasanigasau* (literally meaning 'arrow'), both of which simultaneously refer to soliciting forgiveness and admitting guilt (Ratuva, 2003).

Sociologically, *veisorosorovi* has a number of salient aspects worth noting. First, it is reciprocal, as the repetition of the term *soro* suggests. Reciprocity is a critical element in the Taukei sense of social balance and cohesion. In peace-building terms, this provides space for reforging broken ties and allowing social synergy to flow between the two conflicting groups and to lock them together in a united mould. This unity of purpose can be temporary and can also be long-lasting, depending very much on the situation. Second, *veisorosorovi* can be restorative through reaffirmation of kinship ties that had been temporarily fractured by an individual committing a wrong. Third, it can be transformative not only through the renewal of relationship but also by making sure that the conditions where these relationships exist change into something better and more peaceful.

In these processes kinship provides a powerful peace-building force because of its capacity to provide a sense of both socially constructed and 'primordial' connection. This is more so within the Taukei community where *veiwekani* (kinship) is valued as both an unquestioned immemorial inheritance and a constantly constructed and reconstructed phenomenon. Although it is a unifying and therefore peace-building force, it also has the capacity to generate tension as a result of competition over land, titles, resources and power.

The pertinent question here is to what extent can the *veisorosorovi* approach, which has been the cornerstone of Taukei peace-building, be used in trans-ethnic conflict? When the Qarase government decided to carry out a national reconciliation program in 2005 based on the *veisorosorovi* approach, there was clearly some uncertainty as to its efficacy in a tense and potentially volatile political situation. In October 2005 a whole week was devoted to workshops and discussions on reconciliation, culminating in a public *veisorosorovi* ceremony at Albert Park in Suva. The ceremony consisted of a multidimensional process that involved presentation of *matanigasau* by the government and Taukei chiefs to various ethnic and religious groups pleading for forgiveness for their suffering during the 2000 coup.

However, behind the veneer of public peace-making lay deeper political and religious interests. The ceremonies, while officially coordinated by the Ministry of National Reconciliation, were largely influenced by a Christian group called the Assembly of Christian Churches in Fiji (ACCF), a fundamentalist interdenominational group whose members included Prime Minister Qarase and other senior officers of the state (Newland, 2007). Also, the reconciliation was meant to be part of a deal to appease the victims of the coup, especially Indo-Fijians, as well as the military, so that agreement could be readily reached to release from prison the 2000 coup perpetrators, who had close ideological links with Qarase's ruling SDL Party.

The initiative ultimately failed because two important players, the military and Fiji Labour Party (which was the main victim of the 2000 coup), refused to participate in the *veisorosorovi*, arguing that legal and retributive justice must take precedence over reconciliation and restorative justice. In other words, the perpetrators of the coup deserved to remain in prison as a deterrent to future potential coup-makers. Nevertheless, the failure to harness consensual support for the reconciliation project was part of its downfall. It was not really a fault of the *veisorosorovi* approach as such, but rather of the way it was used, or rather abused—as leverage to serve ulterior political motives in a highly charged political atmosphere— that undermined its credibility and effectiveness. One of the inherent principles of the *veisorosorovi* approach is that it must be supported by all the parties concerned and that there should be transparency and honesty in people's intention. Using it as leverage for conspiratorial political ends has the potential to undermine its moral value and authority.

This is one of the dilemmas associated with using traditional forms of peace-building mechanisms at the national level outside the local community. Outside the scope of the kinship network, the power dynamics change as relationships become more formal and less personal and are influenced by national political ideas and processes. In such a strange atmosphere, local peace-building mechanisms such as *veisorosorovi*, which were meant for community-based conflict resolution, are bound to be confronted by challenges. Adaptation of local peace-building systems to a trans-ethnic national context is still possible, but preconditions such as consensus among those involved on both perpetrator and victim sides as to what needs to be done, and the rationale behind it, must first be met. The process can also be tailored to suit the circumstances.

Civil society peace-building and security

Apart from the culture-based systems, the role of civil society organisations in peace-building in Fiji is well established. Religious organisations, women's organisations, human rights and peace organisations have been active in urban areas for decades. In some cases these groups operate on their own within their particular constituencies, and in other cases they collaborate under a common umbrella.

The period of peace activism in the 1970s set the tone for the proliferation of peace groups in Fiji. The anti-French nuclear testing at Moruroa Atoll in French Polynesia sparked an international outcry. In Fiji a number of citizen groups, including church groups, student organisations and other civil society groups such as the Young Women's Christian Association (YWCA), joined hands to form an umbrella organisation called ATOM (Against Atomic Testing on Moruroa). A major regional peace conference in Suva in 1975 saw the establishment of a region-wide peace movement whose agenda extended from opposition to nuclear testing to other issues including decolonisation, land rights, indigenous emancipation, demilitarisation and development. This, as we noted in Chapter 3, saw the birth of the Nuclear Free and Independent Pacific movement (NFIP), whose geographical coverage included the Pacific Islands states, Australia and New Zealand, and Pacific Rim countries such as Japan, Philippines, Indonesia and the United States.

The NFIP had a significant influence on Fiji's peace movement. It influenced the setting up in 1983 of the Fiji Anti-Nuclear Group (FANG), which became the focal point for peace activism in Fiji for decades. When the Pacific Concerns Resources Centre (PCRC), the secretariat of the NFIP, was relocated to Suva from Auckland in 1993, peace activism in Fiji was given a further boost as peace groups and other civil society organisations in Fiji benefited from the organisation's resources and expertise.

In addition to the YWCA and FANG, a number of peace organisations emerged in the 1990s and 2000s. Among these were women's-based organisations such as Women's Action for Change, which used plays and other forms of dramatisation to publicise peace messages; the Fiji Women's Rights Movement, which mobilised women for political action; the Fiji Women's Crisis Centre, which provided support for female victims of domestic violence; Femlink, which engaged in media outreach programs for urban and rural women; and the Foundation for Rural Integrated Enterprises and Development, whose fundamental responsibility is to empower poor rural women through development of local and family-based industries. Femlink was also the local focal point for Pacific People Building Peace (PPBP), the Pacific arm of the Global Project for the Prevention of Armed Conflict. Collectively, these organisations contributed to women's empowerment, peace-building and stability in different ways.

Other peace-based organisations include the Citizens Constitutional Forum (CCF), set up after the 1987 coups to facilitate dialogue between competing political groups in Fiji. Later the CCF became a human rights advocacy group. The Fiji Dialogue emerged in response to the 2006 coup. Its role was to provide space for dialogue between the perpetrators and victims of the coup. Perhaps the very first professional peace-building organisation was the Pacific Centre for Peace-Building, which has been carrying out training, workshops and consultancies for various government departments and community groups.

The role of religious organisations has been critical in providing a spiritual dimension to peace in a country where religion takes centre stage in most cultures. The Interfaith, an initiative for multireligious engagement, brought together various religious groups such as Christians, Hindus, Muslims, Buddhists and Sikhs to worship and pray for the nation. The fundamentalist leaders of the Methodist Church were often reluctant to join the Interfaith movement because of its close connections to ethnonationalists and saw worshipping beside 'heathens' as sacrilegious. However, the more progressive leaders enthusiastically joined the Interfaith. The Methodists and a number of Pentecostal churches were active members of the ACCF, which was instrumental in the failed 2004 *veisorosorovi* initiative. The Ecumenical Centre for Research Education and Advocacy, a research and advocacy group set up within the Catholic Church, was actively involved in peace-building programs together with other groups like the CCF.

The United Nations Development Program (UNDP) was proactive in peace-building through its Peace, Stability and Development Analysis project, which attempted to link various institutions and organisations for a unified framework for national peace-building. Another UNDP project was the National Initiative on Civic Education, which was based on a national public education process on the issues of human rights, democracy, elections and governance. The idea was that through civic education, national consciousness about unity and peace could be attained. The Pacific Conference of Churches has also been a stalwart for peace-building in Fiji, where it is based.

Given Fiji's small size, civil society space is quite crowded and highly contested. While attempts have been made to bring some organisations under a common umbrella, such as the Fiji Human Rights Coalition, Fiji Anti-Nuclear Group, PPBP, Dialogue Fiji and Interfaith, the power dynamics between them and the desire to maintain their distinctive identities in a highly charged political climate continue to be major defining factors in their relationships. This is further complicated by the political alignment of different organisations. At the time of the 1987 coups, the division was blatantly ethnic and ideological. Taukei-led organisations such as the Methodist Church and those with right-wing leanings such as the indigenous Fijian-based Soqosoqo Vakamarama (Women's Organisation) supported the ethnonationalist coup. Opposition to the coup came from non-Taukei and left-leaning organisations. Although the CCF was largely Taukei-dominated, it had a multi-ethnic and centre-left position and was opposed to the use of political violence for ethnic ends. FANG, which had a centre-left political position, came into direct collision with its parent organisation, the PCRC, which was supportive of indigenous rights. While FANG supported indigenous rights, it believed that they were not to be supported at the cost of other communities' rights, a position that the 1987 coups undermined.

This division was exacerbated by the political alignment of civil society leaders with political parties, government or aid donors. This in some ways shaped the power dynamics within the political party space and often created tension, suspicion and sometimes outright opposition. Some civil society organisations evolved their ideological position in relation to the political climate. The CCF leadership, which initially had sympathy for the 2006 coup because of its attack on ethnonationalism, later evolved into a strong critic of the military-supported government because of its human rights stance at a time when government security forces were involved in serious human rights abuses. The chief executive officer of CCF was later charged and convicted under the Media Industry Development Decree of 2010 for contempt of court for republishing an article that was critical of the justice system in Fiji.

Some civil society organisations drew self-gratifying inspiration from being self-styled warriors in a politically divided political space while others tried to bridge the gap by engaging with the 'enemies' such as the security forces. While some of these organisations were seen as opportunist fraternisers by others in the field, they saw it as an opportunity to soften the hyper-militaristic psychology of the security forces from within. Some of these organisations included the Women's Crisis Centre, which was involved in gender violence training, and the Pacific Centre for Peacebuilding, which carried out post-traumatic response training with the military.

Despite the 2014 democratic elections, the feeling of insecurity has not totally abated, and therefore the role of the civil society organisations as champions of peace and human rights will continue. As agents of conflict resolution and peace-building, the role of civil society in contributing to lessening insecurity in the community cannot be overemphasised.

Conclusion: Addressing the security dilemmas

It would be naïve to think of Fiji's security primarily in terms of coups and the role of the military as projected in popular imagery. Fiji is a complex country where ethnic, religious, cultural, gender, regional and class issues intersect in multiple ways, shaping social, economic and political security at different levels. Hence security in Fiji needs to be framed using multiple lenses; in this case the simultaneous use of postcolonial, securitisation and human security approaches.

It is true that the coups exacerbated poverty, ethnic tension, political instability, social alienation, human rights abuse and feelings of vulnerability; however, it is also true that the same forces were involved in each of the coups. A focus on the coups tends to divert our attention from mundane security issues, some of which are manifest and some latent. Hard and human security issues are closely intertwined and in many ways cannot be separated. Sometimes the line between hard and human security cannot be neatly demarcated. A classic case is the relationship between coups and socioeconomic dislocation, where one contributes in indirect ways to causing or influencing the other.

The nature of security and the response mechanisms in Fiji have evolved significantly from the precolonial, colonial and postcolonial epochs. These were shaped largely by constantly changing political dynamics, socioeconomic structures, cultural systems and shifting perceptions and behaviour patterns. The largely tribal and subsistence precolonial communities revolved around the charismatic and authoritarian power of the warrior chiefs, whose political power pervaded the entire society. Intra- and inter-tribal contestation over power was common, and often the smartest and most tactical survived, although physical strength was also important.

Colonialism transformed Fijian society in fundamental ways, including reconfiguration of the sociopolitical structure, the land tenure system and socioeconomic way of life. Resistance to colonial hegemony took the form of passive resistance and latent counterhegemonic forms, with occasional violent episodes. The British responded through the use of force, and the reciprocal response was the use of similar force. Many people died, many were executed by the British, and leading opponents of British colonialism were banished and exiled. The British contained resistance through tactical use of the Fijian administration structure and the vital role of chiefs as colonial compradors to keep the Taukei subservient and docile. This paternalistic system contributed to the retarded economic situation of the Taukei and, upon independence, the resultant inequality contributed to the ethnopolitical tension that culminated in later political instability.

Fiji's security situation after independence flowed from colonial experiences. The ethnopolitical contestation for power, economic inequality and the role of ethnic entrepreneurs in communal mobilisation were amplified by higher demands for progress, newfound freedom of expression and mobility, and globalisation and all its influences in people's views, expectations and behaviour. The coups became ruptures through which these complex vortexes of issues were vented. These transformed Fijian society in critical ways as responses and counter-responses to security became centripetal forces in the country's evolution.

The future security of the country lies in how Fiji's new democracy can be reconfigured to facilitate consensus rather than adversarial politics. While Fiji has a democratic system in place, it is still sitting on fragile political foundations. Fiji's recent political history, characterised by layers of dialectical synergies—hegemony and counterhegemony, repression and counter-repression, vengeance and countervengeance, and coups and countercoups—has not been automatically counteracted by electoral democracy. Rather, electoral democracy has simply relegated those synergies to a less visible level where they will hibernate until circumstances induce them to rear their ugly heads again. Sometimes formal democratic contestation can contribute to this possibility, as aggrieved minority political groups who feel alienated and disempowered by formal democracy might resort to extraparliamentary means to achieve their aims, or at least to satisfy their personal vendettas and vengeful urges. Creating a moderate middle-ground space where extreme positions on both sides can converge and conduct dialogue is critical to achieving sustainable stability in the long run.

As Fiji's drive towards modernisation and economic growth along the path of the Asian developmental state model intensifies, emerging issues of inequality, poverty, environmental degradation through mining and other forms of pollution, land disputes and crime will likely also intensify. These will affect Fiji's future security in unprecedented ways, and any collective reaction to the neoliberal developmental policies of the state will be met with authoritarian means, as in Singapore, whose developmental strategy Fiji is trying to religiously emulate. If this happens, the security–countersecurity cycle could continue unabated for some time yet.

Nevertheless, the people of Fiji have a great sense of resilience, as demonstrated by their capacity to adapt to dramatically changing circumstances as well as to withstand the excesses of coups and political repression. The capacity for resilience as well as the people's potential for peaceful transformation are at the heart of Fiji's future stability and security. The Fijian people have proven this time and time again.

5

Thy kingdom burn:
Hegemony, resistance and
securitisation in Tonga

There will be no end to the troubles of states, or of humanity itself, till philosophers become kings in this world, or till those we now call kings and rulers really and truly become philosophers, and political power and philosophy thus come into the same hands.

Plato

Although Tonga and Fiji have very close historical and cultural links (Geraghty, 1994), their political architecture and security dynamics are very different. As we saw in Chapter 4, Fiji's security configuration is complicated by its multicultural make-up, in which ethnicity, religion and culture interplay with sociopolitical and socioeconomic factors in complex ways. This is in contrast to Tonga, a culturally homogenous society, where security has been largely shaped by intracommunal sociopolitical and socioeconomic class cleavages consisting of contending vertically stratified groups; on the one hand, the majority—commoners with subaltern status and privileges; on the other hand, the minority—an hereditary monarch and nobles, who by virtue of their control over land also wield significant political and economic power (Campbell, 2015).

The dissolution of Parliament by King Tupou VI on 24 August 2017 sent shockwaves around the region because it signalled a rather gloomy prospect about the promise of sustainable democracy in the young bourgeoning Pacific island state. Although the government of Prime Minister Akilisi

Pohiva, the target of the disolution, returned to power after new elections were called, the King's unilateral intervention in democratic politics has fundamental implications for Tonga's security environment. This is manifested in a contested relationship between the monarch and the interests of commoners, as this chapter attempts to explore. This chapter focuses largely on the deteriorating security situation building up to riots in Nuku'alofa (the capital) on 16 November 2006 and its implications for security dynamics in Tonga, in particular the way they redefined the political culture and democratic process and the implications they have for the future security of the kingdom. The riot was a watershed event in Tonga's modern history, and it is important to see it in the context of the big picture, including the growth of the democracy movement. This involves examining the multilayered relationships between authoritarian monarchical rule, feudalistic restrictions of political rights, depressed socioeconomic conditions, inequality, corruption, cultural patronage, the pro-democracy movement and the demand for reform. The interplay between these forces provided the energy that had built up over the years before the final spark that led to rioting, looting and burning.

Before Tonga became unified under the current Tupou dynasty, in the 1870s, Tonga consisted of warring chiefdoms until Tupou I conquered the country and imposed his rule on it for a long time; however, its internal dynamics and contradictions intensified and the system was bound to give way. The so-called 'stability' that existed was not entirely due to the benevolence of the monarch, who sits at the apex of the cultural and political hierarchy, as suggested by Campbell (2011a), but must be seen in the context of complex factors, including the use of cultural, ideological and political leveraging and hegemony as means of manufacturing consent. For instance, the monarchy derived its legitimacy from the Church, which bestowed on it a 'divine right'. This justificatory ideology is reinforced by collective cultural loyalty; and central to this is the belief that the monarch is the embodiment of sacredness, whose demigod status is part of the cosmological order of things, which dictates profane social life and the secular state. These complex layers of cultural hegemony provided the ideological mysticism that sustained an authoritarian system of rule for some time. The first organised counterhegemonic resistance to the monarchy was by educated individuals who began questioning the privileges of the traditional elites. The critical exposé of these 'organic intellectuals', to use a term coined by Gramsci (1971), inspired generations of Tongans to demand their political as well as their economic rights in an authoritarian and impoverished country.

Rather than being imported from outside, the security situation in Tonga was largely brewed, sustained and controlled from home. The accompanying reactions and counter-reactions were manifestations of the local political dynamics that helped to shape the historical trajectory of the country. Contrary to popular belief, the period between 1875 (when Tonga was unified) and 2006 (when the riot took place) was not one of 'stability' but rather one of effective control and hegemony that kept the population in a state of willing submission under the ideologically pacifying spell of religious and cultural conformity. Over time, this nurtured the conditions for resistance, which needed the right trigger and right circumstances to reach the threshold of action.

This chapter makes the argument that instead of looking at the riot of 16 November 2006 in terms of spontaneous lawlessness (Campbell, 2012), it must be understood in the broader context of transformational social consciousness manifested in resistance against the monarch and the establishment. In 'rethinking' Tonga's security dynamics, it is important to look at the broader 'habitus', to use Bourdieu's term, referring to the interplay between structures and agencies to shape people's thinking, behaviour and responses. This relationship, according to Bourdieu (1984), reproduces power in symbolic but asymmetric fashion, whereby dominant classes impose their values as natural and legitimate. In the case of Tonga, the institution of the monarchy has been able to harness and impose its power through the use of overbearing ideological and institutional mechanisms to shape people's consciousness and responses. However, consent to hegemony, as Gramsci (1971) advises, cannot be total. The pro-democracy movement and the riot in November 2006 showed the limitations of hegemony as attempts by the ruling elites to domesticate consciousness may invoke counterconsciousness.

To understand this counterconsciousness, this chapter, using the postcolonial, securitisation and human security lenses, unpacks the surface impression of stability, which often sheltered deeper structures of inequality, political and ideological hegemony and feudalistic patronage. These are often framed and justified by both religion and dominant cultural discourse as 'divine' and 'natural'. The chapter then examines the counterforces at play, focusing on the people's resistance movement, the riot and, finally, on the implications of the riot for the political culture and future security of the kingdom.

The evolution and contestation of political power

Archaeological evidence suggests that around 3,000 years ago Tonga might have been first settled by Austronesian Lapita people who originated from South-East Asia and who had migrated through the western Pacific over several centuries. Carbon dating suggests that Tongatapu was settled before any of the other islands in the Tongan group (Daly, 2009).

Oral records further suggest that the first Tu'i Tonga (High Chief or King of Tonga), 'Aho'eitu, emerged around 950 AD. He was believed to have originated from the sun god Tangaloa, and he was considered to be sacred. He possessed *mana* (divine right to rule) and was the head of a society based on *tapu* (prohibition, restriction, sacredness). In ancient Tongan cosmology, *mana* was not in the blood but in the head and genitals of chiefs (Van der Grijp, 2014: 23). The *mana*, which possessed both political and religious power, provided the cosmological prism that defined one's place in society and the ideological glue that bound the community together. The residues of this belief have been passed down over the years and still exist today, although the source of *mana* is now the Christian god and the religious conduit is the Free Wesleyan Church, the official Church of the monarch. We will address this point further later, when we consider the ideological means for sustaining the monarchical hegemony in the face of the anti-monarchical struggle by the pro-democracy movement.

According to oral history, there was a continuous dynastic line until European contact, when the written record started. The thirty-ninth and last Tu'i Tonga, Laufilitonga, died in 1865. The second dynasty, the Tui Ha'atakalaua, assumed the temporal authority of the Tu'i Tonga, which meant that the Tu'i Tonga was left only with the sacred role. The third dynasty, Tu'i Kanokupolu, was a temporal line and, by the mid-19th century, had become the most powerful of the three. Through marriages, the three lines converged under the current Tupou dynasty (Spurway, 2015). An important aspect of Tongan culture and lineage that is often overlooked is the interface between gender and rank and the way the convergence of lineages helps to reinforce rather than water down women's rank (Herda, 2008).

The successive reigns of the Tu'i Tonga were often turbulent, and violent deaths occurred. There were also cases of trans-Pacific contact and exchanges with Niue, Samoa, Rotuma, Wallis and Futuna, Rotuma, Fiji, and New Caledonia; and Tikopia, in Solomon Islands, was quite prominent in the 12th century under the Tui Tonga. Under successive Tu'i Tonga, the trilithon at Ha'amonga, used for astronomical purposes, was built, in addition to the *langi*, the terraced tombs at Mu'a, the old capital.

The arrival of the Dutch trading vessel *Eendracht* in 1616 signalled the first European contact and also marked the beginning of external, European-initiated changes to Tongan society. In 1643 Abel Tasman, another Dutch explorer, landed in Tongatapu. But it was really Captain Cook who put Tonga prominently on the then world map by giving it the name 'Friendly Islands' after his visits in 1773, 1774 and 1777. Alessandro Malaspina, a Spanish sailor, visited in 1793 and in 1797. The first London missionaries arrived in 1797, followed in 1822 by the Revd Walter Lawry, a Wesleyan missionary. The missionaries were to have a lasting influence on the social and political landscape of Tonga (Wood, 1938).

In 1831, Taufa'ahau, who also assumed the title of Tu'i Kanokupolu, was baptised with the name Siaosi (George) after King George IV of Britain. The reign of Taufa'ahau, who also took the name of Tupou, was characterised by a trail of conquest, which included taking over power in Ha'apai and Va'avau and the defeat of Tu'i Tonga. The unification of Tonga was a result of a power struggle resulting in wars and the usurpation of titles and territories. Siaosi brought about significant changes, including the abolition of serfdom in Vava'u in 1835, and the publication of the Vava'u Code in 1838, the first written laws in Tonga and the Pacific generally. With the help of the missionary Shirley Baker (incidentally a male), he declared Tonga a constitutional monarchy in 1875; incorporated the European royal style; provided emancipation for the 'serfs'; instituted land tenure, a code of law and freedom of the press; and weakened the power of chiefs who posed a threat to his position. The so-called 'emancipation' was really a way of transferring the loyalty of people away from their chiefs, thus weakening their legitimate powerbase while strengthening his own hegemony in the process.

Tupou I's tactical manoeuvres saved Tonga from foreign colonial rule. At the end of the 19th century he called a meeting of chiefs of Va'avau, Niufo'ou, Niuatoputapu, Tongatapu, 'Eua and Ha'apai and urged them not to give up Tongan sovereignty to any foreign power but only to God.

Problems began when the British High Commission deported Shirley Baker, a British subject who had become Tonga's premier, and appointed Tuku'alo, a competitor for the royal throne, to the post. Infuriated, Tupou I moved to Ha'apai and ignored the new government under Tuku'aho. In protest at what was seen as British arrogance, a large part of the Tonga population refused to pay tax. Although Tuku'aho was dismissed as premier by the Privy Council in 1893, the unilateral imposition of power by the British, including Tukua'ho's appointment, contributed to diminishing the authority of the King. At the time of his death in 1893, Tupou I's *mana* had declined considerably. Tukua'ho's misfortune was exacerbated after he was accused of introducing a flu pandemic from New Zealand. The population was reduced by 10 per cent as a result of the disease (Rutherford, 1977).

A major irony is that while Tupou I fought to keep European imperial powers out of Tonga, he himself remodelled the Tongan Tu'i institution after the British monarchy. He was named after King George of England, transformed the chiefly position of Tu'i Kanakupolu to a fully fledged European-style monarch, including the formal ceremonies, state institutions, official dress and other symbols. This was fine-tuned over the years by generations of the Tupou dynasty to include their general lifestyle and even accents, to the extent that the institution became more European than Tongan, ironically at a time when some European countries had done away with the archaic institution of a monarchy. It was and still is probably the most ridiculous case of superficial political imitation of Europeans anywhere in the world.

European influence, especially the direct involvement of missionaries in local social and political transformation, also strengthened Tupou I's power through the use of British-style laws and the 1875 constitution to legitimise his rule. The irony was that, while this transformed Tonga into a modern monarchy at a time when Pacific states were still under colonial rule, it also locked Tonga into a historical time warp, a situation that was to haunt the kingdom later. As other Pacific states gained independence and embraced democracy towards the end of the 1900s, the Tongan political system had hardly evolved and remained relatively static until constitutional reforms almost 120 years later. The rigid system served the monarch and nobles well by institutionalising their power as well as providing for their dynastic continuity (Herda, Terrell & Gunson, 1990). To further bolster the power and perpetuity of the elite, children of royalty and nobles were sent overseas, especially to Australia, to study.

Despite there being a number of contenders for the throne, Tupou I, who died aged 96, was succeeded by his great-grandson, Tupou II. The new King immediately faced continuing controversy, including criticism of his womanising ways, choice of wife, abuse of state fund, and poor governance. This led to financial crises in 1895 and 1897, and the government was forced to borrow externally from Deutsche Handels und Plantagen Gesellschaft, a German trading company based in Samoa. The King was very unpopular among Tongans, and there was widespread resentment—perhaps the first recorded mass grievances in the history of modern Tonga. People complained that, although they paid taxes, there was no visible improvement in their lives. However, Tongans, including nobles (who feared losing status and land) were afraid to publicise their views about the King who has been described as a 'vain and egotistical man' (Van der Grijp, 2014: 235).

The crisis provided Britain with the option of annexation. Many commoners wanted British rule as a way of removing the scourge of chiefly oppression. On the other hand, the nobles detested any idea of British rule because of the certainty of losing power and land, a situation similar to Fiji under British rule. Amid the internal power struggle, on 18 May 1900, Tonga became a protected state by the Treaty of Friendship with Britain. Despite its protectorate status, Tonga maintained its sovereignty, and a British consul became the representative of Britain from 1901 to 1970 (Bott, 1981).

Europeans lobbied for the removal of the monarch's power and a reduction in significance to a symbolic institution with a flag but no governing or judicial power. Europeans were frustrated with government policies such as blockages on free trade, curbing of copra exports, difficulty in extension of land leases, ineffectiveness of the police and lack of protection against theft of trade goods. There was also fear among the British that what they saw as the lack of discipline and the rebelliousness of the Tongans might influence Fijians, who also had their share of resistance against British rule, as we saw in Chapter 4.

The British decided that the best way to deal with the unpopular King was to give him an ultimatum: cooperate with the British in reforming the operation of the state or be deported to Fiji. Tupou II opted for the former and carried out a number of important reforms, such as the appointment of locals and Europeans to the civil service. The reforms benefited Tonga through the building of hospitals, water towers and other public amenities. The King was saved from the humiliation of deportation and instead the Premier, Sateki, and the Minister of Finance, Fatu, were deported to Fiji.

The British bullying tactic manifested a rather odd political arrangement where, despite the fact that Tonga was not a full British colony, British interest still prevailed in various circumstances. To ensure Tongan compliance with British imperial interests, the Treaty of Friendship was renewed in 1905, 1958, 1965 and 1968 in preparation for eventual 'independence' (from its protectorate status) on 4 June 1970 (Rutherford, 1977). This was part of the familiar evolutionary process towards independence in British colonies. Because Fiji was the centre of British imperial rule in the Pacific, political developments in Fiji would also have repercussions in other colonies or protectorates. It was hardly coincidental that Tonga as a protectorate was also granted self-rule in 1970, the same year that Fiji gained independence, although in different months. It needs to be stated here that Tonga was a protectorate of Britain and not a colony like Fiji.

As was to be the case in Fiji, resistance to British rule in Tonga took the form of economic self-empowerment. A copra growers' cooperative called the Ma'a Tonga Kautaha was formed. The idea was that Tongans as producers could produce and market their produce directly rather than going through European intermediaries and traders. Started by a failed British businessman, Alister Cameron, and supported by Vaema, a noble from Houma, the cooperative was an instant success, with 1,300 members on Tongatapu in May 1909 and 2,000 in Ha'apai and Vava'u in July 1909. This was an amazing feat for a population of only 22,000 and with 5,000 adult taxpayers (Hempenstall & Rutherford, 1984). The Ma'a Tonga Kautaha inspired the Viti Kabani, the Fijian version, led by Apolosi Nawai, who was later arrested and exiled by the British to Rotuma, as we saw in Chapter 4. The movement died out around 1914 after a dispute over Cameron's bookkeeping practices, amid hostility towards cooperative endeavours by the Europeans and the British. The British saw the Ma'a Tonga Kautaha as an attempt to undermine European capital, which the imperial system was supposed to protect, as well as a direct threat to British authority itself.

After the collapse of the Ma'a Tonga Kautaha, European-owned companies such as Burns Philp (BP) suddenly made large profits. The BP inspector of companies for Tonga had earlier complained that Tongan workers were not to be trusted because they refused to make copra when the price was low. Instead they withheld and accumulated their copra, forcing the price up. The company complained that Tongans were only prepared to work for the meagre amount of 10 shillings a day (Hove, Kiste & Lal, 1994: 77). Tongan economic resistance was quite sophisticated and effective, and demonstrated the potential for collective people's action against overwhelming odds, a political virtue that was to be useful in future pro-democracy protests.

Tupou II was succeeded by his 18-year-old daughter Salote Tupou III, who ruled for 48 years from 5 April 1918 to 16 December 1965. Although Salote's early years were quite challenging, her reign inspired great interest in the institution of the monarch as she embarked on ambitious projects to modernise Tonga through improved economic development, health and education, and, at the same time, sought to record and resurrect cultural aspects of Tongan identity, literature and philosophy. She was very closely connected with the people through her village visits, scholarly endeavours such as poetry, helping to mediate differences between churches and her involvement with American soldiers during World War II. Her visit to London for Queen Elizabeth II's coronation exposed Tonga on the global stage. Queen Salote's reign was a 'romantic' yet nostalgic period in Tonga's collective consciousness. The queen was an accomplished composer of songs and poetry (Wood-Ellem, 1999). Her paternalistic political style reinforced Tongan loyalty and strengthened the ideological legitimacy of the monarchy, which had been threatened by opposition to Tupou II's rule.

Queen Salote was succeeded by her son Taufa'au Tupou IV, whom she appointed prime minister during her reign. Under Tupou IV, the Treaty of Friendship and Tonga's protectorate status ended in 1970 in accordance with the arrangements put in place by Queen Salote Tupou III before her death in 1965 (Wood-Ellem, 1999). Following this, Tonga became part of the Commonwealth of Nations in 1970 and a member of the United Nations in 1999. As part of its cost-cutting measures, the British Government closed the British High Commission in Nuku'alofa in March 2006, and all responsibility was shifted to the British High Commission in Fiji.

After Tupou IV's death in September 2006, he was succeeded by Tupou V, who had been minister for foreign affairs and defence for 25 years until 1998. Tupou V, who had lived the life of an unmarried international playboy, was more independent minded and was in a much better position to open the floodgates of political reform. Barely two months into his new role, even before the official coronation, the riot of November 2006 took place, providing a catalyst for reform. In the middle of the reform, Tupou V passed away on 18 March 2012. The process of reform culminated in a major amendment to the constitution in 2010. Tupou V was succeeded by his younger brother, Crown Prince Tupouto'a 'Ulukalala or Tupou VI, a more conservative and less popular figure than his elder brother.

Competing security discourses: Dynastic hegemony versus people's resistance

Perhaps the two most ideologically incongruent forces in contemporary Tongan political history, whose competing interests defined Tongan political security from the 1970s onwards, were the institution of the monarchy (together with the *nopele*) and the pro-democracy movement. These groups held divergent ideological discourses about Tongan politics and society. One relied on the appeal to cosmological *mana* and divine will for societal consent and legitimacy whereas the other relied on principles of equality and human rights as the basis for political action and social transformation (Herda, Terrell & Gunson, , 1990). The only thing in between was the shared collective identity of being Tongan, but even then there are still very clear distinctions between the cultural worlds of royal and commoner Tongans.

The power differential is reinforced by landownership; constitutionally the monarch literally 'owns' all the land, and he or she has the power to distribute it to the nobles or *matapule* (talking chiefs) as part of their hereditary estates. The ordinary people have no land of their own but have to rely on the landed gentry to provide them with lots when required.

Mana, divinity and royalty

The end of the Tu'i Tonga dynasty in the 19th century did not necessarily end the sacred and divine disposition associated with the Tu'i Tonga's position. In fact, notions of sacredness and divine origin were reinvented and institutionalised by Tupou I, who merged the three dynasties— Tu'i Tonga, Tu'i Ha'atakalaua and Tu'i Kanokupolu—under his own Tu'i Kanokupolu title (Bott, 1981). The mythical ideology of spirituality was a powerful lever to gain consent, which Tupou I and his descendants used strategically to maintain their unrivalled rule when the use of force—last used by Tupou I as a tool of unification—to ensure submission, was no longer necessary.

The unification process allowed Tupou I to reconstruct Tongan history and cosmology to his and his descendants' advantage. It ensured that the Tupou dynasty could claim not only direct descent along the Tu'i Tonga line but also the heritage of its associated sacredness. Moreover, the role of the sun god, Tangaloa, as the direct guardian of the monarch was supplemented and not totally replaced by the Christian God. Christianity became the new opium that reified the divine origin of the monarch as well as instilled mass consent in Tongans, who saw their culture as part of that divine obligation of submission. This reification process was integrated into the Tongan socialisation process to strengthen people's sense of belonging within the divinely ordained three-tier sociopolitical structure.

Thus the syncretic coexistence of traditional cosmology embodied in *mana* and Christian cosmology manifested in divinity became a powerful ideological force and at the same time a legitimising tool for the monarch. This means that any other social or political grouping or institution, including the state, must remain subservient to this cosmological discourse. For instance, modern state governance was ultimately subject to monarchical endorsement, as Section 41 of the 1875 constitution stated:

> The King is the Sovereign of all the Chiefs and all the people. The person of the King is sacred. He governs the country but his ministers are responsible. All Acts that have passed the Legislative Assembly must bear the King's signature before they become law. (Kingdom of Tonga, 1875: 13)

The constitutionalisation of the 'sacred' status of the King transcends the human and makes the political status of the monarch irreproachable. In the domain of secular politics, the nobles, who acted as the comprador class for the monarch, elected nine members out of the 33 members of the nobility compared to only nine members elected by the rest of the population. The supremacy of the monarch was endorsed by the constitutionally prescribed oath of councillors and representatives, which states: 'I solemnly swear before God that I will be truly loyal to His Majesty King Taufa'ahau Tupou IV the rightful King of Tonga' (Kingdom of Tonga, 1875: 20). The name had been amended to reflect the current monarch in power. Nevertheless the oath of allegiance and the emphasis on the claim to 'the rightful King of Tonga' made the Tupou dynasty impermeable to counterclaims and attempts to question its legitimacy.

Land is also a powerful hegemonic and social control mechanism. Section 104 of the 1875 constitution stated that: 'All the land is the property of the King and he may at pleasure grant to the nobles and titular chiefs or *matabules* one or more estates to become their hereditary estates' (Kingdom of Tonga, 1875: 24). The line of control over land from the King to the nobles and eventually the people creates a power hierarchy that gives the nobles and monarch significant control over people's livelihood, identity and sense of loyalty. This system of feudalistic patronage was given divine approval by the Church and remains one of the most powerful sociocultural forces in Tongan society.

Apart from this religious, cultural and cosmological appeal, the powers of the monarch were fully entrenched in the 1875 constitution. It guaranteed perpetual dynastic succession and provided for absolute authority to govern the kingdom. The monarch appointed the prime minister and ministers and had authority over them, and had the power to dismiss as he or she wished. Laws were legislated by Parliament under his or her authority. Also, the monarch had unrestricted power to make treaties with foreign states and to grant hereditary noble titles and estates, and could not be impeached. The constitution itself could not be changed without the monarch's consent (Kingdom of Tonga, 1875). Although the day-to-day running of the kingdom was in the hands of the government, the monarch could intervene at will (Powles, 2007).

One must situate the pro-democracy movement in the context of such a monolithic sociopolitical structure. According to Gramsci, hegemony can never be total because of what he refers to as 'dual consciousness', or the capacity of people to think and act independently of the dominant ideological forces. The inability of the feudal patronage system to evolve and adapt to changing aspirations and expectations of the newly educated and globalised young generation became its own nemesis. Paradoxically, education since Tupou I and his predecessors was meant to breed conformity to Tongan identity as constructed by the Tupou dynasty. By the 1980s, a new breed of critical thinkers was able to look beyond the ideological blinkers and started what came to be known as the pro-democracy movement. Power asymmetry created its own contradictions and conditions for resistance.

Counterhegemony: People's movement

Resistance to feudal patronage and the excesses of the monarch caused rumblings within the Tongan community, but these were largely absorbed by a collective sense of cultural loyalty and, for the more religious, the subconscious fear of committing sin by being anti-monarch. Queen Salote's efforts in creating a Tongan cultural renaissance through education, poetry, and mythologisation and romanticisation of Tongan royal genealogy gave the royal institution a regenerated populist image and provided Tongans with a resurgence of cultural euphoria and belief in the benevolence of the monarchy. However, the era of romanticism quickly faded under Tupou IV, who, unlike his poetic mother, Queen Salote, was an enthusiastic economic dreamer who wanted to drive Tonga towards a technocratic path of modernity and development. In the process, he committed one economic blunder after another and thus allowed cocooned grievances to emerge.

Possessed of an overly ambitious entrepreneurial streak, Tupou IV embarked on a modernisation process and vowed to integrate Tonga more deeply into the global economy through education, resource development, an improved health system, transport, tourism and communication, although he was reluctant to carry out political reforms. As part of this plan, Tongans were also encouraged to migrate overseas and send back remittances to relatives to improve their standard of living. These modernisation initiatives had minimal impact because of the misuse of state funds, the unilateral control of investments by royalty in ill-conceived investments and the unequal distribution of resources such as land, wealth and power, which were concentrated largely in the hands of the nobles and monarch. One by one, Tupou IV's entrepreneurial ambitions were thwarted by incompetence and unethical deals and the list of failures became a source of embarrassment for the government: the collapse of Royal Tonga Airlines, sale of Tongan passports, loss of funds in an American insurance scam, and establishment of a ship registry that was misused and generated no income. Under his watch, members of the royal family expanded their business empire to control state assets such as electricity and Tongasat, a company that 'owns' Tonga's satellite slots and is run by Princess Pilolevu, Tupou IV's daughter. In recent years, the *Tonga Herald*, an online paper, was created to defend and promote the Tongan establishment and the royal family against critics. These were the circumstances that galvanised people's grievances and inspired the clamour for greater democratic reforms.

Although the desire for democratisation of Tonga had been nurtured over the years, debates became public in the 1980s and it was not until the pro-democratic national convention in 1992 that the Tonga Pro-Democracy Movement (TPDM) was officially launched as an organised political movement based on the demand for a more egalitarian political system and a greater share of political power by the people. Some pioneers of the pro-democracy movement are Dr Langi Kavaliku, a prominent scholar; the Revd Dr Siupeli Taliai, a respected educator; the late Revd Dr Sione 'Amanaki Havea, former president of the Free Wesleyan Church of Tonga; the late Bishop Patelisio Finau,[1] the first Tongan leader of the Catholic Church in Tonga; and the late Professor Futa Helu,[2] prominent scholar and founder of the Atenisi University. Over the years the younger generation took control of the leadership and future direction of the movement. Samuela 'Akilisi Pohiva, a graduate of the University of the South Pacific and former educator with a very charismatic and outspoken personality, became the public face and symbol of the movement.[3] Others, like Dr Feleti Sevele, the former prime minister, and Lopeti Senituli, former director of the Suva-based Pacific Concerns Resources Center, were also among the leading lights.

The name of the TPDM was changed to Tonga Human Rights and Democracy Movement in 1998, in recognition of the need to emphasise the significance of human rights in the movement. The name was changed to the Friendly Islands Human Rights and Democracy Movement

---

1   A number of Bishop Finau's contemporaries in the Pacific, like the Revd Akuila Yabaki in Fiji, also adhered to the liberation theology movement, which began in Latin America and spread to other developing countries because of its appeal to those seeking social change, especially its focus on the liberation of the oppressed from the powerful classes of society. In my interview with Bishop Finau in 1994, he talked at length about his love for liberation theology and the need for a 'social revolution' in Tonga; that is, significant transformation of the cultural and political structures.

2   Professor Helu described his trip to Italy with his performance group as being 'in the footsteps of Gramsci tour'. Gramsci (1891–1937) is well known to sociologists and political scientists as a major exponent of the theory of 'hegemony', which refers to the way the state and those in power use social, cultural and economic mechanisms to generate consent and domination of the population. Hence the best response is to use 'counterhegemonic' strategies. Gramsci's ideas have influenced generations of revolutionaries and social reformists over the years, including some Pacific activists and scholars. See Gramsci (1971).

3   Mr Pohiva was controversially dismissed from his teaching position by the government, which set his colourful political career in motion.

(FIHRDM) in 2005, when the movement was registered under the Incorporated Societies Act. One of the demands of the government was that the word 'Tonga' should be dropped, because the pro-democracy movement had no right to use it unilaterally but needed the permission of the government.[4]

Like any other new political organisation, there were external as well as internal pressures as the FIHRDM attempted to consolidate its political position amid differences. Jockeying by members for endorsement as candidates for the 2005 election led to internal rifts within the FIHRDM, and some members, such as Professor Helu, deputy chairperson of the organisation, were expelled. The Tonga Democratic Party (TDP), which was formed by the dissident group, became incorporated under the Incorporated Societies Act and emerged as an alternative pro-democracy political grouping. The members of the TDP consisted of strong supporters of the FIHRDM like Father Seluini 'Akau'ola, Teisina Fuko, Semisi Tapueluelu and former minister of police and acting Deputy Prime Minister, William Clive Edwards, whose pro-democracy credentials have often been questioned because of his previous links with the establishment.[5]

Nevertheless, the FIHRDM was the leading political voice in a much larger loose alliance of pro-democracy groups, which included the Friendly Islands Teachers Association, with Finua Tutone as president, the Tonga National Council of Churches, with the Revd Simote Vea as its general secretary until the end of 2005, and the Legal Literacy Project Team, with Betty Blake as its coordinator.[6] The line of demarcation between these organisations and the FIHRDM was blurred, since their

---

4   Tonga, unlike its neighbours Fiji and Samoa, does not have a history of political movements and political parties. The FIHRDM was probably the first organised political group. The refusal of the government to allow use of the word 'Tonga' in the FIHRDM's name was seen as a way of taking away the legitimacy and national status of the pro-democracy movement.

5   As Minister of Police in the 1990s, Edwards was a strong opponent of the pro-democracy movement. He banned the *Times of Tonga* newspaper, ordered surveillance of pro-democracy meetings and brought civil actions against 'Akilisi Pohiva and other democracy activists for defamation. Pohiva and two *Times of Tonga* journalists, Kalafi Moala and Filokalafi 'Akauola, were found guilty by the Tongan Parliament of contempt of Parliament in 1996 and were jailed for 30 days. However, the three were later awarded US$26,000 for wrongful imprisonment. As Minister of Police and Prisons, Edwards was responsible for their imprisonment. The turning point for Edwards was when he was sacked as minister by the Prime Minister, Ulukālala Lavaka, in 2004. Edwards then joined the pro-democracy camp.

6   Over the years, the number of Tongan civil society organisations taking up the pro-democracy cause increased. They provided greater diversity in terms issues relating to of trade union rights, women's rights and community health and community development to the broader pro-democracy agenda.

leaders held key positions in both organisations. For instance, the Revd Simote Vea was chairperson and Finau Tutone the deputy secretary of the FIHRDM for a number of years. Also, Professor Helu, while head of Atenisi University, was also deputy chairperson when he was expelled. In an interesting development, during the September 2005 annual general meeting, HRH Prince Tu'ipelehake was appointed patron of FIHRDM.[7]

Although pro-democracy sentiments had a long period of development and consolidation, between the September 2005 civil service strike and the 16 November 2006 riot, the pro-democracy movement developed into a stronger, more proactive and more assertive nationwide network of politicians, civil servants, business people, journalists, churches, lawyers, villagers, schoolchildren, the unemployed and even royalty in the form of Prince Tu'ipalehake. Senituli describes the situation thus:

> These new emergent organisations, together with the more established member organisations of the 'pro-democracy movement', and individuals, including the People's Representatives to the Legislative Assembly and individual members of the clergy and of the legal profession, had formed a loose coalition of political actors looking for a cause. It included a number of people who felt personally aggrieved by some government policy or decisions and were intent on seeking revenge. It also included a large group of aspiring politicians who had failed in numerous attempts to win a seat in the Legislative Assembly or had lost seats they once held and saw the opportunity to stake early claims for seats in a reformed Parliament. (Senituli, 2006: 3–4)

The need for a more unified front was apparent, and this led to the formation of the People's Committee for Political Reform (PCPR).

The broad pro-democracy alliance swelled after the 22 July 2005 public servants' strike with the inclusion of the Public Servants Association Interim Committee, Tonga National Business Association (TNBA) and the Oceania Broadcasting Network Television (OBN-TV), whose general manager was Sangster Saulala, a government minister, who was later

---

7   Dubbed the 'prince of the people', Prince Tu'ipelehake's pro-democracy stance gave a moral boost to the pro-democracy movement. He was the first member of the royal family who publicly pronounced his support for political reform in support of the commoners' demands.

suspected as being one of the organisers of the riot. However, it should be noted that because of their professional and personal interests, some key members of these associations were ambivalent about, or even opposed to, alignment with the FIHRDM in case it should undermine their demands for better pay and work conditions.[8]

The involvement of the TNBA was of interest because it comprised entrepreneurs who owned small- to medium-sized businesses and who supported the public service strike. The strikers were members of the Tongan middle class who made up a significant portion of the customer base of these businessmen. Any increase in pay would also have a positive flow-on effect to their businesses. In addition, the TNBA saw the proliferation of foreign businesses, especially those belonging to Chinese, Indians and Europeans, as a threat to their survival in the constricted Tongan market. They were also against Tonga's attempt to join the World Trade Organization (WTO) because of its potential impact in allowing an unrestricted flow of cheap foreign goods into Tonga, which they would find difficult to compete against.[9] In addition, they were also opposed to the government's anti-corruption policy, because of its clampdown on businesses.[10] Key players in the TNBA included Dr Tu'i Uata, 'Ofa Simiki and Peseti Ma'afu who, with others in the association, were members of either the FIHRDM or TDP.

OBN-TV played a key role in raising public consciousness through direct live coverage of the activities and speeches at Pangai Si'i. Set up in the early 1990s as a Christian station by Christopher Racine, an American businessman, OBN-TV was a strong advocate of the pro-monarchy and anti-democracy Tonga Kotoa Movement but later changed political allegiance as the wave of pro-democracy sentiment became

8   The 2005 strike was the largest in the history of the kingdom. While it was seen by some as part of the pro-democracy mobilisation, the strike had its own rationale and dynamics, which were industrial in nature and independent of the pro-democracy agenda. However, the strikers' demands, which included higher pay, were fully supported by pro-democracy supporters. Many strikers were also members of the movement.
9   Tonga's membership of the WTO affected local business as well as the Tongan economy generally in a profoundly negative way. The TNBA saw the pro-democracy movement as a useful political mechanism through which they could articulate their commercial interests.
10   The government's anti-corruption policies, which targeted the business community, were viewed with cynicism, especially given the number of highly publicised scandals and cases of corruption involving the government and the royal family.

insurmountable.[11] In assuming the role of the 'CNN of Pangai Si'i', OBN-TV became the media link between Pangai Si'i, which was the centre of political action, and the rest of the country.[12]

The electoral successes of the pro-democracy campaigners were stunning. For instance, the HRDM won seven of the nine people's seats during the 2002 election. They won the same number of seats in 2005 and proceeded to introduce reform proposals in the Legislative Assembly. These electoral gains posed a direct threat to the establishment. They brought into question the long-held assumption that, in the symbiotic relationship between cultural and political loyalty, the two elements are immutably related. The voting pattern showed that ordinary Tongans were able to express their independent political choice against the political establishment under the patronage of the monarch. While people still revere the monarchy as a cultural institution, they were eager to see changes in the political realm.

The anti-establishment votes could also be seen as a way of directly demystifying the perceived 'sacredness' of the Tupou dynasty. One may also say that it was a referendum against the feudal patronage system that gave the nobles uncontested privileges. It affirmed in the minds of the people that they had the power to exercise freedom of choice and to transform society. It was a liberating process that opened up opportunities for rethinking alternatives outside the hegemonic order created through Tupou I's appropriation of Tu'i Tonga's *mana*, Queen Salote's cultural renaissance and Tupou IV's globalisation strategies.

Maintaining state security: Repression of pro-democracy movement

The autocratic leverage of the monarchy through the mysticism of *mana* and divinity and the political and ideological appeal of the constitutional supremacy of the monarch were not sufficient to contain the chorus

---

11   The Tonga Kotoa movement was set up as a pro-monarchical organisation in the face of the call for political change by the pro-democracy movement. Nevertheless it supported the ousting of Prince Ulukalala as prime minister in 2005.

12   One of the strengths of the pro-democracy movement is its very effective use of the media. Apart from the Kele'a, it also uses other papers like *Matangi Tonga*, an independent and critical medium under the guidance of one of the Pacific's most experienced journalists, Pesi Fonua, and *Taimi Tonga Media*, under the direction of Kalafi Moala, a well-respected journalist. Radio and TV were also well utilised. OBN-TV became the most important mobilising medium at Pangai Si'i on 16 November 2006.

of pro-democracy voices and their revolutionary fervour. Hence the monarch and the state had to resort to more secular and psychologically coercive means.

As far back as the 1980s, at the time of the Cold War, Pacific states like Fiji and Tonga that felt threatened by potential internal resistance to the status quo (in the form of the Fiji Labour Party and the demand for democracy in Tonga) were attracted to the Asia-Pacific Anti-Communist League (APACL), formed in Taiwan to keep Chinese communism at bay in the Pacific. A leading supporter of the APACL, Tongan nobleman Fusitua, a former speaker of the Tongan Parliament, made the link between the demand for democracy and communism thus: 'Anybody who tries to move the people against the established order, causing chaos, anarchy, that's the first degree of communism' (Crocombe, 2005: 266). In an APACL meeting in Tonga in 1985, the pro-democracy advocates were branded 'communist' conspirators as a way of discrediting them. Bishop Finau was once labelled a 'Marxist' by the King for his support of the pro-democracy movement (Bain, 1993). A favourite strategy, as in Singapore, was the use of defamation against the pro-democracy supporters as a retaliatory and punitive response. A number of selected cases are given below as examples.

In September 1996, Pohiva, Kalafi Moala and Filokalafi 'Akau'ola, *Times of Tonga* editor, publisher and deputy editor, respectively, were imprisoned after being convicted of alleged contempt of the Legislative Assembly following the publication in *Taimi Tonga*, a weekly newspaper, of an impeachment motion against the minister of justice that had not been tabled in the legislature (Robie, 1996). They were released after serving 24 days of a 30-day sentence after the Supreme Court ruled that the assembly, which overwhelmingly consisted of pro-monarchy supporters, breached a number of constitutional provisions in the conviction of the three. This decision was later upheld by the Tonga Court of Appeal.

In early March 1998, the Supreme Court acquitted Pohiva in a libel case brought against him by the government regarding his claims in an interview with the *Wall Street Journal* and reprinted in *Kele'a*, in which he called Tupou IV a 'dictator'. In the interview, Pohiva alleged that the King was involved in 'financial legerdemain' in relation to the proceeds from the sales of Tongan passports to foreigners as well as revenues generated by Tongasat, a company run by the King's daughter, Pilolevu, which leased global satellite positions Tonga claimed (*Matangi Tonga*, 1998).

Later in the month, on 30 March 1998, the Magistrate's Court convicted and fined 'Akilisi Pohiva US$336 or in default ordered six months imprisonment for defamatory remarks about the minister of police published in *Taimi Tonga*. Pohiva was also convicted and fined US$336 or in default imprisoned for six months for an article published in *Kele'a* (PINA, 1998).

In another case the editor of *Kele'a*, Mateni Tapueluelu, and his wife, Laucala Pohiva, were fined almost T$70,000 in damages and costs for defamation after publishing a letter to the editor that alleged corruption by a particular minister (Stuff NZ, 2013). The case had ramifications for the 2014 election, as Tapueluelu later lost the seat he won after the supervisor of elections ruled that he did not declare his pending court fine when he submitted his application for candidacy.

It began to dawn on the establishment that the constitution to which they declared allegiance in their oath was paradoxically a liability as far as provisions related to free speech were concerned. To remedy the situation and to erect a firewall against the media onslaught, the government initiated restrictive measures such as the Media Operator's Bill as well as, in 2003, a constitutional amendment to restrict media freedom. The legislation gave the government the power to control coverage of 'cultural' and 'moral' issues, ban publications it deemed offensive and ban foreign ownership of the media. This was a big blow to the pro-democracy movement because of its heavy reliance on the media, including ownership of *Kele'a*, as part of its mobilisation campaign.

The intended legislation provoked thousands of people to take part in a protest march through the streets of Nuku'alofa in October 2003 in the first demonstration of its kind in the kingdom. Oblivious to the people's demands and the international outcry, and despite a hot debate in Parliament, the Media Operator's Bill and the constitutional amendment were passed in 2004, and the new licensing process started in earnest. All the papers that were critical of the excesses and corruption of the monarch and government, including *Taimi 'o Tonga* (*Tongan Times*), *Kele'a* and *Matangi Tonga*, were denied licences, while those granted licences were church-based or pro-government. The constitutionality of the amendment was contested in the Supreme Court, and the chief justice struck out most of the clauses in the amendment. This was just one in a series of judgements in which the Supreme Court declared attempts to control the media unconstitutional.

The paradox was that the monarch's attempt to use the constitution that had served its hegemonic interests for generations to undermine free speech was declared unconstitutional. This was a serious blow to the monarch's claim to sacredness. It also raised fundamental issues about the empowering role of the judiciary as an independent organ of the state on which people could rely to confront the overriding political powers of the monarchical juggernaut.

In the broader context of security, the Supreme Court's decision had two implications. First, it provided people with a sense of sociopolitical security in the face of authoritarianism, and second, the court's legal declaration as a secular institution of the state demystified some of the divine and sacred images associated with the monarch. As the ideological veil lifted, people could then see the nakedness of the monarch's control over state power, which was often hidden under the veil of cultural *mana* and Christian divinity. By resorting to legal and other secular means of control and coercion, the monarchy might have felt that its unquestioned acceptance by the people could no longer be guaranteed and might no longer have felt secure simply by using ideological leverage such as *mana* to cultivate and perpetuate what Marx refers to as 'false consciousness'.

Maintaining security through concessions

The failed attempt to weaken the pro-democracy movement through constitutional reform and passage of the anti-media legislation gave way to the only other available option, cooption and 'taming' of the opposition through reform. In 2004, responding to public demand for reform, Prince Tu'ipelehake suggested that a parliamentary committee be set up to facilitate consultations and discussions on possible constitutional reform. This was approved by Parliament. Although its implementation was resisted by some entrenched interests, it was given renewed vigour by the 2005 civil service strike.

With the support of the monarch, the National Committee for Political Reform (NCPR) was set up with Tu'ipelehake as chair, assisted by Dr Sitiveni Halapua, a prominent Tongan scholar based at the East-West Center in Hawaii. After the untimely death of Tu'ipelehake in the United States, the chair of the NCPR was taken over by Halapua, who, on 31 August 2006, presented the report, written in the Tongan language, to the ailing King Tupou IV. Meanwhile, among the signals that changes were afoot, two HRDM supporters, Dr Feleti Sevele and Sione Haukinima, were appointed Cabinet ministers. In 2006 Sevele became the first commoner to be appointed prime minister. He succeeded 'Ulukalala Lavaka-Ata, the King's younger son, whose term was rocked by scandal.

The death of Tupou IV in 2006 signalled a new era in political change for Tonga, as his son and successor, King George Tupou V, seemed more attuned to reform. However, before Parliament could enact any reform agenda, the riot took place and fear of more violence became the major catalyst for speedy change. The King promised wide reforms in political representation, the power of the monarch and other areas of state governance. This led to the establishment in 2008 of the Constitutional and Electoral Commission, whose task was to engage in wide consultation with the Tongan people and propose changes to the constitution. The amendments to the constitution were passed by the assembly in April 2010 and enacted five months later.

Some of the significant reforms included changes in parliamentary representation, the appointment of the prime minister and the appointment of Cabinet. Previously, the unicameral Legislative Assembly consisted of the King's nominees in the form of privy councillors and Cabinet ministers, nine representatives of the nobles and six representatives of the people. Under the new changes, the number of seats for the people's representatives increased from nine out of 30 (30 per cent) to 17 out of 26 (65.4 per cent) and the number of seats for the 33 nobles remained at nine. While previously the monarch appointed the prime minister and Cabinet, the new changes gave power to Parliament to elect a prime minister, who then appointed Cabinet. The prime minister may choose up to 12 ministers for Cabinet, including up to four non-elected persons from outside Parliament. While the coopted Cabinet members became part of and responsible to Parliament, they could not, however, take part in parliamentary votes. In a limited way, the executive authority of the monarch shifted to Cabinet, which was accountable to Parliament.

However, there were differences between the government and pro-democracy group in their approaches to reform. The pro-democracy group claimed that '60 per cent of our proposal was in line with Tu'ipelehake's Committee' (Pohiva, 2007: 3). In their original proposal to the assembly on 9 November 2006, the people's representatives argued for six nobles' representatives and 17 people's representatives. On 13 November this was changed to nine seats for nobles and 21 for the people's representatives. The government's proposal was for 14 people's representatives and 9 nobles' representatives. However, the government wanted to retain the monarch's prerogative of appointing a third of a Cabinet of 14 ministers from the 14 people's representatives and nine nobles' representatives in the assembly or from outside. There were other differences, including views on the electoral system (Senituli, 2006). Some of these differences also helped to fuel the tension that had already built up.

In 2010 the first election under the new electoral system took place. Optimism reigned that at last, and for the first time, Tonga would see an elected commoner-led government. Although Pohiva's party, the Democratic Party of the Friendly Islands (DPFI), won 12 out of 17 seats, they could not form a government because the other five independent parliamentarians opted to join the nobles, who had nine seats, to form a 14-seat government. This power dynamic changed after the 2014 election. Although the DPFI won only nine seats (a decrease of three seats) and independents won eight seats (an increase of three), six of the independent parliamentarians joined the DPFI to form the government. The dramatic U-turn by the independents was probably out of fear of further violence if the DPFI did not come to power (Akilisi Pohiva, personal communication). This enabled Pohiva to become prime minister (Ratuva, 2015b). This became the pinnacle of Tonga's political reform—the leader of the pro-democracy movement becoming prime minister of the kingdom.

But how substantive and sustainable was the reform? Despite the reforms, the monarch still reigns supreme politically as head of state with veto powers, and culturally as the highest symbol of Tongan social cosmology. Although King George V provided the much-needed blessing for the reform, the power of the monarch was not actually reduced. Rather, the exercise of those powers was to be limited. This means that, rather than directly making executive decisions, the monarch would seek the advice of the prime minister as well as the law lords. King George V emphasised this when he said in a press release:

> Officially, the sovereign's powers remain unchanged. Because we are a monarchy, we have a unity of power as opposed to a separation of power. The difference in future is that I shall not be able to exercise any of my powers at will, but all the sovereign's powers must be exercised solely on the advice of the Prime Minister in most things, and in traditional matters the law lords who advise

exercise of power. In that case, I suppose we are different from other nominal monarchies which retain the trappings of monarchy, but actually govern themselves as republics. (King George V, 2012)

The King still retains veto power as well as the power to dismiss the government. One of the conceptual changes in the constitution in relation to 'King's powers' was the deletion of the word 'governs' and substitution of the word 'reigns' (Government of Tonga, 2010a). This is to shift the emphasis from an authoritarian to a ceremonial image. However, questions are still being asked as to whether the reform of the monarch's role is substantively genuine or merely symbolic.

The reformist King George Tupou V died in March 2012. He was succeeded by his brother Crown Prince Tupouto'a Lavaka, who was sworn in as King Tupou VI. The new King is considered less amenable to reform, and questions are already being asked as to whether his reactionary political demeanour might provoke future upheavals.

The riot and ensuing debates

The build-up towards the riots followed a series of developments in a tense and high-pressure atmosphere. The long-awaited report of the National Committee on Political Reform (NCPR) was presented to the Legislative Assembly in October 2006, together with two other reports, one from Cabinet and the other from the People's Committee for Political Reform (PCPR), which was submitted by the people's representatives. After some deliberation, the Legislative Assembly adopted the report and recommendations of the NCPR 'in principle' and, following this, the government proposed that a tripartite committee, consisting of equal numbers of representatives from Cabinet, the people's representatives and the noble's representatives, be formed to try to arrive at a consensus regarding a model that would combine all three reports (Senituli, 2017).

This suggestion for a tripartite committee was opposed by the people's representatives, who insisted that the Legislative Assembly conduct a vote on the PCPR report and recommendations. Further action on the issue was to proceed during the scheduled 6 November 2006 session but, due to concerns about the security of members of the assembly, the speaker decided to adjourn the house for the year. This deference was the last trigger that sparked the riots.

The pro-democracy supporters who had camped at Pangai Si'i Park in central Nuku'alofa for days marched to the Legislative Assembly and threw coconuts at the building. The crowd later scattered and became uncontrollable as people ran amok around the capital, burning, looting, tipping over cars and throwing rocks and other objects.

The riot started around 3.30pm. The destruction of properties was not indiscriminate but well targeted. The businesses destroyed belonged to the government, prime minister, royalty and foreign entrepreneurs, mostly Europeans, Chinese and Indian. As we have seen earlier, the pro-democracy grievances were linked to political rights and economic exploitation. By and large, these were reflected in the choice of targets for smashing, burning and looting. There was 'collateral' damage to other properties as the rioters went out of control.

In subsequent Court of Appeal cases, a number of individuals were singled out as potential ring leaders. One of them was Isileli Pulu, a pro-democracy leader, who was heard by witnesses yelling out: 'Proceed to plan number four' when the government-owned Leiola Duty Free store was being vandalised. He reportedly thanked the rioters saying, 'Thank you, thank you, we have accomplished what we wanted' (Court of Appeal, 2009b: 9). A video tape of the riot shows Pulu in the midst of the destruction directing people in the manner of a 'field commander' (Matavesi, 2006).[13]

The same film showed that the rioters seemed to be aware of which shops to attack and which ones to miss. Those that were targeted were stoned and plundered. The 'onlookers' seemed to be aware also of the 'appropriate targets'. Another film on YouTube showed a woman yelling to the camera, 'We are free', perhaps referring to her newfound political status, real or imagined, symbolised by the free-for-all destruction, as she, together with other bystanders, cheered on the rioters.

Unemployed youths, some of whom were sent home for 'cultural education' from overseas, notably the United States, took advantage of the opportunity to vent their frustrations by joining the fracas. The destruction of businesses by ordinary protesters was a classic example of how political protests could create conditions for the development of multiple expressions of grievances. In the broader context of their

---

13 A Fijian sports administrator filmed the build-up to the riots and the riots themselves, and this video was used as a significant source of evidence during the trial.

demand for equality and reform, people singled out businesses belonging to the monarch as evidence of greed and corruption that contributed to inequality. In the same way, Chinese were seen as contributing to the ordinary Tongan's lack of socioeconomic progress through control of retail and merchandise trading. As we have seen elsewhere, socioeconomic grievances readily transform into ethnopolitical grievances and ethnic scapegoating when the circumstances are favourable (Ratuva, 2013).

About 80 per cent of the central business district (CBD) was destroyed, and about 10 people, mostly looters, died in the fire. Footage of the riot taken by a Tonga-based Fijian sports administrator showed a number of interesting scenarios. It appeared that the riot was pre-planned. Not only were particular shops targeted but also certain individuals were seen organising rioters. Many bystanders also joined in and helped themselves in the looting spree. There were a lot of opportunistic activities by small groups of looters targeting alcohol, which contributed to more drunkenness and fuelled the free-for-all destruction.

The looting and the burning were symbolic political acts. In my field interviews in Tonga, several views were suggested. Some said that the riots provided protesters with an opportunity to express their repugnance at a system they saw as being unfair and exploitative. Some saw the riots as a cleansing act for Tonga, to clear out the dirt-filled past and restart with a new future and identity. Some also saw the incident as a moment of empowerment when, in a hitherto unthinkable way, the people finally 'took control' of the country's capital, albeit in an extralegal way.

State security responses

In the beginning, the police and His Majesty's Armed Forces (HMAF) were caught off guard by the spontaneous eruption of violence. Later, as things began to calm down, they regained control and cordoned off the CBD, ensuring that no one entered the 'crime scene'. The day after, a state of emergency was declared, and only fire-fighters, police, utility workers and those involved in essential services were allowed inside a defined perimeter. Residents within the perimeter had to undergo searches. The emergency laws were wide-ranging, including prohibiting the gathering of more than five people within the area. Security forces were given the right to stop and search people without a warrant (Radio New Zealand, 2006b).

Fearing further escalation, the government's major response on 17 November was to promise prompt democratic reforms, including the guarantee that elections that would ensure the dominance of people's representation would be held in 2008. Meanwhile, the Chinese embassy started evacuating Chinese nationals who were victims of the riot on a chartered plane. There were also chartered flights for people of other nationalities who wanted to leave Tonga.

The post-riot security situation in Tonga was still unpredictable and potentially volatile, and the government sought help from Australia and New Zealand, under the provisions of the Biketawa Declaration. The two countries obliged by providing 110 soldiers and 44 police officers to act as peace-keepers. There was a clear division of labour for the Australian and New Zealand security personnel. The Australians were directly involved in patrolling the streets to assist the Tongan police while the New Zealand soldiers were deployed to look after airport security and the New Zealand police were in charge of the New Zealand High Commission's security. The involvement of security forces from Australia and New Zealand raised a number of questions. Pohiva himself criticised the involvement of foreign troops, stating that it was further proof of the ineffectiveness of the government and its security apparatus under Sevele, which failed to heed the warning signs of the people's anger and did not intervene in time to stop the riots (ABC, 2006).

On 19 November, the restrictions surrounding the CBD were relaxed and access was granted for the Sunday church service, but only on foot. Meanwhile, police investigations were under way, and some looted goods were returned. Part of the investigation was to examine the call logs at the telecommunication centre, hoping to find some clues as to who was involved in organising the riot. By 22 November, police had arrested about 26 people. At last it appeared that the security forces were in control and the security of the country was being normalised. Some shops and commercial centres were open in town as well as in the suburbs.

In early December the Australian and New Zealand forces began withdrawing, and the local security forces took firm control of the situation. The police had by then made about 571 arrests, some in controversial circumstances. There were allegations of police brutality associated with the investigation, codenamed 'Operation Kaliloa'. Pro-democracy MP and former police minister Clive Edwards alleged that police brutality was widespread, with an estimated 300 people, including himself, being brutalised. He was quoted as saying:

> We are trying to get the medical certificates and photographs of these and we are hoping to be processing and publishing them, because instead of having a state of trying to restore peace and order, the soldiers are causing problems [for] the people, and attacking people. It's very bad over here at the moment. (Radio New Zealand, 2006a)

Under the state of emergency law, a number of high-profile individuals were arrested and charged with inciting violence. These included Edwards and Pohiva. The state of emergency was renewed several times. In January 2008, one year and four months after the state of emergency was first declared, a Proclamation of Public Order was once again declared on the grounds that 'there exists a state of danger' in Nuku'alofa. The proclamation further stated that central Nuku'alofa would be 'controlled and maintained by the Tonga Police Force and Tonga Defence Force for the sole purpose of maintaining public order for all people of the country' (Fonua, 2008: 1). This drew heavy criticism from the pro-democracy leaders, who saw no need for it because of a lack of threat to security. The state of emergency was finally lifted in January 2011 after the 2010 election, which saw Siale Tu'ivakano, a *nopele*, become prime minister.

Most of the post-riot cases were tried in the Court of Appeal. The court quashed a number of cases, such as the charges of uttering seditious comments and inciting violence, against five leading pro-democracy campaigners, 'Akilisi Pohiva, Isileli Pulu, William Clive Edwards, 'Uliti Uata and Lepolo Taunisila. It stated that 'it would be impossible for a reasonable jury to conclude that the appellants were uttering threats rather than legitimate warnings'; however, it also suggested that the warnings pertained to 'what would inevitably happen if no heed were taken of the people's will' (Court of Appeal, 2009a: 21). The term 'inevitably' is significant because it is an endorsement of the fact that violence was unavoidable in the circumstances if the political demands were not met. The 'people's will' in this case refers to what the people at Pangai Si'i wanted, which was the proposal for 30 parliamentary seats, consisting of 21 representatives for the people and nine for the nobles. The inability of the government to promptly agree to this spawned what Pohiva referred to as the 'people's upheaval'. The judgement quoted Pohiva saying that: 'The people are waiting if it's a yes or no … the rule of law is a fraud …

The law is in the hands of the people' (Court of Appeal, 2009a: 15). Although this might not have been an 'order' to carry out the riot, it was a direct endorsement and pre-empting of the riot.

Thus the judgement acknowledged that while there was no prima facie evidence of the pro-democracy leaders uttering seditious comments or inciting people to riot, they did acknowledge that the leaders were aware of the potentially explosive situation if their political demands were not met. It was probably a case of not directly ordering an 'attack' but indirectly prodding and encouraging until the threshold of patience was reached.

The court cases reduced the tension and anxiety considerably as people realised that the rule of law had once again taken charge of the once chaotic situation, although the security threat had not totally disappeared. The riot was no doubt the climax of decades of seismic relationships between the contesting classes and the accumulating grievances. The build-up of tension, anger, anxiety and impatience for change was going to erupt at any moment when the circumstances were favourable and the right triggers were in place. The delay by the Legislative Assembly in passing the PCPR's recommendation for reform was the last straw.

All the King's men: The role of His Majesty's Armed Forces

Where does HMAF fit into all these? Perhaps a brief discussion of the emergency powers of the military would throw more light on the state's responses.

Despite the growing political tension and demands for greater democracy, HMAF (known as the Tongan Defence Force until 2013) was not deployed locally in the 1980s and 1990s during the formative years of the pro-democracy movement, although it might have been involved in secret surveillance operations and might have also developed strategies to protect the monarch in times of emergency. It was only during the riot in November 2006 that it was actively used and, even then, because of the time taken for the decision-making process for deployment to be reached (as we shall later discuss), there were delays and it was powerless to do anything during the actual period of riot and burning.

***

Although Tongan soldiers served in World War I as members of the New Zealand Expeditionary Force, it was not until 1939, at the beginning of World War II, that the then Tongan Defence Force (TDF) came into existence. Tongan soldiers, trained by the New Zealand military, saw active service in Solomon Islands in 1943 at a time when American and New Zealand troops were also stationed on Tongatapu. The TDF was disbanded after the war and was reactivated in 1946, remaining for a long time a ceremonial military for the monarch.

Constitutionally, the King is the commander-in-chief of HMAF. That position gives him total authority over the security mechanism of the state. HMAF has been virtually an extension of the monarchy by acting as its ceremonial and coercive arm. Both Tupou V and Tupou VI, the current King, had military training, the former at Royal Military Academy Sandhurst in the UK and the latter at the US Naval War College. Their military training was symbolic of the close integration of the monarch, the state and the military. Tupou VI started as a naval officer in 1982, and rose to the rank of lieutenant commander in 1987. He commanded the naval vessel *Pangai* from 1990 to 1995 and later became military commander. During his term as commander, Tongan forces participated in the regional peace-keeping mission in Bougainville. He completed his military career in 1998 and was appointed minister for defence and minister for foreign affairs. He was later appointed prime minister on 3 January 2000 until his sudden resignation on 11 February 2006 amid increasing pro-democracy protests.

Tongan soldiers were deployed as part of the regional peace-keeping force under the Regional Mission Assistance Mission (RAMSI) in Solomon Islands from 2004 to 2005. Tongan troops also joined the 'coalition of the willing' in Iraq from 2004 to 2008. They were also deployed in Afghanistan under a Royal Air Force regiment from February 2011 to April 2014.

The name His Majesty's Armed Forces was conferred in September 2013, a politically symbolic move that subtly, yet clearly signalled where the control and loyalty of the armed forces must lie. This was ironic in a time of reform and the loosening of certain powers of the monarch in the affairs of the state. On the other hand, it might have been a deliberate act to consolidate the military's accountability to the monarch at a time when the latter's power was being threatened by greater democracy represented by an elected government. It appears that, more and more, as Tonga's political dynamics unfold in an uncertain direction, the monarchy is eager to protect its institutional interests and ultimately its perpetuity through reliance on HMAF. The new name signalled in an unambiguous way the close security alliance between the monarch and the military.

With a total of about 450 personnel, HMAF, whose official mission is to 'defend the sovereignty of the Kingdom of Tonga', consists of three operational command components and two support elements (logistics and training groups). It is partially supported by Australia, the United States, China, the United Kingdom, India and New Zealand through defence cooperation agreements. This security cooperation was activated after the Nuku'alofa riot and resulted in the deployment of New Zealand and Australian troops. The three major components, organised in a unified command system, are the regular force, the territorial force and the active reserve, and the three major units of the regular force are the land force, Her majesty's Defence Force (HMDF) and the navy.

The governance and command structure of the force consists of a number of components, including HMAF Headquarters, Joint Force Headquarters, Territorial Forces, Land Force, Tonga Royal Guards, Tongan Navy, Royal Tongan Marines, Air Wing, Training Wing and Support Unit. In recent years, the HMAF has forged links with relevant international defence organisations for training and operations purposes. These include the Pacific Armies Management Seminar, Pacific Area Senior Officers Logistics Seminar, Western Pacific Naval Symposium (WPNS), International Hydrographic Organisation, South Pacific Hydrographic Commission, NATO Codification and the United Nations. These engagements and alliances have helped to expand and deepen Tonga's security capability, both regionally and internally.

The Tonga Defence Service Act 1992 (Section 5 [1]) defines the roles of the HMAF as:

> The defence of the Kingdom; the aid of the civil authorities in the maintenance of order in the Kingdom; the support of the civil authorities; and, those other functions and duties that His Majesty may from time to time determine.

Clearly there is provision for the military to act as an internal security mechanism in the 'maintenance of order'. In fact Subsections 2 and 3 endorse the use of force, which might even lead to death, if it is necessary in the circumstances, under 'lawful orders', as long as such an order complies with international law (Government of Tonga, 1992). Furthermore, the Public Order Preservation Act 1988 (POP; Government of Tonga, 1988b), enacted four years earlier, provides the legal scenario for intervention of the military in times of emergencies. There is an administrative and political process to be followed in the declaration of a 'state of danger to public order', starting with the determination by the prime minister through the advice of the minister of police or minister responsible for internal security whether, given the state of security, an emergency needs to be declared. This declaration is then submitted to the Privy Council, which will then make the final decision before it is gazetted and takes effect.

Sections 5–18 of the POP give wide-ranging powers to the police and HMAF, ranging from setting up roadblocks to arrest and use of lethal force. This is supplemented by the Emergency Powers Act 1959, which provides the King with emergency powers to make regulations:

> Subject to the provisions of this Act, His Majesty in Council may in an emergency make such Regulations as appear to him to be necessary or expedient for securing the public safety, the defence of the Kingdom, the maintenance of public order and for the maintaining of supplies and services essential to the life of the community. (Government of Tonga, 1988a: 5)

The emergency powers of the military and police were used to arrest suspected rioters and, by 17 January 2007, two months after the riots, 678 people, ranging from nine to 70 years old and including 54 women, had been arrested and charged with offences relating to the violence (Senituli, 2017). There were altogether 320 related prosecutions, accompanied by allegations of widespread brutality by the security forces. The state of emergency was renewed every 30 days, until it was eventually lifted in 2011.

One of the dilemmas of the HMAF is that, although, as an institution, it is controlled by the monarch, the individual soldiers of the rank and file are still closely linked to the community as members of the *kainga*. They are often torn between, on one hand, their professional loyalty to the Crown and, on the other, their obligation to their families and communities. Sometimes their own families and local communities might be supporters of the pro-democracy movement. To be caught in a situation where a soldier's sense of commitment is being pulled by opposing forces can be a psychologically intimidating and unsettling experience. Hence the strongest weapon that the HMAF has is not so much its praetorian militaristic strategy but its community engagement role as community peace-keepers. This is despite allegations of brutality by soldiers, which were denied by the military (Radio New Zealand, 2006c).

Competing narratives of security

The smoke had hardly cleared when the debate as to who was responsible for the violence started in earnest. There was a clear division of competing narratives between those who were part of the government and those who were not, with each group accusing the other of being responsible.

Writing in 2005, Lopeti Senituli, the then prime minister's political adviser, said: 'Political transitions are frequently occasions for violence; Tonga, however, has so far managed change and conflict with a notable lack of violence' (Senituli, 2005: 1). However, after the riot of 16 November 2006, he forthrightly declared that an 'attempted coup' had taken place (Senituli, 2006: 1). On the other hand, Pohiva, the leading people's representative in Parliament, referred to the same incident as a 'people's upheaval' (Pohiva, 2007: 1). The language used by the two sides diverged considerably and represented their different positions in the political divide.

From his vantage point, Senituli, a former secretary of the pro-democracy movement who later joined the government as adviser to the prime minister, accused the pro-democracy supporters of attempting to overthrow the government, Fiji-style. He stated that the members of the pro-democracy PCPR must bear the full responsibility for the violence and deaths of 16 November and added that:

> The People's Representatives (and the PCPR's) plan was to call for a ballot anyway, which they knew they would lose, which would then provide the people in Pangai Si'i with the excuse to storm the Legislative Assembly and inflict injury, if not death, on the Prime Minister and the Cabinet ministers, which would then be the justification for their Petition to His Majesty on the day after, to appoint a new Prime Minister and Cabinet. (I accidentally witnessed part of the preparation of this Petition on Wednesday, 15 November by 'Akilisi Pohiva, 'Uliti Uata and Lepolo Taunisila at the Offices of the Legislative Assembly.) (Senituli, 2006: 20)

This was disputed by Akilisi Pohiva, who argued that:

> It was rather a people's upheaval caused and consistently activated by suppressive and dictatorial measures and continuous refusal of government to listen and respond to people's grievances over a long period of time. The exercise of suppressive methods and delay tactics to avoid the vote on the people representatives' proposals in the last session of Parliament for the year sparked people's anger and discontent. (Pohiva, 2007: 1)

For Pohiva, the collective angry mood was beyond his control. Whether or not the PCPR leaders gave direct 'orders' to demonstrators to 'attack' is not clear, although Pohiva himself admitted that he was 'in front of an angry mob that surrounded the Prime Minister's office to stop them from attacking him and from invading the Cabinet room where the Prime Minister, and a few others, including the speaker of the House, remained' (Pohiva, 2007: 1). An eyewitness and editor of *Kele'a*, the pro-democracy movement newspaper, Mateni Tapueluelu (Pohiva's son-in-law, now a government minister), affirmed that rioters 'were pro-democracy supporters, and some had been at a rally at which thousands of people demanded that a vote approving democratic reforms take place in the Legislative Assembly before the House rose for the year'. He added that 'they demanded that if the Government did not agree to political reform by 2008, they would do something—nobody knew what they meant' (*New Zealand Herald*, 2006).

In a further response to Senituli's suggestion that what happened was tantamount to a 'coup', as we saw earlier, Pohiva countered that 'the crisis of November 16 was not a *coup d'état*' because, if it was, 'we would all have witnessed a totally different picture of the situation' (Pohiva, 2007: 1). If there was 'a plan to harm the Prime Minister and other Ministers and/or even kill them … it could have come from a different group of people unknown to our committee' (Pohiva, 2007: 2).

The NCPR was also blamed for undermining the power of the monarch and inciting the riot, but a member of the NCPR, Dr Ana Taufe'ulungaki, defended the committee by arguing that the recommendations of the committee were merely constitutional and not structural:

In essence, there were no changes recommended to the existing political and social structures but there were recommendations for some shifts in the powers of the King and greater participation of the people in political decisions. The reforms would occur at the Constitutional level, not in the political system as such. (Taufe'ulungaki, 2006: 3)

This was disputed by Senituli, who argued:

The changes that the NCPR recommended amounted to the total overhaul of the constitution and of the country's political system and turning a uniquely Tongan, and a uniquely tripartite but unicameral Legislative Assembly into a bipartisan Westminster-type Parliament and in the process disenfranchising His Majesty the King. (Senituli, 2006: 9)

For instance, one of the key recommendations was the increase in the people's representation in the Legislative Assembly from nine to 17, while the number of noble representatives remained at nine, and the King lost his prerogative to select his nine representatives as well as the appointment of the Cabinet (NCPR, 2006).

Dr Taufe'ulungaki also blamed the pro-democracy movement for inciting the protesters during the build-up to 16 November:

The abusive language, charges of corruption, and threats, targeting Government leaders and the Royal Family, continued unabated in these public meetings. Their members also continued to protest and occupy Pangai Si'i, and held panel discussions almost every night on OBNTV, which was more of the same kind of content as their public meetings around Tongatapu. (Taufe'ulungaki, 2006: 6–7)

The then director of the Friendly Islands Human Rights and Democracy Movement, 'Akenete Lauti, a close associate of Pohiva, retorted that they advocated 'non-violence' but blamed the government for the riot (AIMC, 2006). Both sides blamed each other for the violence and, understandably, no one was prepared to take responsibility. From the pro-democracy side, the blame lay squarely with the government for being too slow in responding to the people's wishes, whereas, from the government side, the blame lay with the pro-democracy forces for deliberately instigating the violence to force regime change.

Dr Sitiveni Halapua, the deputy chair and later chair of the NCPR, concurred with Pohiva that the prime minister should shoulder the blame for the crisis. Dr Halapua accused the government of not responding positively to the NCPR's and the people's proposals and instead tried to put forward its own counter proposals (*New Zealand Herald*, 2006).

In response to the spontaneous violence, the prime minister, under immense duress, convened a meeting with the nobles and people's representatives in the hope of making some concessions to help quell public anger. He wrote in a letter:

> A meeting was held between the Prime Minister, Nobles and the People's Representatives today the 16th November 2006. They agreed to have the people elect 21 representatives and Nobles to elect 9 representatives commencing in 2008, and the total seats in Parliament will be 30. (Court of Appeal, 2009a: 16)

This agreement had little influence on stopping the wave of political anger, which had spilled onto the streets of Nuku'alofa. Perhaps the disturbances could have been avoided had the agreement been reached earlier.

Given their minority position in Parliament, PCPR deployed the strategy of using people power as political leverage. In his letter to the secretary general of the Pacific Islands Forum in Suva in July 2006 (four months before the riot), Pohiva wrote that the PCPR had devised a strategy of demonstrations and civil disobedience, which they planned to use until the Forum meeting, and added that:

> Because the Tonga Government has been ignoring the will of its people for a considerable number of years, it now feels it can no longer ignore nor tolerate the continuation of the present despotic regime therefore would like to warn the Forum Secretariat that the demonstration cannot be guaranteed to be peaceful. (Pohiva, 2006: 1)

The warning to the Forum that 'the demonstration cannot be guaranteed to be peaceful' was a veiled threat to attract the attention of the regional organisation and the region generally to the lack of democracy in Tonga.

In a way, Pohiva claimed victory by the people. Although he did not have the numbers in the Legislative Assembly, his use of people power to pressure the government might have worked:

The only chance lay with people outside Parliament. It was proved true when the Prime Minister was forced by pressure from the angry mob outside the Prime Minister's building to agree to our proposals. Despite that, why did they want the people, our power base, to leave Pangai si'i and allow them, as the majority to win the game inside Parliament by default? We appealed to the people to come to Pangai si'i to show their support to our proposals and to demonstrate that we are the majority outside. And we had the right to do that. And ministers had nothing to worry about if they were willing to listen to the majority. (Pohiva, 2007: 1)

The PCPR's strategy was quite clear. Tongan democracy was unfair and unjust, and provided little potential for the majority of the population to realise political transformation through Parliament. The only viable option they had was the use of extraparliamentary means; that is, as Pohiva argues, the use of 'pressure from the angry mob' to force Parliament 'to agree to our proposals' (Pohiva, 2007: 2).

The contending security narratives shows the wide political divide in a culturally homogenous society. The riot had unleashed the genie of political grievances and social gripes that had been bottled up for decades. One of the positive consequences of the riots, as we have seen in this section, is that it forced the debates to become more rigorous and arrive at a conclusion quite fast. The government's decision to engage in a lengthy process of deliberation to arrive at a consensus was not a very smart strategy in the circumstances. The post-riot debate was a time to reflect on where things went wrong and how the destruction could have been avoided. Whether the crisis constituted a coup or whether it was a 'people's upheaval' or both, the government and pro-democracy forces both played a part in heightening the political tension, which eventually exploded into Tonga's worst case of political violence in the modern era.

Fanning the fire of insecurity: The security symbolism of Si'i Park

Any discussion of the 16 November 2006 event must necessarily include an analysis of the significance of Pangai Si'i Park, which over the years had been used as 'ground zero', as it were, of agitation, mobilisation and activism. For the protesters, the park was strategically located because it was adjacent to the offices of the prime minister and the Ministry of Finance—two important symbols of state power.

In the years leading to the 2006 riot, the park had become a symbol of protest, democracy and free expression in the political life of the kingdom. It was where the 2005 civil service strike was organised and for days became 'home' to strikers and their supporters. Again, in 2006 it was the gathering centre of the pro-democracy supporters throughout the year. It was a hive of festivities, cultural performance and political mobilisation. For days before 16 November, it was where people converged, political banners were hung, political speeches made, prayers dedicated and a feeling of common bonds forged. It was a safe space where people could feel protected by the presence of other fellow pro-democracy supporters. It was also a source of information on what was happening and instructions on what needed to be done. It was where the pro-democracy identity was defined and vision articulated. There was a public appeal by the pro-democracy leaders for people to come to Pangai Si'i Park, which had acted as a kind of people's alternative assembly, outside the parliamentary process. Pohiva stated:

> To me it was part of the process of continuous events of the last 15–20 years. My role is to speak on behalf of the people. Government kept telling us that we didn't have the support of the people. So we had to show the government we have the support of the people. We called them. Just to show that we have the support of the people. That's why they said we didn't have the support. So we appeared on TV and appealed to people to come to Pangai Si'i to show support. We had come to a point in Parliament where we were asking people to support us … during the Parliament's discussions, just to show support. (Fonua, 2006: 1)

Loudspeakers were directed at Parliament to drown out proceedings. On 7 November, for instance, Parliament had to stop its session for the day as a result of abusive language and threats emanating from Pangai Si'i. A parliamentary subcommittee was set up to look into the matter, and it was decided to shift the speakers to the far end of the park.

The fiery speeches leading up to the riot would have nurtured an atmosphere of collective anger and anticipation of collective action, as reported in *Tonga Now*:

> During the daily Pangai Sii protest, people were led to believe that everything was going to be held peacefully and in accordance with the law. However, if you analyse the events of the last two weeks—you will find that the rhetoric and abusive words used at Pangai Si'i was increasing on a daily basis and up to a point

where supporters were swearing in the open though this was very disrespectful. Many prominent individuals as well as People's Representatives were on-hand to cheer and urge the speakers on.

Pangia Si'i was where the people's parliamentary representatives generated legitimacy and support and the base from which they consulted the people as they engaged in talks with Parliament and the government. In a speech captured on film on 16 November, before the riot, Mr Pohiva said:

> Before we return to Parliament and pass onto the chair and the nobles the things that we want and the things we are waiting for, I want the news media of Tonga today to tell the world the truth. The will of the people is here in Pangai Si'i today. My ministers, we have visited all the villages and have had meetings. How many Misi? Thirty-four meetings. And we have spread this issue to the people of this country … We are not going to change our minds. We represent 98 per cent of the population.

The collective synergy, group dynamics and political solidarity that the Pangai Si'i environment created was to have a very powerful impact on crowd behaviour during the day. The 'route' of the riot began and ended at Pangai Si'i. A film of the riot showed many who were at Pangai Si'i being involved in the riot and then returning to Pangai Si'i later. The park symbolised resistance, democratisation, transformation and indeed security. It is now part of Tonga's security narrative. Some of the sentiments fermented at Pangai Si'i could be seen around Nuku'aloka in the form of graffiti such as: 'The nu face of youth rebellion', 'Revolutionary not evolutionary', 'Freedomfighter', 'Fight the Power', 'Democracy not Hypocrisy', 'You had it coming' and 'F … Prime Minister'.

Tongan masculinity and security

Like any other political organisation with an overtly transformative agenda, the pro-democracy movement consisted of diverse individuals and subgroups with different political positions relating to strategies for change. By and large the movement, under the leadership and ideological direction of Pohiva, advocated peaceful reform. However, there was a very small minority who advocated extremist methods in the form of violence. While researching the pro-democracy movement in Tonga, I encountered rumblings about the potential for deliberate use of violence to bring about change. For instance, in 1994, a Tongan scholar (name withheld), now residing in Australia, talked of the possibility of Tongans who were Vietnam War veterans being mobilised to carry out a Fiji-style coup.[14] During a public lecture on Tongan pro-democracy in 2002, which I chaired at The Australian National University in Canberra, where I worked, the same pro-democracy supporter expressed his desire to see the monarchy totally eradicated. Discussions in some of the international Tongan blogs also raised similar sentiments. The use of military-style violence might have been based on speculation; however, given the experiences of some countries where foreign mercenaries have been used to topple governments, there was reason to take note of its seriousness at the time.

The second violent option was spontaneous public expression of anger. This was always seen as an alternative in the minds of some pro-democracy campaigners, and this was often used as a warning to those resisting change. Speeches by pro-democracy leaders have often included threats of possible violence if demands were not met.

Culturally, Tongans have profound respect for authority and community values, a factor that provides political restraint and mitigates against the potential for violence. However, the threshold for violent action had been lowered considerably by the increasing grievances and anger of the people, the national campaign for democracy through the media, village meetings and international and public campaigns over a period of more than two decades by the pro-democracy movement.

While the pro-democracy leaders did not explicitly preach about violence, the tense environment and the interpretation of speeches in this politically charged atmosphere made violence almost imperative. At the same time, there were also elements of masculinity, which found expression in the politically volatile situation. Within the Tongan framing of masculinity, the image of the warrior (*to'a*) personality features strongly. This is often represented in traditional mythology, songs and male dances (*kailao*). A version of warrior dancing (*sipi tau*) is now being used as a 'pre-war' psyching challenge before an international rugby match. Tongans pride themselves on being natural warriors whose ancestors defeated their Fijian

---

14   The Fiji coup in 1987 redefined new parameters for extralegal options for political change in the Pacific. It provided inspiration for some Maori activists, and in the 1990s some Tongans I spoke to showed enthusiasm about a similar coup in Tonga. These were based more on speculative thinking rather than serious political strategising.

and Samoan neighbours in fierce battles of the past.[15] This masculine identity is often masked by the Tongans' calm and humorous disposition. However, when threatened, the Tongan spirit of *to'a* can be manifested in the form of threats or sometimes violent behaviour.

This expression of masculinity was very much identifiable in the fiery speeches and challenges to the government by the pro-democracy leaders during village gatherings and at Pangai Si'i. Moreover, the occasional festive environment at Pangai Si'i kept the peace for a certain period before the riot began. This is not to say that the *to'a* sprit caused the riot. Rather, the *to'a* spirit might have provided some psychological boost to the male participants in the riot. Having said this, it is important to note that Tongan culture has a powerful peace-building mechanism where anger and conflict can be easily mitigated through traditional forms of reconciliation. This became obvious after the riot as the reconciliation process started.

Hence, despite the appeal for peaceful orderly demonstrations, pro-democracy leaders were fully aware that beneath the veneer of a Christian and law-abiding friendly citizen was a proud Tongan warrior ready to defend his honour when his human and political rights were trampled on. All that was needed was the right political environment, appropriate political psyching and a trigger, before an explosion took place. Most of those involved in the riots were males, although some females were also seen participating.

Individual criminality or collective political action: Implications for security

It has been argued that the riots of 16 November 2006 in Tonga need to be understood in relation to the criminal behaviour of the individual rioters rather than the political context. Campbell (2012: 20) contends that the 'arson was the work of criminal elements separate from the larger political events going on around them'. This argument was used in a court case involving insurance payout to a number of businesses that were burnt during the riots. How valid is Campbell's position?

---

15   Some of these past victories are still referred to today as a way of asserting Tongan identity and pride.

Over the years, sociologists studying crowd psychology have shifted the focus of their work from the classical psychological reductionist approach (CPR) to the sociocontextual approach. CPR, first advocated by French sociologist Gastave Le Bon (1895), argued that in a situation of crowd conflict, people must be seen as individualised, irrational and regressive beings acting robotically without any coherent thinking. This approach has been criticised for being too mechanical and simplistic because it reduces rioters to thoughtless packs of potentially destructive beings inspired by primordial (or inborn) and irrational criminal urges. It portrays rioters as unrelated and autonomous individuals driven by self-gratifying instincts (Waddington & King, 2005). These explanations do not stand up to the results of sociological research on human behaviour and crowd psychology over the years.

Sociologists now accept the sociocontextual approach as the most appropriate way to understand the complex nature and dynamics of crowd behaviour and individual responses in a situation of conflict and riot. The importance of the political context, collective social identity and the role of beliefs and ideologies are crucial in shaping crowd behaviour. A leading British and world expert on street riots and crowd behaviour, Professor Steven Reicher, wrote:

> Indeed, understanding social identity is the key to understanding crowds and how to deal with them. It is not simply that social identity shapes the values and standards on which we act, it also determines, amongst other things, who can influence us and how, the nature of our goals and priorities, how we view others and interpret their behavior, and, more specifically, the conditions under which we enter into conflict with others. (Reicher et al., 2004: 556)

Reicher developed the now widely used Elaborated Social Identity Model of crowd psychology and conflict as a result of years of careful research into riots in British cities and other parts of the world. This approach is now widely used by police forces around the world as a guide to riot control. The approach concluded that, in the context of British riots, participants shared common social attributes and definitions of themselves and others: (a) they unanimously considered themselves exploited and impoverished by the government and financial institutions, and perceived themselves as victims of regular police discrimination; (b) they suffered constant humiliation due to their dependency on the welfare system; (c) they were resentful of local retailers who were taking advantage of low local rental costs but whose goods were not affordable to the community; and (d) they felt that they had lost the capacity to exert any control over community matters (Waddington & King, 2005: 496).

The above assessment sounds uncannily similar to the Nuku'alofa situation on 16 November 2006. The Nuku'alofa rioters shared some common immediate goals: (a) a collective desire for reform, (b) a guarantee that reform be visible and real, and (c) that reform be prompt. There were broader shared attributes as well: (a) they collectively saw themselves as exploited, poor, commoner Tongans; (b) they were resentful of nepotism, corruption and business monopolies by royals; (c) they were resentful of government allowing foreign entrepreneurs to operate locally at the cost of Tongan business; (d) given their politically disadvantaged position in a highly rigid feudal-type sociopolitical hierarchy dominated by the privileged few, they felt a sense of alienation, powerlessness and lack of control over their future and the future of their children; and (e) given the lack of meaningful reform after more than 20 years of demands for change, many were beginning to lose patience. These shared attributes provided the potentially explosive cocktail for spontaneous collective action.

Sociologically, the broader and specific contexts of riots have to be understood because human beings do not behave responsively in a vacuum but in a cultural, social or political context.

While the political and cultural contexts of riots differ from society to society, the group dynamics and the way they shape people's behaviour and the outcome of the violence have similar characteristics. The analyses of the situation by eyewitnesses from both sides of the political divide (Senituli and Pohiva for instance), despite disagreement as to who was responsible, agree that collective identification with the political cause of reform spawned the wave of grievances that reached a flashpoint leading to the riot.

Sociologists and social psychologists doing research on crowd psychology will reject in no uncertain terms the assumption that individual criminal intent led to or inspired the Nuku'alofa riot. In fact there is no *prima facie* evidence from research carried out on crowd riots around the world in recent times to suggest this conclusion. While there would be individuals joining in to be part of the crowd, the common goal is the overriding factor. As Reicher (2008) argues, the driving force, the momentum of the crowd and even the targets of the riots often become part of the collective synergy and identity. While it might appear that certain individuals are acting on their own, they are still part of the group, and their behaviour is shaped by what sociologists refer to as 'group dynamics', defined as the roles, relationships, collective goals, collective identity, collective expectations and behaviour of people in a group (Pettigrew & Tropp, 2006). If you remove the situation of group dynamics, then individuals would not be rioting publicly on their own as they did in Nuku'alofa.

Although the riot itself appeared to be spontaneous, the build-up took years of political resentment and anger. The expressions of political grievances spanning almost two decades of demand for political reform had reached a flashpoint, which inevitably manifested itself in the form of the riot. This was a case of political expression overriding communal and cultural ethos, which revolved around the community and *kainga* (family). The autocratic rule of the monarch, the widely publicised corruption, the violation of human rights and free speech and the increase in poverty and inequality nurtured widespread dissatisfaction over time and changed people's perception of and attitude to authority.

The riot needs to be understood in the context of a number of factors, including the broader political climate of demand for reform over a period of almost two decades; the extensive campaign by the pro-democracy movement in mobilising people's opinions, sentiments and anger through the media and village meetings weeks before 16 November; the way the campaign became intensified as people converged on Panagai Si'i Park days before the riot and on the day of the riot; and the perceived 'delay' in adopting the pro-democracy proposal for constitutional change.

The constitutional reform process had heightened expectations as people realised that it was the only option for political reform available to them. This high expectation, built up by months of country-wide mobilisation of opinion through village meetings, media hype and fiery speeches at Pangai Si'i, provided a politically combustible condition for crowd psychology. Although the law was broken and there were sporadic acts of criminality, the wider mobilising and motivating force was political.

Socioeconomic deprivation: A future security threat?

One of the major threats to the future security of Tonga is growing poverty, inequality and lack of opportunity. Although political reform has always been highlighted as being of the utmost importance, economic reform is equally significant. The monarchy might have relinquished some political power, but its control over wealth and resources such as land will continue to be problematic and might cause even more friction in the future as people's expectations grow rapidly as a result of globalisation in the context of retarded socioeconomic development.

The deprived economic situation of ordinary Tongans fed into the swelling vortex of grievances that fuelled the riot. The inequality between the monarch and the nobles on the one hand and the ordinary people on the other was made worse by the monarchy's monopoly of some major national business operations such as power, airlines and geostationary satellite slots.[16] Many Tongans relied on remittances from their relatives working overseas, but this source of income was badly affected by the global economic crisis in 2008.[17]

The GDP per capita for Tonga in 2004–05, the period leading up to the riot, was US$2,350. Comparatively, around the same period, close neighbour Samoa had a GDP per capita of US$5,125. The growth rate for Tonga in the 20 years between 1990 and 2010 was 1.6 per cent, compared to Samoa's 3 per cent. The 2009 Tonga Household Income and Expenditure Survey showed that absolute poverty in Tonga increased from 2.8 per cent in 2001 to 3.1 per cent in 2009 and that the proportion of people living below the basic needs poverty line jumped from 16.2 per cent in 2001 to 22.5 per cent of the population in 2009 (Government of Tonga, 2010b). The United Nations Millennium

---

16 The distinction between property and wealth belonging to the state and those belonging to the royal family personally has not been very clear. This was brought out into the open when the late King tried to sell a property in Auckland. The controversial sale led to a debate between royal ownership and people/state ownership. The lack of clear distinction between the state and the monarch's assets and the behaviour of members of the royal family using state resources and privileges for family business has been a major concern of the pro-democracy advocates.

17 The global crisis led to a reduction in remittances, and Tonga's membership of the WTO undermined local business as well as depriving the government of income worth millions of dollars. These factors have contributed to increased poverty.

Development Goal Report states that more than 3,000 Tongans live in 'absolute poverty' or 'food poverty'—having less than T$24.12 per person per week (UN, 2010).

There was an increase in the Poverty Gap Index (the average gap between poor people's standard of living and the basic needs poverty line) from 4.4 in 2001 to 6.3 in 2009. Poverty in the outer islands almost doubled from 11.8 per cent of the population in 2001 to 22.9 per cent in 2009. The very low growth in Tonga's economy (0.9 per cent in 2009 and 1.2 per cent in 2010) compares unfavourably with 3.9 per cent in growth for the rest of the Pacific.

The lack of socioeconomic opportunities is a major factor for migration of Tongans to New Zealand, Australia and the United States. Although Tonga had for a number of years achieved a high Human Development Index, it was more an indication of the level of universal access to education and life expectancy supported by subsistence farming and kinship support systems than a measure of disposable income and wealth in the country. Economic production and investment in Tonga has been low, and many people have had to rely on the subsistence economy for sustenance. What kept the economy going was remittances from overseas, but even this source declined over the years as a result of the 2008 global financial crisis. The growing business of a few elites, including members of the royal family and foreigners, made the disparity more obvious, and this was a cause of resentment. The targeted burning of some shops reflected that anger. Political discourse and action became a means by which economic grievances were articulated.

Frustrations emanating from socioeconomic conditions were exacerbated by the visible inequality manifested by the opulent lifestyle of royalty and nobles. Over the years, the increase in the number of European, Chinese and Indian business immigrants has added to the socioeconomic grievances of locals, and this was expressed in a violent way during the riot, when Chinese shops were burnt and looted.[18]

---

18 Anti-foreigner feelings were also aimed at the government for allowing Tonga to be flooded with foreign entrepreneurs with whom local Tongan shopkeepers and businessmen could not compete.

Unfinished revolution? Implications of the riot for Tonga's security

Have reforms in Tonga been sufficient to ensure the sustainability of Tonga's security in the future? Was November 2006 an unfinished revolution that has not completed the process of democratisation? A starting point is to examine more carefully the statement by Tupou V, the reformist monarch, who, as we saw earlier, categorically stated: 'Officially, the sovereign's powers remain unchanged. Because we are a monarchy, we have a unity of power as opposed to a separation of power.' The notion of 'unity of power' is another way of articulating the subservience of all state institutions under the supreme authority of the monarch.

One of the changes is that, instead of exercising his power 'at will', the monarch would rely on the advice of the prime minister or the law lords. Despite this public declaration, the monarch still retains veto powers over bills adopted by the Legislative Assembly. The first test of the new doctrine was in relation to the adoption, by a vote of 10 to eight, of the Arms and Ammunition (Amendment) Bill in October 2012, which aimed to reduce criminal sentences for illicit possession of firearms. Members of the government, including the prime minister, voted for the Bill in support of two government members who had been charged under the law. The Opposition was incensed with what they saw as political nepotism and conflict of interest, and asked the King to veto the decision of the Legislative Assembly. The King agreed and vetoed the Bill. Although ethically it could be argued that the King might have made the right decision in vetoing a highly questionable bill, the broader principle relating to the exercise of veto power by the monarch could be problematic in future.

Although commoners now have 17 representatives in Parliament, this expression of democratic representation is still overshadowed by the uncontested supreme power of the monarch. As demonstrated during the 2010 election, the reform did not guarantee a functional democratic process whereby all members of the Legislative Assembly are elected through popular votes. The 33 nobles are still represented by nine members and 40,736 voters are represented by a mere 17 members. This is a startling contrast of seat-to-voter ratio of 1:2,396 as opposed to 1:4 for the nobles. The reform has simply brought down the people's seat-to-voter ratio from 1:4,526, a reduction of almost 50 per cent.

However, despite the changes in favour of the people's representatives, the nobles still hold the balance of power and, as we saw during the 2010 election, they can leverage their position to return to power and maintain the status quo. The role of the independents is also critical in shifting the balance of power, as we saw in the last two elections. The shift in the centre of political gravity from the nobles after the 2010 election to Pohiva's pro-democracy group after the 2014 election signifies a see-saw tendency, which could become a permanent feature of Tongan politics. If at some point the nobles are able to claw their way back into power and maintain their rule, there might be counter-reaction by the new generation, who would feel that their high expectations and hopes for democratisation had been dashed by the self-serving nobles. This is a long-term security dilemma for Tonga.

At the same time, what holds the pro-democracy group together is the charisma and leadership skills of Pohiva, who is now sickly and frail. When he steps down, the political dynamics will change quickly. Because his son, who has been groomed as his successor, might not have the same charisma, there is bound to be a leadership struggle, and there will no doubt be casualties. This will probably divide the pro-democracy group further and thus make Tongan politics more unstable. Pohiva's rule as prime minister has been a challenge because of lack of policy experience, inability to maintain a coherent stance and pressures from the nobles to undermine his rule. The suspension of Parliament in August 2017 shows that the democratic transformation is far from over.

Another major security issue is the role of the military. The military is directly under the control of the monarch and, as in Thailand, it can be used against an 'unwanted' government. This might sound far-fetched, but any attempt to weaken the real power of the monarch into mere titular authority, such as in Britain, through large-scale reform, could provoke stiff resistance from the nobles and monarch; and the military could be used either to directly suppress any disturbance or even to remove a government bent on neutralising the power of the monarch.

The dilemma for Tonga is that on the one hand the unfinished revolution provides a breathing space and hope, but it also raises expectations that could unfold into a 16 November-type scenario if expectations are not fulfilled. On the other hand, attempts to execute a 'complete' change have the potential to invoke the wrath of the ruling classes, as we have seen in the King's intervention to suspend Parliament on the pretext that the government under Pohiva was trying to undermine the King's power.

Conclusion

Although Tonga was never formally colonised, the British influence was similar to other colonies. The political structure, economic system and class structure are very much reflective of postcolonial realities. The history and sociology of conflict in Tonga might not be as complex as that of Fiji, but it is unique in the sense that is shows a classical intracommunal class tension in a way that has not been seen in the Pacific. Tonga's rigid class structure, consisting of the monarch, nobles and commoners, had been sustained and reproduced through Christianity, the constitution, education, political hegemony, cultural loyalty and social mythology. The contradictions began to unravel as subaltern social class forces began to exert their demands. As commoners attempted to express their grievances as a subaltern group, the establishment was not in a position to accommodate their demands by instituting necessary changes. It was really after George Tupou V came to the throne that reforms began in earnest. The reforms gave the pro-democracy movement an added political thrust and heightened people's expectations of greater things to come. The high expectations and rising tension, coupled with the slow pace of reform, triggered the riot. The violence, although politically driven, also became an opportunity for unemployed, disgruntled young people and poor sections of the community to vent their anger and appropriate goods from burning shops.

The violence, the worst in Tonga's contemporary history, redefined Tonga's historical trajectory in an unprecedented way. It showed how formal state authority and hegemony, which had been the cornerstone of Tongan 'stability', could easily be usurped by collective expressions of power by the people. Resorting to violence is often an unstated option in situations of political contestation and, as in the case of Tonga, it became a latent result of the ongoing power struggle between the people and the establishment. Often, as in the case of Fiji's first coup in 1987, the first case of extralegal violence sometimes opens the floodgate, as extra-violence becomes a recognised option in regime change when legal mechanisms are seen as ineffective. The possibility of further political violence resurfacing in Tonga will depend on the right circumstances and triggers occurring. As poverty and inequality increases and as economic and political reforms stall amid high expectations and repressed grievances, a repetition of 16 November is not impossible.

The role of the Tongan military will increasingly become important in future as the vanguard of Tonga's security. Although it was largely ineffective during the 2006 riot, its symbolic presence and the rearticulation of its role might help to consolidate the state's capacity to respond to national emergencies. The expansion of the military coincided with the rise and expansion of the pro-democracy movement. The fact that the military is directly under the control of the monarch creates an ironic situation akin to Thailand, where the government can be constantly threatened by a military it does not control.

Nevertheless, perhaps the most powerful forces that have kept the peace in Tonga are religion and culture, which in everyday life are inseparably tied together. Tongan communal life is resilient and adaptive and, despite the violence, relationships have normalised as people have moved on as they embrace the future. However, the ghosts of 16 November 2006 have not completely disappeared, and there is constant fear that history might return for another eerie visit. In a country where human security factors like socioeconomic difficulties are prevalent, and where the hegemonic role of the monarch and lords still dominate political power and wealth, this is not a remote possibility.

6

Longing for peace: Transformation of the Solomon Islands security environment

An eye for an eye only ends up making the whole world blind.

Mahatma Gandhi

The formal termination of the mandate of the Regional Assistance Mission to Solomon Islands (RAMSI) on 30 June 2017 marked the end of a significant phase in the Solomon Islands peace-building and rehabilitation process, although it did not necessarily mean the 'end' of conflict itself and the 'beginning' of long-term peace. This is because some of the fundamental issues emanating from an interplay between identity, land dispute, poverty and inequality, intercommunal perception, political governance, corruption and behaviour of political elites, which contributed to nurturing the tension in the first place, are still shimmering. This was perhaps one of the factors that inspired the security treaty of 14 August 2017 between Australia and Solomon Islands, which would enable the rapid deployment of Australian security forces in case of civil unrest (Batley, 2017). This in itself is symbolic of a shared feeling of caution (just in case) and trepidation by the two sides on the potential sustainability of the post-RAMSI security environment. This chapter explores some of the factors that shaped the evolving security climate in Solomon Islands and the effectiveness of RAMSI as a security response mechanism.

The security environment—and indeed the conflict in Solomon Islands— was different from the case studies of Fiji and Tonga (in Chapters 4 and 5, respectively) because of a number of historical and sociopolitical factors. The tension in Fiji revolved around a diaspora group and the indigenous community and the way these groups interplayed with economic, cultural and political factors, whereas in Tonga, the tension was largely been two social classes. In Solomon Islands, the tension was between two indigenous groups whose respective histories were connected to political, socioeconomic and cultural developments that over time led to conflict. These differences make these case studies historically unique in their own ways, a salient aspect that one needs to take into consideration while doing comparative analysis.

The conflict in Solomon Islands from 1999 to 2001 was complex, with multiple dimensions—local, national, regional and international—and had a profound impact on the country, whose population numbers about half a million people. It transformed a largely subsistence society in a significant way and left scars, which have been the subject of peace-building efforts. Attempts to address the conflict in Solomon Islands took various forms, ranging from community-based reconciliation predicated on indigenous notions of balance and harmony to external intervention in the form of RAMSI. There were other formal initiatives, such as the Townsville Peace Agreement and the Truth and Reconciliation Commission, as well as peace projects, which consisted of shades of customary and introduced peace-building mechanisms, which some have referred to as 'hybrid' (Clements et al., 2007). Although their strategic focus, ideological assumptions and methodological tools were different, they were, by and large, preoccupied with creating a stable and peaceful society.

One of the interesting challenges in the debates around the Solomon Islands conflict is the contending theoretical positions held by different authors, based largely on different interpretations of historical events, trends and changes. This is nothing new in the study of conflicts in which the complex interplay between ethnicity, class, power, resources and culture can be overwhelming for observers and researchers. In the face of such complexity, some are compelled to emphasise certain aspects that they feel intellectually competent and comfortable to deal with. One of the approaches that has been dominant in debates on the conflict in Solomon Islands was the 'failed state' and 'arc of instability' discourse, discussed in Chapter 2.

Solomon Islands is often depicted as possessing unsophisticated cultures, norms and structures. Frequently accompanied by doses of social Darwinism and racism, such a view does more to obfuscate than enlighten us as to the trends of history, realities of society and dynamics of conflict. On the other hand, the increasingly popular hybrid discourse, which is meant to be a counter to the deficit approach, provides an overly simplistic assumption about the complexity of cultural engagements (Richmond, 2011; Wallis, Jeffery & Kent, 2015). It is assumed by advocates of the hybrid approach that cultures create an instant 'mix' when they come together. Contrary to this simplistic framework, the sociological reality is far more complex; the encounter between two different cultural forces involves a spontaneous process of accommodation, resistance/opposition, synthesis and coexistence, rather than just creating a new hybrid.

This chapter moves away from the deficit and hybrid approaches and instead focuses on the broader dialectics between the colonial economic and political systems and the local cultures and people, and examines some of the resulting contradictions that articulated themselves during the colonial and postcolonial periods in the context of postcolonial theory. The argument made here is that, to understand the Solomon Islands conflict of 1999 to 2001 better, one needs to use postcolonial lenses to capture some of the dynamics of the colonial state: human relationships, including the development policies that led to internal labour migration; the shabby and ineffective governance structure; the paternalistic attitude of the British; the issues of land and lack of autonomy; and participation of local cultural groups. These issues were firmly entrenched in the structural and normative life of the country and spilled over into the postcolonial period and fermented conditions for the conflicts. The grievances and conditions for conflict built up over time, and, although there were accommodating factors such as kinship, religion, intermarriage and the *wantok* ideology,[1] which moderated the rising tension, other external factors, such as the demands of the market economy for the commodification of land and employment, and rising poverty, inequality and economic marginalisation, intensified the tension and eventually sparked the conflict. Solomon Islands is a classic example of the way in which the denial and lack of human security among certain

---

1   *Wantok*, a pidgin term that literally means 'one language', refers to common identity, common origin and shared culture.

parts of the population has led to conflict. The approach here will weave together postcolonial, securitisation and human security approaches to understand some of the complex issues relating to conflict.

Genesis and transformation

Settled about 30,000 years ago, Solomon Islands was, apart from the island of New Guinea and other surrounding archipelagos, the earliest inhabited place in the South Pacific. A culturally diverse society with around 86 languages, the population of the Solomon Islands consisted of independent kinship-based communities operating within defined localities (Bennett, 2002). Beyond the local social boundaries, interisland and intertribal trade enabled the exchange and circulation of goods while maintaining social networks and peaceful relationships. Although there were inter- and intra-tribal skirmishes, these were mostly localised and were due to disputes over territory, resources, women, relationships and other factors. Culture-based conflict mitigation and resolution systems were in place to maintain a sense of balance, continuity and perpetuity of peaceful and stable relations. Community life revolved around kinship and division of labour, based on gender and age, with females involved largely with looking after the domestic duties and gardening while males were engaged in more 'prestigious' political matters such as decision-making, as well as 'masculine' activities such as hunting and acting as protectors of the family and community. Although, in many communities, land was allocated through matrilineal lines, political power still rested largely with older men (Bennett, 1987).

Trading in the form of barter and the use of traditional currency such as shell money took place between islands, and intermarriage consolidated relationships and created alliances between island tribes (Naitoro, 2000). Loyalty and identity revolved around localised kinship groups, and there was a clear distinction between 'insiders' and 'outsiders', although the line of demarcation shifted as a result of intermarriage and greater integration with neighbouring and faraway communities. The identity boundary was maintained and guarded through constant intra- and inter-tribal negotiation, war or sorcery, and the practice of compensation was a way of restoring balance and goodwill between groups and individuals. Social relations and identities were defined at both the social and cosmological levels, in which people and spiritual existence were intricately linked. In his study of the Kwara'ae people, Ben Burt observed that:

> This dialectic is quite transparent in the way the Kwara'ae created relationships of authority and power, extended beyond the living to include the dead. Through these relationships, their society participated in a cosmic order of religious power which provided a religious legitimation of the social order by transcending and denying its human construction. (Burt, 2001: 2)

Land, which later became a central issue in the tension in Solomon Islands, was part of the broader kinship and cosmological relationship that connected individuals and defined collective identity and relationships. This played out in different ways in different localities. For instance, in Morovo, rights to fishing, planting and access to land for various purposes depended on their claim to access through recognised consanguineal and affinal ties with tribal groups that controlled the land (Hviding & Baines, 1994).

Christianity later transformed this relationship through imposition of a highly structured and globalised organisation, characterised by a new set of morals and a new eschatological paradigm, which, just as before, put humans at a lower level of the cosmic order below the revered deity. Christianity attempted to undermine the traditional cosmic world and in the process also created conditions for the emergence of new forms of resistance as locals attempted to articulate their identities in a changing environment. However, at the same time, aspects of Christianity were indigenised and incorporated into the local culture and vice versa. As in other parts of the Pacific such as Fiji and Tonga, the distinction between customary ways and the Christian ethos became blurred as the two systems morphed into each other. As we shall see later, the Christian notion of peace was later incorporated into the local peace-building approaches to address future conflicts (Brown, 2004).

Even before the missionaries arrived, some of the early contact with Europeans in the form of whalers, shell and bêche-de-mer collectors and beachcombers had made their mark on hitherto autonomous communities. There was a series of contacts with Europeans, some substantive and some minimal. There was a period of 325 years between the first contact with Europeans in the form of the Spanish explorer Alvaro de Mendana de Neira in 1568, and the start of British annexation. The British annexed the South Solomons (Guadalcanal, Savo, Malaita, San Cristobal, the New Georgia group) in 1893, the Santa Cruz group in 1898 and 1899, and the Shortlands group (Santa Isabel, Choiseul and Ontong Java) in 1900.

They decided to take over Solomon Islands not for economic gain but for strategic reasons: to keep German influence, now entrenched in nearby New Guinea, at bay.

The forced recruitment of labour, through what came to be known as 'blackbirding', had started in 1870, about two decades before British annexation, and many Solomon Islanders, together with some workers from Vanuatu and New Caledonia, were sent to Fiji, Queensland and Samoa as plantation labourers (Corris, 1970). This was probably the first large-scale and permanent encounter between many local communities and global capitalism and was probably the single most transformative external force for Solomon Islands, aside from Christianity and colonialism.

The Malaitans were the most widely recruited group during the labour trade, with a total of 14,335 involved in contracts to Queensland and Fiji between the 1870s and 1911 and 35,596 contracts internally in Solomon Islands between 1913 and 1940. While this labour system was exacting and exploitative, it also allowed for voluntary labour and some workers willingly embraced it, as they valued the European goods they were given as part of their payment. Guns, especially, were highly valued, since they were effective in subduing competing tribes and chiefs in local disputes and helped to expand the power and influence of some chiefs. Internal labour migration, especially involving Malaitans in Guadalcanal, was encouraged and supervised by the colonial administration, and contributed to tension over land in later years. Malaitans mostly worked as contract labourers on copra plantations, the most important source of revenue for the protectorate.

Breeding insecurity: Half-hearted British colonial hegemony

Solomon Islands was not a full-fledged British colony but a protectorate under supervision from Fiji, the only British Crown colony in the Pacific Islands. The governor of Fiji also acted as high commissioner for the western Pacific and oversaw other Pacific protectorates such as Solomon Islands, Vanuatu (a condominium with France), Tonga (a British protected state since 1900), Tuvalu and Kiribati (Scarr, 1968). The local Solomon Islands representative, called the resident commissioner, looked after the day-to-day operation of the protectorate and was in charge of all British personnel. This arrangement lasted for 60 years, ending when the high commissioner's headquarters was moved to Solomon Islands in 1953 after the other British protectorates in the Pacific were removed from its supervision. The title was changed to governor in 1974 as the country moved closer to independence.

The British had a half-hearted presence and a reserved policy stance in Solomon Islands. With their headquarters 2,129 kilometres away in Fiji, the colonial state implanted a shabbily constructed administrative structure by 'remote control', consisting of a hierarchy of positions and government stations that were far removed both from the centre and from the local social structures and people. This was in significant contrast with British policies in Fiji, where the central colonial state assumed a hegemonic presence at different levels of the local social structures through a patronage system that included chieftocrats acting as comprador agents for the British colonial state, as we saw in Chapter 4. In the case of Solomon Islands, the 'state' assumed the form of a resident commissioner who held supreme authority, below whom was a resident magistrate (sometimes referred to as district magistrate), whose title changed to district officer in 1914.

To extend their nationwide reach, the British progressively created a network of government stations over the years, starting with Gizo Island in 1899, Shortland Islands in 1907, Malaita at Rarasu (now called Auki) in 1909, a temporary base at Masi (New Georgia) in 1910, Aola (Guadalcanal) in 1914, Makira (San Cristoval) and Isabel in 1918, and Peu (Vanikolo) in 1923 to administer the new Santa Cruz District on Savo and in the Nggela Islands (separate from Tulagi). A total of eight administrative areas, each with at least one district officer and sometimes additional officers, were set up by 1934 in Mala (Malaita), Guadalcanal, Gizo, Shortlands, Isabel and Russell, Eastern Solomons, Santa Cruz and Tulagi (British High Commission Protectorate, 1911; 1926; 1934).

This state governance 'structure' was in practice a network of positions superimposed on communities without there necessarily being any coherent system of communication, administration and operation to link to each other effectively or to connect with the people. At one level this system had a symbolic role in affirming a sense of British 'presence' and colonial 'legitimacy'. At a more mundane level, it also acted as a system of social control to consolidate colonial hegemony and respond to situations that were deemed threatening to the colonial establishment. The governance structure was disconnected from ordinary citizens, who in turn saw it as something of minimal or even no relevance to their everyday existence.

The colonial presence was a distant and strange phenomenon and, despite some development projects and social changes, local life hardly changed for years during the colonial and postcolonial periods. In addition to this disconnect was the paternalistic and racist attitudes in the minds of British officials. Young field officials in Solomon Islands and senior administrators in faraway Fiji and London were ignorant of local cultures and perceptions and imposed their will in insensitive and often racially prejudiced ways.

Let us not forget that the first governor of Fiji, Sir Arthur Gordon, as we saw in Chapter 4, was an adherent of social Darwinism. This influenced his policies towards indigenous Fijians, whom he thought could be saved by cocooning them in their traditional social system to ensure their slow evolution and survival in the face of cultural onslaught by the 'superior' European race (Ratuva, 2005). This patronising world view would have also influenced the way in which Solomon Islands was administered. The difference, however, was that, in the case of Fiji, the native administration, run on the basis of separate development (which they referred to as 'indirect rule'), was based on a complex state bureaucracy from the village level to the governor, supported by rigid rules and regulations, unlike Solomon Islands, where the reach of the state was minimal or even non-existent in most localities.

The period from annexation to the 1920s was characterised largely by consolidation of British hegemony through pacification and by ensuring a steady supply of labourers for plantations, which were central to the colonial economy. In response to emerging circumstances, some changes were made in the 1920s, starting with the setting up of an advisory council in 1921 to provide the resident commissioner with advice on issues relating to the administration of the protectorate. The advisory council included Solomon Islanders, and for the first time locals were involved in the decision-making process in the country. In addition to this, in 1925 a structure like that of the Fijian Native Administration was established with the appointment of the first native clerks, subdistrict headmen, village headmen and village constables. There was also some emphasis on medical services as well as, as in Fiji, the introduction of taxation of the indigenous population in 1921. The introduction of taxation was very unpopular and, as we shall see later, helped to fuel anti-colonial resistance. Education and training were also emphasised in the 1920s in response to the need for more locals to run lower positions in the civil service, as well as professional positions such as teachers and medical officers.

It was not until 1937 that attempts were made to create a more coherent 'native administration', in response both to demands for more local participation and to growing grievances relating to taxation and other issues. The changes included the setting up of native courts in several districts in 1940 to enforce law and order in communities, most of which were in rural areas. World War II put a stop to reforms and, after the war, in 1945, the two main issues faced by the protectorate were reconstruction and development. The capital was shifted from Tulagi to Honiara, and it was also suggested that local government councils be set up, to be responsible for local administration, development, justice, health, education and agriculture. An attempt was made to divide the protectorate into two divisions, but this was deemed too cumbersome and impractical. In late 1948 four districts were created instead, each under the responsibility of a district commissioner. These were the Western district, Central district, Malaita district and the Eastern district. Further changes were made to the membership of these districts in the 1950s. The districts were further divided into subdistricts, run by district commissioners and their district officers, who were assisted by headmen and assistant headmen. This system was purely administrative rather than developmental and participatory, and lacked any direct link with the communities. These administrative measures were, at best, symbols of state authority rather than effective tools of state service. This was an unwieldy undertaking because the idea was to construct a series of administrative entities from a collection of heterogenous communities with different languages, cultures and world views. This was just one of a series of superficial institutional structures set up by the protectorate that were incompatible with local social realities.

The relocation of the western Pacific high commissioner to Solomon Islands in 1953 was the first time the country had its own central government with more new substantive positions, although advisory links with the Fiji administration were maintained in health, education and agriculture. Following the proclamation of the British Solomon Islands constitution on 10 October 1960, the Legislative Council, with 21 members, was created. Thus, a national representative body was set up for the first time. Eleven members were to be government officials, and 10 were nominees. Six of the 10 were to be Solomon Islanders. A new constitution was introduced in 1964, with the council having 25 members. Representation by Solomon Islanders was through electoral colleges, formed by local district councils. This nurtured the culture of patronage that was to characterise the Solomon Islands political culture in future years.

As independence drew closer, the policy of localisation in the civil service increased in tempo. This included the district officer and district commissioner positions, which were filled after independence in 1978 by people who later became national leaders, such as Peter Kenilorea, Francis Talasasa, Francis Billy Hilly and Nathaniel Waena. A new pre-independence constitution was approved in 1974, which, among other new initiatives, provided for a governor and an elected Legislative Assembly. As a prelude to independence, the country acquired internal self-governing status on 2 January 1976. It became independent on 7 July 1978 under the leadership of Peter Kenilorea, who served three terms in office. Kenilorea was succeeded by his deputy, Ezekiel Alebua, in 1986. Other prime ministers since independence and before the conflict were Solomon Mamaloni, who had three terms, Francis Billy Hilly and Bartholomew Ulufa'alu.

Although the above description of the colonial system might sound mechanical, there are a number of salient points that I need to raise as part of the security analysis here. The state architecture had a fundamentally hegemonic role in advancing the pacification role of the colonial state. The state's presence in the rural communities was meant to make the statement that colonial authority was supreme and dissent would not be tolerated. This was consistent with British colonial subjugation in other parts of the world. Furthermore, the colonial structures were intended to facilitate the ready appropriation of cheap local labour to produce a surplus for the colonial economy. Money was needed to run the colonial system, and labour recruitment was seen as an economic imperative. Most of the labourers were recruited from Malaita, and many of these were relocated to various parts of Solomon Islands, where they were involved in commercial labour and other market-based activities. This provoked the wrath of the largely subsistence-based local population and planted the seeds of future tension.

To help fund the colonial structure, taxation was introduced as a compulsory imposition. Apart from this economic role, it also had a hegemonic role in controlling people's political choices, or rather lack of choices, because failure to pay tax could lead to imprisonment. What might have looked like an innocent administrative structure, justified as a system to provide law and order and to maintain stability, created contradictions that alerted people to the injustices of colonialism, as we shall see later.

Increasing insecurity: Resistance against colonial hegemony

Even before colonial rule, resistance to external intervention took many forms, including skirmishes with explorers, missionaries, traders and later with colonial officials as Solomon Islanders found their way of life, identity, well-being and even their territories threatened by foreigners. Some of this resistance ended in deaths on both sides. In 1872 six crew members of the schooner *Lavinia* were killed on Nggela Island while collecting bêche-de-mer. Eight years later, Lieutenant Bower, commander of HMS *Sandfly*, and three crewmen were killed on the same island. On 20 May 1886, six crewmen and six Malaitans on the schooner *Young Dick* were killed while involved in a blackbirding mission.

The accumulation of grievances over the years came to the fore in late 1927 when William Bell, district officer in Malaita, together with some assistants, killed while on a tax-collection trip on Malaita (Keesing & Corris, 1980). The labour recruitment policies of the British, the imposition of tax, and the uneven development and marginalisation of locals had spawned widespread grievances and anti-colonial resentment. The head tax was one of the most notorious and unpopular policies because locals could not understand why they should be paying for something from their meagre resources that did not benefit them at all. Besides, taxation, which was extractive and non-reciprocal, unlike local economic exchanges, was seen as an affront to their culture. Government public services were practically non-existent, and the patronising attitude of colonial officials fuelled the tension further. In response to Bell's death, the British sent a punitive expedition that carried out a brutal retribution, resulting in the death of about 60 Malaitans and the incarceration of almost 200 people (Swinden, 1998). This was part of the broader 'pacification' process whereby sacred sites were desecrated and cultural relics were burned and destroyed as a way of forcing people to accept Christianity and to submit to colonial rule.

The incident was historically significant in a number of ways. The attack on Bell and his group, which was well planned and widely supported by locals, manifested the deep-seated revulsion to the British style of rule, which was aloof, condescending and exploitative, with virtually no return to the people in the form of health services, education or development. The legal system could not be relied on for recourse, nor were there local representatives to take up their cause with the authorities, based far away in Suva. The locals realised that taking the law in to their own hands, although seen as a last resort, was a form of self-empowerment to express their will in the most direct and explicit way. The harsh response by the British was characteristic of a power that no longer had any sense of control of the situation and therefore resorted to extreme violence as a form of deterrence to other potential dissent. It was symbolic of the colonial state's failure to address the fundamental issues of development, governance, security and justice in a humane way. The ability of the British to exert control was due in part to their tactical use of locals to kill and arrest their own people, a technique they used effectively, as part of their pacification program in other colonies, as we saw in the case of Fiji.

The incident made both sides realise that better and more effective means of rule were important to create and maintain trust between the people and the colonial administration. For the British, it revealed how little they knew about the local cultures or the aspirations and feelings of the local people, and showed the need to change their attitudes and approaches. The colonial administration had a strong alliance with the European planters who volunteered to be part of the punitive expedition. The planters' participation in the incident served their interest in appropriating land and local resources for business. For the locals, there was clamour for a more efficient and humane system to protect their interests, identity, culture and future against what they saw as impending usurpation of their customary way of life.

The trial was used to show the unquestionable dominance of British justice. Of those arrested, 11 were charged with murder and, of these, six were convicted; of the 71 charged with lesser offences, 21 were convicted. The leader of the resistance, Basiana, who also killed Bell, was executed by hanging on 29 June 1928, while his two sons watched. Repressive regulations were also put in place to legalise arrests as well as detention to maintain order.

The pacification program had its limitations. Instead of nipping rebellion in the bud, it merely inflamed greater passion for autonomy. The issues that led to the killing of Bell and the clamour for protection of local customs and greater political and economic empowerment led to the emergence of the Maasina movement, which started in Malaita and spread to other nearby islands. Its central demand was the creation of an alternative, indigenous-led economic development policy and a politically autonomous system separate from the colonial state. It called for an increase in pay for plantation labourers and demanded the reform of the exploitative labour contract system. In addition, it also called for a more democratic system with indigenous representation in the decision-making process (Keesing, 1978).

There were external factors, too, which helped to catalyse the process. These included the 1930s Depression, which saw the collapse of copra prices. This meant that many Malaitans (who, since the inception of the Queensland and Fiji labour trade, had come to depend on plantation labour) lost their jobs, and those who continued working had their pay reduced. There was widespread disenchantment, expressed in sporadic cases of plantation rebellion and withdrawal of labour. Another important factor was the influence of World War II in raising the consciousness of people about the need for liberation from the British. There was hope that the Americans, who treated the locals better, would help the Solomon Islanders displace the British, but when this did not eventuate the Solomon Islanders proceeded to organise their new liberation strategy (Laracy, 1983).

The Maasina publicly manifested itself during the war in 1943 and 1944 and was symbolic of both political resistance and economic liberation, ideals that the Malaitans have engaged with and nurtured as a result of their grim experiences in labour migration and plantation work over decades. They had learnt how vulnerable they were to global capitalism and colonial rule, the two most powerful foreign forces they had to deal with every day. Their only option was to create their own independent system, which they could control to serve their interests and maximise benefits for themselves (Akin, 2013). They set up their own system of government, which won widespread support and which extended to various other parts of the country.

Needless to say, the Maasina movement was seen as a direct threat to the colonial administration, and in response the British launched Operation De-Louse to arrest the leaders of the movement for violation of the British Unlawful Societies Act of 1799 and the Seditious Meetings Act of 1817. Both these acts were invoked, and the leading chiefs were arrested and sentenced to six years hard labour for secretly conspiring to overthrow the government and holding illegal courts. The people responded by refusing to pay tax, submit to the census or cooperate in any way. This led to the arrest and imprisonment of thousands of people in 1948 and 1949. This softened the islanders' urge for further resistance and, when the first island council was set up in Malaita in 1952, the last bastion of resistance ceased (Frazer, 1990).

In his book *Colonialism, Maasina Rule and the Origins of Malaitan Kastom*, Akin (2013) provides a historical as well as ethnographic analysis of the Maasina rule using the postcolonial lenses to focus on how economic exploitation, political subjugation and ethnic marginalisation created conditions for resistance. The British colonial policy of pacification and coerced imposition under unilateral centralised rule was 'an alien imposition' (Akin, 2013: 87), which came into contradiction with the cultural world of a group of people who lived in relatively egalitarian, subsistence-based and autonomous kinship systems. The early reactions were 'against taxation, unpaid labour, loss of dignity' (Akin, 2013: 87).

Inequality in a structural, ethnic and economic form was an inevitable result of British colonial rule. It permeated the entire society from the level of institutionalised political power to the level of everyday interaction. As an example, reflecting on the issue of unequal justice, Akin says:

> There was also anger that when Europeans committed crimes such as murder, severe assault, or rape they were most always deported rather than punished in the Solomons (if at all) in order to avoid embarrassing the white community by a local trial and imprisonment. And when an Islander fought a European, it was always the Islander who went to jail. (Akin, 2013: 86)

The locals found solace in *kastom*, the locally constructed cultural norms to help define their community identity and help them adapt to the changing circumstances. These became the prisms for self-identification, intragroup relationships and engagement with the outside world. *Kastom* became a multipurpose system to provide moral and ethical guidance and collective protection against outside usurpation, a tool of cultural socialisation as well as a framework for social transformation, adaptation and engagement with the outside world.

The anti-colonial resistance shown by Bell's killing and the Maasina movement set the tone for future conflicts, because some of the same forces that contributed to these events manifested themselves in those conflicts. Among these was the creation of a new proletarian class of Malaitans, who participated in labour migration. In later years, this created tension with the people of Guadalcanal, who felt threatened by their more mobile and commercially experienced island neighbours. Another significant factor was the uneven and socially disruptive development strategies of the British, which created conditions for both the anti-British rebellion and the Malaita/Guadalcanal conflict. The lack of an effective state system to ameliorate tension was also a common feature of colonial and postcolonial conflicts. Both participatory governance and people-centred development were minimal or non-existent in many cases, and this bred animosity.

The colonial hegemony and transformation of the Solomon Islands under the British bred its own contradictions, created in part by an incompetent colonial administration. An ineffective administrative system that boasted neither a central state as a locus of authority nor entrenched local community support was constructed and implanted. The British were more concerned with simply making a physical 'presence' in Solomon Islands as a buffer against German interest in nearby New Guinea than in taking any genuine interest in developing the protectorate.

The colonial administrative structure had neither the capacity nor the intent to unite the culturally diverse country. If anything, it merely exacerbated differences and tensions. For instance, carving up the country into four districts meant that different tribes were forced into administrative units with others and, in the process, separated from cognate tribes in other districts. The role of the districts in acting as electoral colleges for the Legislative Council encouraged patronage at the local level. This allowed district officers and powerful individuals to leverage power to achieve their own political and economic interests. The structure of the state was thin and superficial, and its role was purely administrative rather than policy-making, developmental and legislative.

Although reforms to create a more representative legislative system took place in the 1960s and 1970s, these did very little to enhance people's participation and promote democratic values and culture. The system failed to incorporate Solomon Islands' communities effectively into the administrative structure and vice versa. The reach of the state was limited; there was a huge gap between local identities and loyalties, and national identity and local identities often supplanted national identity. In fact, the idea of a national identity was contested and continues to be so.

Thus it would be nonsensical to talk of Solomon Islands as a 'failed state', fundamentally because the state itself was not sufficiently developed into a fully fledged democracy. Rather than being a failed state, the best description would be a 'syncretic state', where there was a complex ensemble of forces interacting with each other in a situation of contradiction, accommodation or synthesis (Ratuva, 2004). In the case of Solomon Islands, as with many postcolonial societies, there was a constant interaction (action and reaction) between tradition and modernity, subsistence and market economy, communalism and individualism, and Western bureaucracy and indigenous power structures. Sometimes one overrode the other or contradicted one another, and at other times they accommodated each other or integrated to form a new mode of behaviour and a new structure. Hence this complex process of interaction cannot be simplistically explained as being 'failed' or artificially framed as 'hybrid'.

The Malaita/Guadalcanal conflict

In the earlier part of the chapter, we discussed some of the broader forces that nurtured the conditions for future conflict between the Guadalcanal and Malaitan communities. Strained relations led to the eruption of violence around the latter part of 1998, although some Guadalcanal youths had been collecting arms since 1996 as anti-Malaitan grievances gradually built up over the years. The attack on Malaita settlements by a group of Guadalcanal youths in November 1998 was the catalyst that set in train an almost inevitable process of intercommunal violence. Sentiments were further heightened by the nationalistic utterance by Ezekiel Alebua, premier of Guadalcanal province, who proclaimed that non-Guadalcanal people should respect their hosts, pay rent to Honiara landowners and pay compensation for the Guadalcanal people murdered in Honiara (Kabutaulaka, 2001).

The attack sent shockwaves around the country and sparked further escalation, which saw the shooting of a Guadalcanal youth by the police in December 1998. Guadalcanal youths formed themselves into an organised paramilitary group with different labels, including the Guadalcanal Revolutionary Army (GRA), the Isatabu Freedom Fighters (IFF) and later the Isatabu Freedom Movement (IFM). Attacks on settlers continued and, by June 1999, about 50 people had been killed and about 20,000 people from Malaita and other provinces were displaced from areas around Honiara. The police responded violently and, as a result, 13 members of the IFM were killed. This tit-for-tat killing spawned more violence that consumed the communities around the Honiara area.

In response to the IFM's violent tactics, the Malaita Eagle Force (MEF) was formed by Malaitan youth to protect the displaced Malaitans, seek vengeance for their treatment at the hands of the IFM, and compensation for the damages to properties and for Malaitan deaths. Their raids on Guadalcanal villages led to a number of deaths, including of women and children. The initial skirmishes turned into full-blown confrontations, with both sides inflicting and suffering casualties.

Without an effective security apparatus for law enforcement, the state lacked the authority and power to maintain stability. The security situation deteriorated further after the MEF and other Malaitans in the Royal Solomon Islands Police Force (RSIPF) took over the police armoury in Roveand. Prime Minister Ulufa'alu was forced to resign after a coup led by Malaitan lawyer Andrew Nori, and, in the midst of the ensuing confusion, Manasseh Sogavare was elected prime minister under duress (Kabutaulaka, 2001). The violent confrontation between the MEF and IFM worsened and took centre stage, with more than 200 people estimated to have died. The consequences of the conflict were disastrous for a country that had not been able to frame a coherent national identity to unify the different ethnocultural groups since independence.

The situation in Solomon Islands at the time of the conflict was much more complex than the ethnic and tribal factors that have been popularly articulated by the media and other commentators (Kabutaulaka, 2001). The salient factors were multifaceted and in different ways contributed to the grievances, tension and eventual violence. First, as mentioned earlier, the half-hearted colonial policies on governance had consequences that carried over into the postcolonial period. Upon independence, while positions in leadership were localised, the principles of governance and development remained unchanged, and there was little attempt to redirect development towards what was relevant to the local population. The state became a conduit for cronyism and patronage. Rather than encouraging unity and common identity, the political elites were more focused on their local constituencies and their own political careers. There was, since independence, optimism about creating a new national consciousness and identity, particularly among the urban-based elites and the young educated individuals who had acquired a taste of regionalised and globalised life through contact with the outside world. These progressive and globalised views were at odds with the localised loyalties and identities of rural village folk (Jourdan, 1995).

As with other newly independent postcolonial states, the tension between common national consciousness (through education, common pidgin language, common popular cultural expressions such as music and common national symbolism such as the flag and emblem) on the one hand and communal consciousness on the other, became a dominant challenge for the new state. This was a classic situation of a binary relationship between civic nationalism (national consciousness in relation to the state) and communal nationalism (exertion of communal interests), which Stavenhagen (1996) talked about as a potential cause of friction and instability. Creating the balance between the desire to construct a unified national identity and expressions of distinctive communal identity provides a major cultural and political backdrop to the Malaita/ Guadalcanal tension and remains a major issue for Solomon Islands today.

This identity crisis was made more volatile by uneven development and worsening poverty and inequality. The prevalence of inequality and perception of socioeconomic differences between social and cultural groups was a recipe for conflict. The Malaitans were seen to be the 'industrious' ones, acquiring the most lucrative jobs and businesses, thus invoking envy and ethnic stereotypes as 'aggressive' and 'selfish'. The situation was further exacerbated by widespread corruption among politicians, who took bribes from mostly Chinese businessmen and foreign logging companies in return for favours. This also brewed anti-Chinese sentiments, which led to a major riot. The fact that people's expectations in relation to improved livelihood did not match their living standard was a recipe for violence. On top of this was the sensitive issue of land rights, sale and usage. The migration of people into Honiara, especially from Malaita, put considerable pressure on the land and created tension. Many Malaitans married Guadalcanal women and, through matrilineal determination of land rights, were able to acquire land on which they invited other relatives to settle. Settlements mushroomed around Honiara, and the local landowners might have felt crowded out by the new migrants. Many felt that their identity was being trampled on.

Rising unemployment, poverty and alienation among Guadalcanal youths helped to brew grievances. Knowledge of the outside world through education and the media raised the young people's expectations and, when the goods were not forthcoming and dreams remained unfulfilled, grievances turned to anger and eventually mobilisation for violent action. This was further heightened by the intimidation and killing of some Guadalcanal people by Malaitans. The speech by Alebua regarding indiscretions by Malaitans and the need for compensation was seen by some as the 'order' to open the floodgates of violence.

The inability of the government, run by self-serving politicians, to address the above issues was a major problem. The conflict revealed the inability of the state machinery to deal with law and order and, when the crunch came, those in government had to choose between loyalty to national interest or loyalty to their communities. Many chose the latter.

The analysis by Allen (2012) focuses on a critical assessment of competing identity narratives between 'a Malaitan settler narrative and a Guadalcanal landowner narrative' and how this helped transform the conditions for conflict. Malaitans were initially able to acquire rights to use tribal land on northern Guadalcanal 'but subsequently fell victim to a Guale project of exclusion' (Allen, 2012: 163). The Guadalcanal landowners denied Malaitans the use of land as an expression of discontent against what they saw as cultural and economic intrusion into their traditional domain. This reinforced the Guale claim to ownership and denied Malaitans their source of livelihood. This social disequilibrium—based on the dual processes of exclusion and assertion of rights—contributed significantly to the tension. The denial of access to land and associated socioeconomic and political benefits shaped the power relations and provoked violent reaction. Local grievances based on the desire to share the benefits from resource development on their land escalated to become part of the broader autonomy project for Guadalcanal. Filer, McDonnell and Allen (2017) refer to this process as the 'power of exclusion', referring to a dynamic power relationship where a group denies another access to land and resources and associated socioeconomic and political benefits.

Fraenkel (2004) makes the argument that the conflict was made even more complex by what he referred to as the 'manipulation of culture'. According to Fraenkel, one of the significant features of the conflict was the way in which both sides used the traditional practice of compensation as a means of acquiring cash either from each other or from the government. The state was criminally leached and looted to the point of bankruptcy. He argues that 'custom was inevitably remoulded, redefined and selectively styled to meet these new and unfamiliar circumstances. And since there was scope for designing custom, there was also space for manipulation' (Fraenkel, 2004: 11). Ethnographers might disagree with this instrumentalist view of culture since it ignores the sociocultural role of compensation as a means of maintaining social equilibrium in a changing situation.

A significant aspect of the conflict that is not well understood is the way in which the local issues were part of the globalised discussions among the Solomon Islands diaspora through the Iu-Mi-Nao ('It's up to us to do it now') chat group. Discussions ranged from updates of daily events to critical assessment of the political situation back home and how to address these (Moore, 2004). Cyberspace became the connecting mechanism that linked individuals and groups located overseas but who had a strong primordial attachment to and sense of place with Solomon Islands. The indigenous Solomon Islands narratives were globalised and found expressions in an internationalised discursive space through the more mobile and educated citizens based overseas.

Assault on human security: 'Shadow' political economy, corruption and patronage

The potential for instability, exploitation and retarded development was exacerbated by prevalent patronage and corruption, which ranged from 'petty and bureaucratic corruption to grand forms of corruption involving high-level officials' (Chene, 2017). The economy itself has been infested with the scourge of money politics and patronage at different levels from the village to the highest level of politics. Solomon Islands has been described as having a number of 'shadow' states, including a complex system of patronage based on money and power, which linked politicians, their constituencies and businessmen outside the ambit of state control (Braithwaite et al., 2010).

Among the notorious shadowy figures are the Asian logging companies who are able to access logging areas directly by bribing landowners and government officials. For landowners, who live a largely subsistence life and have no direct means of generating income, this is an attractive source of cash. Dawea and Canon (2017) document how Malaysian companies were able to use tens of thousands of dollars to pay off landowners and government officials, including the local police, in order to access the local forests on the Santa Cruz Islands. The corrupted local officials acted as 'consultants' and guides and provided legitimacy for the illegal logging operations. The companies had no legal licences to operate and took advantage of the administrative disconnect between the capital Honiara and the rural areas as well as inefficiency in the enforcement system. To justify receiving the money, the locals argued that they 'have effectively been cut loose by the national government, with little choice but to monetise the islands' natural resources to fill the province's coffers and fund development programs' (Dawea & Canon, 2017). Given the government's inability to fund the provinces, logging money plays a vital role in providing resources for local development. Logging has caused irreversible environmental damage and not only on land but also the reefs and coastal areas as a result of silt being washed down rivers. In addition, logging companies have been involved in illegal logging, tax evasion, money-laundering, under-reporting of export value, price transfer and altering the names of tree species. Government officials are often bribed to look the other way. These issues have caused dismay and grievances among many Solomon Islanders and a threat to human security as well as a potential flashpoint for future tensions.

There is a danger that this culture of patronage and corruption will also undermine the environmental, social and economic viability of the mining industry, now envisaged as a substitute for logging, after the forestry resources have been exhausted. Some of these anomalies have manifested themselves in the Gold Ridge mining operations, where there have been issues of licensing, disputes over the disbursement of royalties and benefit-sharing between Guadalcanal province and the national government, and a corrupt payment made to a member of Parliament. The lack of proper regulation and transparency in the administration of the primary industry, coupled with the predatory nature of unscrupulous foreign businesses in collaboration with local entrepreneurial politicians, has a profound impact on social cohesion, communal trust and human security. The shadowy networks involve state officials and community leaders entrusted with the responsibility of looking after the social and economic security of ordinary citizens, many of whom are not well educated and lack the means for social mobility in a capitalist system.

Another issue that has compromised the integrity of political leaders in a significant way is the discretionary funds allocated to parliamentarians annually. While the official purpose of the fund are for constituency development not covered by the budget, parliamentarians have total discretion as to how the money is used. A significant portion of the money is used for family business, and to build up local patronage and buy off voters. Although a guiding policy for the disbursement and accountability of the discretionary funds exists, this blatant abuse of public money, which is well known, is due to the lack of accountability and regulation because the beneficiaries of the system are the very same people who are supposed to be responsible for enforcement and policing.

In response to concerns about the potential damage that widespread corruption could cause the economy, pressure from the public and international agencies, the National Development Strategy 2016–35 prioritises the battle against corruption in logging and mining. This includes strengthening of anti-bribery laws, creating a special anti-corruption agency and enacting accountability laws (Chene, 2017). The challenges to achieving the aim of reduced corruption are hampered by a number of factors, including weak government capacity, lack of state presence in the outer communities, limited opportunities for public participation as well as the fluidity and instability in state policy due to constant changes in government.

Corruption and patronage pose a direct threat to people's human security due to the arbitrary appropriation of wealth by certain individuals linked to state power, diversion of bribery money from public use, misdistribution of resources, deprivation of a large section of the population and undermining of the developmental potential of the country. Grievances could lead to distrust and tension. The attempts by the government to address corruption can be viable only if the politicians themselves take the lead in adhering to the rules and there is greater cooperation between the state and the people to ensure equal and just distribution of power over resources and decision-making.

Desecuritisation through peace-building initiatives

The conflict went through several phases: the expression of communal grievances, which built up to sporadic violence; the formation of rival militia groups (1998–2000); internecine conflict (2000–01); and more criminalised disturbances (2000–03). At different stages, there were futile attempts to intervene as the dividing line between warring groups became sharper and the tension more intense.

As the conflict subsided and life slowly returned to 'normal', perhaps the biggest challenges for Solomon Islands were how to rebuild destroyed infrastructure, reshape collapsed state institutions, reconstruct shattered social relations and, more importantly, avoid future conflicts of a similar nature. When the state security apparatus failed to stop—or at least manage—the conflict, the responsibility fell on the local and international communities. Wars have the paradoxical effect of expressing both the most inhuman and the most humane form of behavioural dispositions. While there is a desire to destroy, there is also a desire for peace and rebuilding.

In Solomon Islands, there were various levels of peace-building efforts at the regional, national and local levels. Some of these were formally linked, some were informally associated and some operated independently of each other. We cannot dismiss them as being ineffective because, in their own ways, in particular contexts and at particular times, they had their own impact in engaging people and created their own synergy, even if carried out in a limited space and with limited reach and effectiveness. Some were focused on addressing the manifestations of conflict, some were related to addressing relationships and intergroup trust, some were based on managing conflict to ensure that it did not escalate, some were attempts to heal psychological wounds and some were geared towards addressing the root causes of the tension. The last approach is always the most difficult because it means rewinding history and identifying some of the historical issues, as well as casting analytical eyes far and wide to identify deeper economic, political and sociocultural issues at the heart of the tension.

One of the first major attempts (apart from several earlier initiatives) to bring the conflicting parties together was the Townsville Peace Agreement (TPA), facilitated by Australia. It was, as the TPA document itself proclaims, an agreement for the 'cessation of hostilities between Malaita Eagle Force and the Isatabu Freedom Movement and for the restoration of peace and ethnic harmony in Solomon Islands' (Solomon Islands Government, 2000). This involved a six-day discussion between the rival militia groups and the Solomon Islands Government in October 2000 in Townsville, in order to arrive at some common understanding regarding the way forward. Both sides attempted to articulate conditions and demands based on their own political and historical narratives of the conflict. This posed some difficulties in the beginning, but compromises were made in certain areas and attempts were made to balance sectarian and national interests in a win-win formula. The final agreement was hailed as a significant way forward, but not everyone was happy.

The agreement contained a number of ambitious and almost impractical provisions to reduce the tension, initiate peace-building and facilitate rehabilitation. These included the continued employment of police officers who took sides during the confrontation; restructuring of the police force; provision of weapons and general amnesty for combatants; rehabilitation for combatants, which included repatriation to their villages; demilitarisation; more government autonomy for Malaita and Guadalcanal; appointment of a constitutional council; a land enquiry in Guadalcanal; and increased development projects to provide jobs and support for rehabilitation. On the peace-building side, the agreement encouraged reconciliation and proposed the formation of a peace and reconciliation committee as well as international peace monitors. Above all it proclaimed that: 'The parties hereby agree that they renounce violence and intimidation and will henceforth address their differences through negotiations and develop co-operative processes to fulfil the needs of their communities' (Solomon Island Government, 2000: 29).

The TPA took place in the wake of the deaths of perhaps 2,000 people and the failure of six previous peace initiatives brokered by the Commonwealth Secretariat and Solomon Islands Government between June 1999 and 12 May 2000. Despite being hailed by some as a success story, there were shortcomings in the agreement. These included its inability to address some of the fundamental causes of the conflict, which had been built up over generations. For instance, while the idea of rehabilitation of the former militia members through socioeconomic development was a theoretically sound proposal, it was quite ambitious in as far as availability of resources was concerned. The government was literally bankrupt, and there was a lack of funds for any meaningful development. Furthermore, while the agreement provided proposals for quick solutions to stop the tension, there was no realistic framework for long-term conflict resolution. It has also been argued that the agreement merely 'institutionalises ethnic division' because militia from the two sides were encouraged to go back to their home islands, and this minimised interaction and increased the possible recurrence of violence (Byrne, 2000). Indeed violence continued despite the TPA.

The TPA of 15 October 2000 was followed by the mobilisation of an Australian-led International Peace Monitoring Team to supervise the surrender of weapons. Ironically, instead of ending the conflict as anticipated, the TPA caused further differences and tension. Tension was particularly prevalent around Guadalcanal's Weather Coast, where pro-TPA and anti-TPA factions were engaged in a violent campaign against each other. The pro-TPA faction, led by Harold Keke, was involved in police patrol-boat raids against those opposed to the agreement. There were cases of threats, intimidation and violence, including torture. Keke's rebellious stance and intimidating activities were used by the Malaitan militants as an excuse for refusing to surrender their weapons. Even today, these incidents still provoke grievances among some local communities.

Desecuritising the land: The Regional Assistance Mission to the Solomon Islands

The Regional Assistance Mission to the Solomon Islands (RAMSI) took place under the auspices of the Biketawa Declaration, a regional security agreement by the Pacific Island Forum leaders, as discussed in Chapter 3. The declaration provided for possible intervention by members of the Pacific Island Forum in a member country if invited to do so. Article 2 states:

> Forum Leaders recognised the need in time of crisis or in response to members' request for assistance, for action to be taken on the basis of all members of the Forum being part of the Pacific Islands extended family. (PIF, 2000: 1)

The Solomon Islands Government's request to Australia for help in 1999 was ignored until after 9/11, when Australia reformulated its security approach, which framed neighbouring Pacific Island states as 'failed' and possible bases for terrorists to attack Australia. Thus RAMSI was originally conceived not as a humanitarian gesture but as part of a bigger strategic policy thrust by Australia to create a security buffer around itself against mythical terrorists lurking around Oceania ready to pounce on Australia. Nevertheless, many Solomon Islanders saw RAMSI as a saviour to rid the country of some security threats in the form of armed militants and lawlessness.

The intervention, which started on 24 July 2003, was led by Australia. One of the first tasks was to establish law and order and provide security for citizens. Among other things, one of the approaches was to give an ultimatum to militant groups to surrender their weapons and to back this threat with legal force. The mission's personnel included military and police officers from the member countries of the Pacific Island Forum, together with civilians who worked in advisory and even operational capacities in government departments.

Apart from security, RAMSI's other focus was on state-building by way of institutional reconstruction along the lines of the Australian neoliberal agenda. Almost every ministry had a RAMSI adviser, whose job involved both day-to-day operational matters and broader strategic issues. One of the underlying assumptions was that locals lacked the capacity to operate a modern state system and that external expertise was needed to build professional capacity and work ethic. In some cases, local personnel were displaced from line ministries and remained as symbolic figures while policies and decisions were formulated and carried out by RAMSI officials. This imposing approach created some tension, especially among locals who felt that their capabilities were not being appreciated—in fact were shunned—by another neocolonial establishment.

With RAMSI taking over security, legal and operational matters, a number of security issues emerged. At the political level, the question of Solomon Islands sovereignty was at stake as a new hegemonic force took over operations of important state apparatus. Differences between the Solomon Islands and Australian governments, predicated on opposing perceptions of each other, intensified over the years. Many Australian officials still perceived Solomon Islands through the condescending 'arc of instability' prism, and Solomon Islanders were conscious of this and viewed the Australians with suspicion and distrust. In this situation of mutual psychological distance and suspicion, it was inevitable that particular types of behaviour were interpreted and stereotyped in disparaging ways. The Australian Government's interference in some sensitive local issues heightened the political temperature significantly.

A case in point was the Australian Government's attempt to thwart the appointment of the Fiji-born Attorney General, Julian Moti, whom Australia saw as a threat to their interests. A charge of sexual assault was used to try to prosecute Moti, but eventually the Australian courts dismissed the case. This was an embarrassing case for Australia, whose credibility in Solomon Islands was badly dented. Another case related to the behind-the-scenes involvement of Patrick Cole, the Australian high commissioner, in local politics. The revelations came in an email leaked by a RAMSI officer, and as a consequence Cole was expelled.

RAMSI's patronising approach attracted negative reaction from the Solomon Islands Government. This included a report by six ministers of the government, which recommended that RAMSI be scaled back and its excesses limited. One of the reasons given was that under the accountant general, the Ministry of Finance was slow in delivering services and goods to the people. It recommended that the role of RAMSI officials should be purely advisory and not substantive. RAMSI was accused of being a stooge of Canberra and was alienated from the Solomon Islands Government (Fraenkel, Madraiwiwi & Okole, 2014). The feeling was widespread among local politicians, civil servants and many Solomon Islands citizens themselves, who saw RAMSI as a semi-imperialist force of sorts, imposing its will on the local population.

People's anger was also violently expressed after Snyder Rini was chosen as prime minister during the April 2006 general elections. A demonstration against Rini's appointment turned violent when Australian Federal Police (AFP) personnel fired tear gas at demonstrators. This led to riots and burnings, including the smashing and torching of RAMSI vehicles around the China Town business district. RAMSI personnel were also targeted. A possible vote of no confidence forced Rini to resign, thus opening the door for the selection of Manasseh Sogavare, who was an uncompromising anti-Australian politician. Australian officials loathed him and tried to undermine him when the chance arose (Fraenkel, Madraiwiwi & Okole, 2014).

The relationship between the Solomon Islands Government and RAMSI oscillated between tension and cordiality, depending very much on the circumstances and who was at the helm. Different prime ministers had different attitudes towards RAMSI but, by and large, there was some agreement that it provided the desired security and institutional rehabilitation for a country struggling to find its footing in constantly shifting internal and regional political dynamics. There was also a general feeling that RAMSI's role was finite. The ultimate question related to the exit strategy and the timing of it. New Zealand made it clear that it preferred a bilateral program and the rolling back of RAMSI operations. A transitional strategy was put in place after the 2010 Solomon Islands election, resulting in the withdrawal of military personnel in favour of police-assisted programs by 2013. By then, RAMSI had been sufficiently established for Australia to use it as a supporting reference for its bid for a United Nation's Security Council seat (Fullilove, 2009).

Perspectives on RAMSI vary considerably, depending on the respondents and the context of their responses. Advocates of RAMSI often refer to its significance in removing the security threat from the combatants and for creating a more stable and more peaceful environment for the people, many of whom were displaced or suffered in various ways as a result of the conflict. Opponents of RAMSI see it as a Trojan horse for an Australian neo-imperialist agenda, which was manifested in Australian personnel having control of significant line ministries such as finance and justice and in reforming the state bureaucracy to mirror Australian civil service norms and culture. Australians were often accused of being Aussie-centric due to their alleged cultural arrogance and disdain (latent and sometimes manifest) for the local people and culture.

Discussions between the author and civil servants, Civil Society Organizations (CSOs), academics and other citizens revealed some deep-seated concern and at times anger about what was perceived as the 'racist' attitude of Australian personnel. The locals had developed a means of 'security mapping' representing the various levels of 'reliability' and 'trustworthiness', to use Enloe's (1980) terminology, to categorise the RAMSI personnel and their attitude towards locals. A local guide took the author around Honiara, observing the way soldiers from the different countries carried out their daily patrols, and to confirm his story about the level of security consciousness of, and trust of the local population by, RAMSI military personnel. We observed the Australian soldiers, fully armed with weapons at the ready position, as if prepared at any moment to pounce on unsuspecting terrorists or to respond to any sudden ambush by hidden 'enemies'. One is reminded of nervous and trigger-happy US marines, in full battle gear, cautiously patrolling the streets of Baghdad and at the same time putting up an aggressively menacing look, as if motivated by the belief that every local was a potential terrorist who must not be trusted. The guide explained that the 'Aussies' (as he referred to them) not only had little trust in the local population but also treated them as inferiors. This, he felt, helped to fuel the groundswell of anti-Aussie sentiments.

Next we observed the New Zealand soldiers on patrol. They were far more relaxed and, although fully armed with light weapons, casually held their guns, which were pointed, not horizontally as the Australians, but towards the ground. Many New Zealanders were of Pacific Islands and Maori heritage; they fitted in well with the local culture and community and were generally trusted by locals. Many locals the author talked to were highly appreciative of New Zealanders, who they thought were more understanding and down to earth in contrast to their Australian counterparts.

The guide then told me to watch how the Fijian soldiers carried out their patrol. They were quite unique in their patrolling style, and we observed them walking around unarmed, shaking people's hands, smiling and saying 'bula' (hello) in response to a chorus of 'bula' from locals. The Fijians' level of understanding of the local culture and their degree of integration into local life was relatively deep, and locals saw them as the most trustworthy of the RAMSI military forces. Apart from some areas of similarity in their cultural background with the locals, the Fijian soldiers deployed to Solomon Islands had significant experience in peace-keeping operations in the Middle East and other parts of the world. The different approaches of the other military forces testified to the diversity of RAMSI as well as the differing world views that participating nations brought to the mission.

RAMSI was more than just an operation; it turned out to be a system, a complex of multilayered structures and relationships. It was, to put it rather simplistically, a kind of state within a state. Its role spanned a variety of activities including security, finance, development, rehabilitation, justice, policing, public service reform, electoral support and peace-building. Some of these were formally part of the prescribed functions, and some were auxiliary responsibilities. There were differences in opinion as to what RAMSI should be doing. While RAMSI's main responsibilities were to re-establish and ensure security and state rebuilding, some were concerned about its lack of focus on economic development and peace-building. To be fair to RAMSI, it had neither the mandate nor the expertise to carry out either of these two activities. RAMSI's work was more focused on rebuilding institutions rather than mending people's strained post-conflict relationships. The deep-seated grievances and tensions that helped to spawn the conflict remained relatively untouched. Now that much of RAMSI's security apparatus has been withdrawn, the biggest challenge is how the current 'peace' can hold and for how long. Whether the people of Solomon Islands have reached a stage of conflict fatigue is a critical question. Even if this is the case, there will always be opportunistic individuals and groups who exploit particular situations for their political and economic ends.

What about the role of the Solomon Islands police in future security operations? On the positive side, RAMSI itself has argued that there has been a 'noticeable improvement in the responsiveness and capability of Solomon Islands Police Force (RSIPF)' (RAMSI Media Unit, 2016). How permanent the 'noticeable improvement' is might be debatable. Pessimists could argue that the 'improvement' could just be a temporary expression of enthusiasm by the RSIPF while optimists see it as a promising sign for the future response capability of the force. It will take time before the restructuring and training carried out by RAMSI gels into the institutional norms and behavioural ethics of the force's personnel. Perhaps the biggest question is whether the training was appropriate for the local cultural context and the unique political terrain of the Solomon Islands, especially when the training template was based on the AFP model of policing. The incongruity between the sociocultural appropriateness of the remodelled police force and the changing local sociopolitical realities could be a security challenge in itself. While the police have been trained to address the visible manifestations of conflict, their inability to address the deep-rooted aspects of conflict, something they might not be trained for, could be overwhelming. The fact that the police personnel might still harbour tribal loyalties that mirror the original political fault lines also poses grave threats to future security.

The current move to arm the police force needs careful consideration, given the situation in 2000 when arms were taken from the armoury by the Malaita-aligned faction of the police force. The need for regulatory and control mechanisms to ensure that this is not repeated is critical for the force and national security at large. Because arms may still be illegally kept by some members of the former combatants, there is some validity in the idea of arming the police. The disadvantages, however, are that an armed police can encourage use of arms by those with guns and, second, there is no guarantee that arms cannot be used by factions within the police against other factions in times of crisis, as we saw in 2000. A more sensible approach is to develop a highly disciplined and well-trained special response team who are allowed to use arms only when confronted with a gun-related life-and-death situation.

Lessons of RAMSI

There are a number of critical lessons we can learn from RAMSI. First, in terms of regional security, RAMSI has demonstrated the capacity of regional states to collaborate in an interventionist way, to provide security and help in the post-conflict rebuilding of another neighbouring Pacific state. This was a major regional security project emanating from the Biketawa Declaration, which provided for possible intervention by members of the Pacific Islands Forum if invited by the host country. RAMSI demonstrated that regional security cooperation was possible, given the right circumstances, and if there was a common interest among Forum member countries. However, regional intervention dos not always work, as we saw in the case of Fiji after the 2006 coup. The Forum's Eminent Persons Group mission to Fiji turned out to be disastrously comical and purely tokenistic because Fiji did not take it seriously, and it had no impact on post-2006 coup developments in Fiji.

The flip side of the coin is that any similar intervention has implications concerning resources. Intervention has to be funded, and this is where the major challenge begins. Australia, by virtue of being the richest country in the region, was able to bankroll the operation with ease and efficiency. However, the deeper issue relates to the way this money could be used as a powerful political lever and soft power instrument to reinforce Australia's hegemony, not only in Solomon Islands but also in the region generally. RAMSI was an opportunity for Australia, through the estimated A$2.4 billion poured into the operation, to drive its reform agenda in Solomon Islands and the region, as well as providing opportunities for employment for hundreds of Australian citizens, who worked in various capacities. It was probably Australia's largest single aid project as well as the most high profile and most prestigious in the region.

In a way, in terms of geopolitical psychology, RAMSI would have boosted Australia's ego as a big regional power. To claim a position in the upper echelons of global security stratification, a country needs to 'prove' its capacity to influence and dominate others politically. This has been the basis of big power hegemony such as that of the United States. Australia's ability to exert its power, to buy off or influence Pacific Island states by virtue of its wealth and political leverage, has often worked well in its favour. Interestingly, Australia is not able to demonstrate a similar hegemonic tendency in Asia, which contains equally powerful or more powerful states that can outmanoeuvre Australia.

Another effect of RAMSI was the creation of an artificial and unequal economy, which exacerbated the class divide between locals, who relied largely on a semi-subsistence livelihood, and highly paid expatriate advisers, consultants and other RAMSI personnel. The large amount of money poured into the country caused unprecedented inflation and hikes in the cost of real estate and funded a lifestyle for foreigners that became the envy of locals, some of whom, admittedly, benefited through employment, the sale of produce and other economic activities in the informal sector. However, the substantial flow of monetary benefits was restricted to locals who had established business interests in hotels, shops, real estate and the food industry. TThe sharp disparity between the wealth of foreigners and the income of locals also fed into shimmering anti-foreigner grievances and nationalism that erupted during violence against the Australian police and Chinese businesses during the 2006 riots.

Despite its role in restoring stability, one of the major shortcomings of RAMSI was its inability to establish a long-term conflict resolution strategy for Solomon Islands. The focus of the intervention was largely on rebuilding state institutions, not on nation-building. As a result, the issues of social tension, community fractures, conflict and social dislocation remained. RAMSI had neither the intention nor the expertise to carry out these activities, although some of their personnel were involved in some community-based reconciliation.

Post-conflict transformation requires a process of continuity from conflict to stabilisation and restoration of community trust and relationships. This should involve a restorative and transformative approach. RAMSI's approach was based on retributive rather than restorative justice. In other words, the legal process was paramount in determining who was guilty and what type of punishment was needed. The judicial reforms were largely targeted at ensuring the effectiveness of the retributive system. While the retributive approach provided for short-term stability, it might not be sufficient to guarantee long-term sustainable peace.

In this regard, one of the major tests of cultural inclusivity for RAMSI was its recognition of local peace-building initiatives as a legitimate part of the post-conflict rehabilitation process. RAMSI failed this test because local peace-building initiatives were still seen as culturally distinct and in fact of lesser value, and were not accorded a prominent place in the RAMSI official discourse. What needs to be recognised, however, is that community-based peace initiatives helped to energise the peace process and helped to make RAMSI's work easier to achieve. While RAMSI might have provided the macro and national framework for security, its lack of reach and influence within the villages meant that local communities themselves had to be responsible for local peace-building. The future of sustainable peace in Solomon Islands will depend quite significantly on the social cohesion and harmonious relations emanating from local peace-building initiatives. This reflects the bigger problem of disjuncture between RAMSI and the local communities. RAMSI operated at three different levels: state politics, government bureaucracy and local community. Each had its own identity and operational boundary. Although RAMSI was officially linked to the state elites and bureaucracy, it maintained a certain degree of paternalistic distance. Local state officials were hostile to what they saw as the condescending and haughty attitudes of RAMSI personnel.

This 'cultural gap' might have had a hand in shaping the relationship between local cultural perceptions and the Australian-driven world view of RAMSI. The Australian-centric approach to the intervention was dominant and provided the ideological engine for the entire operation from the policy level to the individual behavioural disposition of Australian RAMSI personnel. Rather than taking a politically 'objective' approach, as often assumed, RAMSI's intervention was highly ideological and culturally driven. It was an extension of Australia's foreign policy discourse and a manifestation of Australia's self-mandated missionising influence in the Pacific. RAMSI was a new missionary enterprise that acted as a conduit for Australian values and Australia's political system and social ethos in a Pacific 'failed state'. RAMSI existed in a different cultural and ideological space from that in which the local people lived, and its aspirations were not really implanted meaningfully into the community.

In their analysis of peace-building in Solomon Islands, Braithwaite et al. (2010: 1) argue that there were issues relating to the framing of the problem and the approaches used. Contrary to the dominant perception that Solomon Islands was a 'failed state', a framework used by RAMSI, the country was not a 'failed' state because it was 'not a "formed state" but a "state in a process of formation"'. They also refer to RAMSI as a 'shadow state' because it operated autonomously, separate from the central state.

Braithwaite et al. (2010: 2) argue that, although RAMSI had some notable successes, it did not really address some of the basic issues that led to conflict. It was in fact a 'crude state-building agenda; it was not about unpicking the specificities of a knot of fragilities'. RAMSI was more interested in state-building than peace-building, and most of its rebuilding activities revolved around urban Honiara, yet more than 80 per cent of the population were hardly affected. Braithwaite et al. (2010) maintain that, although many mistakes were made during the peace-building process, a lot of lessons were also learned, and this is one of the reasons peace-building has not yet failed in Solomon Islands.

Constitutional engineering and security

The proposal for a new federal constitution has been a central political agenda item in the post-conflict era because of the need for a political structure and constitutional system that addresses some of the issues of governance, resource distribution, civic organisation and people's loyalties, which were salient to the conflict. Remember that the TPA had proposed a new political system to facilitate different regional interests; the challenge was how to put in place a constitution that was acceptable to all the provinces and people of the country. The broad idea was that constitutional reform would help in addressing some of the country's issues of security and stability.

In fact, even before independence in 1978, debate as to the best constitutional arrangement to unify a diverse country with about 65 different languages had started. The centralised Westminster system was chosen ahead of the federal one because it was considered to be cheaper and easier to operate and because it was a continuation of the precolonial structure and process. However, postcolonial system did not serve the general interests of the population in terms of political empowerment and participation, as Mae proclaimed:

> The level of participation in Solomon Islands under the Westminster system is far from what was envisaged in the 1978 Independence Constitution. There is a huge gap between the

promise of popular participation and the reality of participation
… Furthermore, the current Westminster system of government
still resembles the colonial system of government—it's just the
personnel serving the system that changed. (Mae, 2010: 5)

The clamour for a federal system was strong even before independence, as
was reflected in the boycott of independence celebrations by the Western
district. Also, in 1988, the Guadalcanal people staged a demonstration
and demanded the formation of state governments in order to protect
their traditional rights, which they believed were being undermined by
migrants from other islands. The seeds of rebellion against the status
quo were already in place. For the people of Guadalcanal, a system that
gave them more autonomy to engage with their own development and
with land rights, and to deal with economic and political domination by
migrants, especially Malaitans, was uppermost in their mind.

The two-tier, post-independence politico-administrative system,
consisting of the central government and the provincial governments, did
not fully address the issue of autonomy. While the Provincial Government
Act of 1981 delegated some power to provincial governments, the central
government retained most of the power to make laws and decisions for the
country. This structure was problematic because, rather than empowering
and encouraging the participation of people in their own governance and
development, it merely created a political and bureaucratic 'gap', which
disconnected the state from the people. The absence of any effective and
trusted mechanism through which people could channel their grievances
merely exacerbated discontent. The structure not only replicated the
colonial administrative architecture but also simulated its intent, which
was based on paternalistic centralised political control rather than
democratic participation.

The issue of federalism dominated Solomon Islands political discourse
in its postcolonial life. It was the subject of a number of reviews and
consultations, including the Provincial Government Review Committee
(Kausimae Report, 1979), the Committee to Review the Provincial
Government System (Lulei Report, 1986), the Constitutional
Review Committee (Mamaloni Report, 1987), the Committee to Review
the Provincial Government System (Tozaka Report, 1999), the Buala
and Auki Communiqués (2000), the State Government Task Force
Report (SGTF, 2000), UNDP Provincial Consultations (2003), MPs
Consultations (2005) and the Constitutional Congress Consultations

(2007–10). A draft of a federal constitution was produced in 2011 and, after wide consultations and review, the final draft was produced in 2014. From 2014 to 2016, the government was involved in wide consultation within the country as well as outside the country in places where Solomon Islands citizens lived, such as in Fiji.

There is a general perception that the new constitution will provide a strong platform for addressing some of the issues of empowerment, autonomy, land rights and development, which had helped fuel discontent in the past. Three pertinent provisions in the Preamble of the 2014 constitutional draft attempt to do this:

> Affirm the indigenous political units of our original society, whose cultures, traditions, customs, practices and social relationships have always existed, based on tribes, clans, lineages; Respect our diversity, even as we are proud of our common identity and conscious of our shared destiny; Desire that those changes will be directed through constitutional and legal channels and not by violent or unlawful means. (Solomon Islands Joint Constitutional Congress, 2014)

These three key principles—affirmation of indigenous culture and linages, respect for diversity and avoidance of the deployment of violence—are central to the ideological foundation of the nation-building process for a country scarred by violence, ethnic displacement and cultural dislocation. The proposed draft constitution attempts to address some of these outstanding grievances by proposing a three-tier governance structure consisting of the federal government, state government and community governments, under the rubric of what is fancifully termed 'cooperative federalism'. A number of critical areas to help bolster nation-building are also proposed. These include equal citizenship, a bill of rights, protection of the natural heritage and environment, provisions concerning civil society, political parties, national security and the election of a unifying president as head of state.

As we have seen in the case of Fiji, the effectiveness of the constitution lies not so much in the enlightening appeal of its principles nor its grand vision for the future, but in how it responds to constantly changing sociopolitical realities and how much legitimacy and respect it is accorded by the people. On the bright side, the federal system has the potential to engage the communities much more closely and meaningfully in relation to issues of socioeconomic development and well-being and to facilitate and enhance direct democratic participation and community empowerment. These benefits might help to moderate some of the conditions and lessen some of the tensions that spawned the Guadalcanal/Malaita conflict. However, one of the dangers of the federal system is that, while it provides for 'autonomy', dispersal of power and localised decision-making, it has the potential to exacerbate the existing divisions. Administrative and political divisions based on ethnocultural factors might generate intranational enclaves. This will further weaken the central state, which, since independence, has had minimal penetration into and influence in the local communities. Because the population is now nationally dispersed, an important issue is how local governments are going to accommodate people from outside the federal 'states'. For instance, what will happen to the numerous Malaitans who hold high positions in other states, such as Guadalcanal? The issue of distribution of resources and wealth is also a critical one, given the obvious differences in the resource base of the various 'states'.

The situation seems to be more complicated than originally realised because of the different positions taken by different regions. Nevertheless, the optimism about the newly proposed constitution is in itself a unifying factor. It is asking a great deal for it to deliver the benefits hoped for in terms of national unity and stability, but that outcome is also a bright possibility.

Truth and Reconciliation Commission

Based on the South African Truth and Reconciliation Commission (TRC) model, the Solomon Islands' localised version was meant to explore and make more explicit some deep-seated issues of communal conflict, individual and collective traumas and grievances as a basis for collective forgiveness and reconciliation. The principle behind TRCs in other countries often revolve around providing a climate conducive to peace-building and national reconciliation, healing some of the wounds inflicted on victims by both sides of the conflict through direct engagement between victims and perpetrators, and re-establishing a long-term environment of nation-building in a politically scarred landscape.

The Solomon Islands Truth and Reconciliation Commission (STRC), consisting of five members, was set up in 2009 under the 2008 Truth and Reconciliation Act, and completed its assignment in 2011, with the aim to 'discover the causes, details and effects of the country's "ethnic tension" crisis of 1998–2003' (STRC, 2012). The Act itself mandated that there should be wide participation of people nationwide in the reconciliation process. The STRC, the Act suggested, should be engaged in the promotion of national unity and reconciliation through identification of the truth about what happened in the conflicts and why (STRC Act, Section 5c). To this end, the STRC conducted public and closed hearings and collected statements from victims and perpetrators alike. It also facilitated focus group interviews with a diverse range of people directly involved in the conflict and carried out research on issues related to the conflict.

To make the process workable, a number of mechanisms were put in place to protect both victims and perpetrators who were able to share their stories. Among these was the rights of witnesses in relation to the provision of personal security and freedom from incrimination for what was said. Confidentiality was strictly adhered to if requested, and no personal information was to be publicised. Furthermore, a number of principles guided the process to ensure its credibility: informed consent of victims and witnesses before interviews, respect for diversity, non-hierarchical ordering of cases, provision of emotional and social support for victims and witnesses, availability of trauma counselling, special attention to the situation of children, transparency, freedom to use any language, and procedural fairness for all those involved. These were restorative justice principles that ensured that the subjective being of the person, not the process, was the central focus of attention. This was necessary in a situation of deeply fractured relationships, communal hostility and mutual distrust, to ensure that the engagement space was welcoming, non-inhibiting and non-partisan.

STRC's comprehensive nationwide engagement with the communities unearthed diverse experiences, views and sentiments of individuals, organisations and communities relating to the conflict. The STRC divided the consultation process into regions, which in themselves were unique in terms of their circumstances, problems and the way they were linked to the conflict. For instance, in the Weather Coast area (one of the strongholds of Guadalcanal nationalism and where 35 per cent of all deaths took place) a significant amount of focus was on Harold Keke, one of the rebel leaders, and the havoc he created. Most of the 70 people who died did so as a result of incursions by the so-called Joint Operation to subdue Keke and his supporters. Guadalcanal was also the birthplace of the Moro group, an anti-colonial movement for self-determination.

It was apparent that some of these earlier nationalistic sentiments rearticulated themselves during the conflict. In the Western province of Solomon Islands, an interesting development was the involvement of the Bougainville Revolutionary Army in providing security for the locals.

The STRC captured personal stories about compensation, vengeance, displacement, violence, personal and collective trauma, despair, fear, silence and intimidation. The 330-page report was itself an interesting study in power by the gun and the powerlessness of citizens in a world of uncertainty and deep anxiety. All these factors had a devastating impact on basic services like health, education and the rule of law. The dismantling of state institutions and usurpation of state power meant that the police force, the most visible manifestation of state authority in the country, and which was also divided by tribal loyalties, was rendered ineffective. Militia members and local warlords like Keke ruled the streets, the villages and the country in partisan and often violent ways.

Caught between the warring militias, and in the absence of any state protection, the general population had to seek refuge in certain 'safe' places, some under the protection of their respective militia groups and some with their kinsfolks on the 'other' side of the divide. Links through intermarriage became a useful means of security; for instance, some Malaitans who married into Guadalcanal families were protected by their kin. Many Malaitans who had bought land, built houses and ran businesses in Guadalcanal lost everything and left Honiara as internal refugees.

Despite the stories of doom and despair, the STRC also heard stories of hope. There were narratives of people helping and caring for each other in times of crisis and tribulation. This was a great sign of promise for the future. Amid death and destruction, there were pockets of peaceful engagement and coexistence among the members of the community, which sustained stability at the local level.

The responses to the conflict, as we have seen with RAMSI and the numerous court cases, were very legalistic. This was also reflected in the rather bureaucratic recommendations of the STRC, which suggested the introduction of community policing to re-establish trust and confidence between the community and police; developing the capacity of local professionals in the Office of the Director of Public Prosecution and the Office of the Public Solicitor; improvement of juvenile rehabilitation programs; provision of mental health facilities for accused persons and prisoners; a provincial quota system for the police force and prisons service; a review of tension trials; and consideration of correctional services redundancies, especially for officers who compromised themselves during the conflict (STRC, 2012: 330–2). These recommendations were quite disappointing because they were not based on restorative justice principles but on legally conceptualised and framed retributive approaches. They hardly addressed the deeper issues of healing community wounds and societal fractures, which truth and reconciliation commissions are supposed to address.

Although the recommendations of the STRC do little to address the bigger issue of nation-building and long-term security, from the point of view of the individuals and communities who shared their stories, narrating their experiences was in itself therapeutic and helped to establish a social space for open dialogue. The future of peace-building in Solomon Islands lies not simply in strengthening the legal process, as the STRC suggested, but in empowering people to establish a culture of peace that flows both vertically to the top and horizontally across communities.

Community-based peace-building

The predominant focus on the role of RAMSI, STRC and high-profile legal cases often overshadowed peace-building initiatives on the ground. Yet, in a society based on kinship and sociocultural bonding, communally based peace initiatives have been part of people's lives for generations. The fact that they usually exist below the radar of state and legal institutions does not render them inferior in any way. Religious, women's and other community organisations were eager to engage with the people and repair the deep-seated impact of the conflict on their community structures, relationships and norms. While some community groups operated independently at the local level, at the national levels, the Ministry of National Unity, Reconciliation and Peace (MNURP) provided an institutional state umbrella within which some of the national peace initiatives were carried out.

One of the lessons learnt from the conflict was the need for multistakeholder cooperation. That was one of the reasons why MNURP has been working closely with churches, such as the Anglican Church of Melanesia, on projects such as training in peace-building (*Solomon*

Star, 2015). As the most influential and powerful institutions outside the state, churches have used their social and spiritual status to involve themselves directly in the social transformation process by promoting communal harmony. Since the conflict, different churches have pursued their own programs using their respective national networks. For instance, from 28 April to 1 May 2008, 90 members of the Church of Melanesia convened for a provincial consultation process in Honiara on the theme 'Healing past hurts: A way forward for the Church of Melanesia'. The participants were from areas badly affected by the conflict, including rural Guadalcanal, Malaita Province and Honiara. The participants included bishops, clergy, the Church's four religious communities, women, youth, chiefs, laymen, ex-militants and ex-police, as well as Provincial Office staff, bishops of other dioceses in Solomon Islands and representatives of the Solomon Islands Government (Solomon Islands Anglican Communion New Service, 2008). The focus of the consultation was to find a common reconciliatory path for those affected by the conflict using the Christian principles of love and forgiveness in a communal setting and to respond to the need to fully understand the deeper impact of the conflict on families. The meeting also endorsed the STRC, which was to be convened later. This was just one of the many conferences, meetings and workshops conducted by civil society organisations on the matter.

International organisations participated in the community rehabilitation and peace process in various ways. For instance, UNICEF was involved in addressing children's needs and UNESCO was directly involved in programs to integrate children's welfare with peace-building and education. This was crucial because of the involvement in the conflict of many young people without formal education and unemployed young people, both as victims and perpetrators (UNESCO, 2014). This went hand in hand with the Ministry of Education's initiative to introduce peace-based modules into its curriculum (Maebuta, 2012). In 2016 the UNDP launched a UN peace-building program designed to support national efforts towards sustainable peace and stability, with emphasis on women's participation, in Solomon Islands (UNDP, 2016). Other international organisations such as the Asian Development Bank, World Bank and European Union were involved in direct or indirect ways through their contribution to development projects as well as social protection.

The role of the international agencies was problematic because of the lack of connection with the local communities. Their links were on a multilateral basis, which, in many instances, were far removed from reality on the ground. From the vantage point of the international agencies, the value of their contribution to peace-building was the publicity they were able to generate to reinforce their status and legitimacy. The photo sessions and news publicity became ends in themselves. Being seen to be concerned and being pictured on the ground was a great publicity opportunity, although the financial contribution and the actual impact was nominal or, at worst, insignificant. In the bigger scheme of things, peace-building has become an industry that has spawned competition and territoriality among international agencies, academics and consulting firms. For some international agencies, their global status and reputation have been used to help cement their claim to relevance and legitimacy in the peace-building world.

The real workhorses in community peace-building in Solomon Islands were women's organisations, whose role as advocates of non-violence, dialogue, disarmament and peace-building spanned the entire period of the conflict. They provided the support system for children and the old, and kept families together amid the crisis. Unfortunately, women were largely excluded from the formal peace dialogue processes, but this did not deter them from being actively involved in grassroots mobilisation and in creating the necessary conditions for peace-building and dialogue processes such as the TPA and other peace-building initiatives during and after the conflict.

Conclusion

The colonial experience of Solomon Islands created an economically uneven, institutionally weak, socially fractious and politically demarcated society in which state structures were wobbly, ineffective and largely tokenistic. The British were not really interested in developing infrastructure because it was a secondary colony, ruled from Fiji, the Crown colony. The only visible manifestation of British colonial rule was the flag and a handful of British officials. This neglect created a distorted sociopolitical structure, and the resulting configuration was not fully modelled on the Westminster or customary system, nor was it a utilitarian combination of both, as was the case in other British colonies like Fiji.

Upon independence, Solomon Islands, with minimal or a complete absence of trained expertise, infrastructure and basic state structure, had to start from scratch, and it was not long before seismic shifts began to be felt. The struggle to keep up with modernity led to overexploitation of resources, corruption, land disputes and maldistribution of wealth, and these put increasing stress on the new country, struggling to create a unified nation amid ethnic and cultural diversity. The syncretic relationship between civic nationalism (the desire to create a unified national identity) and communal nationalism (the desire to maintain communal distinctiveness) formed a fault line, which was exacerbated by socioeconomic disparity and grievances. This intersection between communal mobilisation and socioeconomic disparity became the epicentre of the rippling political quakes.

It was only a matter of time before the inevitable happened. When it happened, the Solomon Island communities were not ready in terms of their conflict resolution responses. They had to adapt to the fast-changing conflict culture and its consequences. The conflict was the single most transformative event in the modern history of Solomon Islands, at least since colonisation, and its long-term effects will be felt for some time yet. Communities were transformed in a fundamental way, and so were the cultural response mechanisms and sense of resilience. Historians will look back and define the conflict as the watershed moment when the country had to come to terms with the complexities of social transformation, a time when indigenous values and colonial cultures intersected and defined each other in a syncretic way.

The conflict in Solomon Islands had a number of significant characteristics that were typical of many postcolonial societies. One major issue was the way in which modernity disrupted and transformed a communal and subsistence culture and created social and political fissures that led to conflict. While local conflicts were taking place as part of normal everyday tension, as in any society, the national conflict in Solomon Islands moved to another level of intensity. The consequences were unprecedented. The growth of the capitalist economy and the subsequent demand for labour and the pressure this put on land and social relations on Guadalcanal provided a recipe for tension. Economic disparity and the corrupt activities of political elites, many of whom were from economically depressed communities and, therefore, wanted quick money for themselves, together with the pressure from their *wantok* for resources, were all juxtaposed in a melting pot of grievances, waiting for a spark to cause an explosion. When it did, it was not easy to stop the genie of aggression, which had been bottled up for some time.

The customary means of reconciliation that had provided for social balance and cultural harmony within kinship groups could not stem the tide of violence and destruction. The extent of violence was national in latitude and impact and was beyond the capacity of local communities to contain using customary means. The setting up of armed groups by warring sides and the mode of engagement and weaponry were modelled on modern militaries or guerrilla armies elsewhere around the world. Clearly these were beyond the cultural knowledge and notion of place of local communities, who found themselves sandwiched between contending forces in a confrontation whose magnitude and intensity were outside the conflict norms of their familiar world. The older generation might have remembered the World War II campaign by the Allies against the Japanese invasion, but these were seen to be instigated from outside and the defeat of the Japanese meant the end of the conflict. This was not the case with the internally generated civil disorder that transformed Honiara and parts of Guadalcanal into 'war zones' of sorts.

The sense of unfamiliarity with the use of firearms and the semi-military organised fighting groups were traumatic for the community collectively as well as for individuals. Relationships were fractured, but this did not dampen the sense of resilience of communities. Often, in times of crisis, collective resilience goes through a phase of resurgence as a protective mechanism to ensure self-preservation. To some extent, mitigating responses might have some links to the subconscious evolutionary intuition for survival. At another level, however, there is an important social rationale for the perpetuation of the human species. For kinship-based societies like that of Solomon Islands, the life of individuals is just as important as the life of the community in general. Life is defined not by the chronological sequence of events from birth to death but by one's consciousness about identity and one's contribution to collective survival. The conflict, and the desire for perpetuity, inspired survival initiatives in the form of community peace-building by community groups such as church and women's organisations. At the more ontological level, in the absence of the capacity for nationwide reach, community peace groups searched more deeply for indigenous modes of reconciliation to address conflicts in neighbourhoods. These pockets of peace-building, scattered around the country, worked well together in diffusing tension at the local level and collectively contributed to national peace, at least for the time being.

For the rest of the Pacific, the Solomon Island conflict was an important lesson in regional intervention, where sovereignty had to be traded for security. For a country desperate to unload the burden of violence, security was the major priority, around which other considerations revolved. RAMSI not only provided the much-needed security but also transformed the security discourse into an Australian-based one. The challenge now is to find ways to build capacity for the local security institutions, principally the police, judiciary, corrections and intelligence, to ensure the sustainability of security and stability. An equally daunting task is to carry out a process of inclusive and consensual nation-building to mend the social fractures and communal rifts that have remained in a state of hibernation since the height of the violence.

Solomon Islands represents a classic postcolonial state where national conflict emanated from the contradiction of its colonial history. The use of postcolonial, securitisation and human security discourses are important in capturing the multilayered factors that have shaped conflict and security during the colonial and postcolonial periods. Although this might be the theoretical approach to explain the past, the narrative for the future is in the hands not of scholars pontificating about what ought to be done but of Solomon Islanders themselves, whose destiny they must take charge of without the paternalistic urgings of neo-imperialist neighbours such as Australia or the patronising whims of international agencies. A future in people's hands is a future in good hands.

7
Contested future: Where to for Pacific security?

I refuse to accept the view that mankind is so tragically bound to the starless midnight of racism and war that the bright daybreak of peace and brotherhood can never become a reality ... I believe that unarmed truth and unconditional love will have the final word.

Martin Luther King, Jr

The three case studies (in Chapters 4, 5 and 6) are meant to demonstrate the wide diversity of historical, sociopolitical and cultural experiences of Pacific countries in the area of security. The 'Pacific' is not a generic or homogenous entity, as is often assumed and reflected in such generalised terms as 'arc of instability'. Rather, the region consists of diverse cultures, political systems and life experiences. Instead of constructing universalised narratives, it is important to delve deeper into the unique experiences of different countries. This book attempts to capture the specific experiences of three different countries, without being limited by the usually mechanical conventional comparative analysis template of identifying similarities and differences, often used by some political scientists. This allows one to study the countries in depth without being confined to superficial comparative variables.

Within the broader analytical eclecticism paradigm, the book employs various conceptual tools, most notably the postcolonial, securitisation and human security lenses, to examine power relationships from precolonial times to the postcolonial period. The three approaches are closely related, and collectively they can shed light on the complex interactions between people's human security and well-being and the perception of security in the postcolonial context.

Critical lessons from the case studies

This study highlights a number of conceptual, methodological and empirical aspects that redefine the notion of security in the Pacific and more broadly. Not only is the notion of security contested in relation to varying schools of thought, it is also contested in terms of contextual application, as we have seen in the very different cases of Fiji, Tonga and Solomon Islands. With this in mind, it is prudent to think of regional Pacific security not in terms of a unifying metanarrative but in terms of multiple narratives. The study has also revealed a number of significant aspects of Pacific security that could be the basis of how we define, conceptualise and operationalise security discourses in the future. Although the case studies are meant to stand on their own to represent the unique situations of different countries, there are some common strands of conceptual and empirical themes that connect them and which are worth considering in the context of the broader analytical eclecticism framework of the book. We look at some of these below.

Importance of the analytical eclecticism approach

At a broad theoretical level, the use of multiconceptual approaches provides a holistic narrative of the situation within countries, especially in relation to social conditions, group relations, power dynamics, resource distribution and conflict as well as phases of their historical development. The postcolonial approach provides a more nuanced view, which, instead of simply documenting the official state-centred perspectives, examines situations from the viewpoint of the subaltern colonised groups in the broader contest of history and the unfolding political economy. This approach is appropriate for postcolonial societies whose state structures, economic development models, cultural institutions and collective national consciousness and identities have been shaped to some degree by the imposed colonial pacification processes. The imposition of taxation, for instance, as we saw in Fiji, Tonga and Solomon Islands, had profound effects on the economic conditions of the locals, thus breeding dissent and opposition to state rule. Even after independence, the colonially constructed and imposed systems remained and evolved in ways that were driven by and served the interests of local elites. Although Tonga was a protectorate and not formally a colony of Britain, British influence was significant, nonetheless, and the monarch assimilated or imitated a lot of the symbolism and state institutions of the British monarch.

The postcolonial narrative has resonance throughout the Pacific. Although formal colonialism has passed (except for the French colonies, Tokelau and Pitcairn Island), new forms of cultural hegemony, the impact of climate change, the global neoliberal agenda, and the influence of big power militarism and corporate interests have further diminished the leveraging power and increased the insecurity of Pacific Island Countries (PICs). In other words, new forms of domination and subalternation have emerged and created a structure that continues to keep PICs at the bottom of the global power strata. One's position in this power hierarchy continues to pose security challenges for the region, as we have seen. For instance, the trade deficit with the Pacific powers of Australia and New Zealand, the imposition of the PACER Plus free trade deal, the latent conditions linked to aid by donors and the challenges of climate change are just some of the ways in which PICs continue to remain 'subservient' in a hostile geopolitical environment. Domination is justified by stereotyping of subaltern communities and countries using negative imagery, a process referred to by Said as orientalism. Subconscious prejudices latently embedded in terms such as 'arc of instability', for instance, have reinforced perceptions of inferiority while justifying interventions as modern forms of civilising missions. The postcolonial discourse provides the methodological tools to illuminate these often hidden dimensions of power, exploitation and inequality, which are often overlooked by security theories such as realism, liberalism and even securitisation.

While the postcolonial discourse analyses and critiques existing modes of dominance and associated problems of marginalisation, it also opens up new windows for alternative narratives and new trajectories for the future. This is critical for understanding regional security where power differentials exist at various levels whereby two dominant countries like New Zealand and Australia occupy the top tier and Fiji and Papua New Guinea are at the second tier and others at the lower tiers. A related question is how to address this unequal power structure, economic disparity and associated stereotyping, as detailed in Chapter 3, to ensure that we have a more egalitarian and just economic and political configuration for the region. This should be a critical question of our time since lack of equality, access and opportunities can pose a serious security challenge for the region.

While the postcolonial discourse provides a useful overarching approach that frames and analyses the historical and political economy of the region and individual states, there is still a gap in analysis in relation to individual perception and psychology. The securitisation theory fills this gap by focusing on the dynamic relationship between language, words and actions and the way they shape the security environment. Rather than just framing security in terms of direct threat, naming and thinking about a potential threat can be profoundly transformative. As we have seen in the case of Fiji, the use of the term 'coup' invokes collective anxiety and fear, and discussions of the riots in Tonga or the 'tension' in Solomon Islands ignite memories of the past and become sources of collective psychological threat.

In Fiji, the perception of inequality, economic deprivation of indigenous Fijians, threat of loss of land and power, and fear of being politically overwhelmed by Indo-Fijians gave rise to ethnonationalist sentiments, open conflict and regime change. Perception and framing of each other (indigenous Fijians and Indo-Fijians) as sources of threat as well as the use of racialised stereotypes such as *jungali pagla* (stupid Fijian bushman) or *Kaidia lawakica* (cunning and untrustworthy Indian) have securitised ethnic relations in a potentially explosive way. In the case of Tonga, behind the veneer of respect for the monarch, the use of the term *temokalati* (democracy) securitised the King and nobles as enemies of the people and dichotomised Tonga into two major competing political camps. In Solomon Islands, words such as 'corruption', 'politicians', 'militants' and 'tension' have become part of the vocabulary of security and, even in the 'post-conflict' era, continue to invoke consciousness of threat because of their association with the 1999–2003 civil conflict.

Generally, in the Pacific, although the threat of climate change may be real, the mental image of the threat and potential for even more destruction in the future has galvanised Pacific countries to engage in international lobbying and leadership, such as Fiji's presidency of climate change process under COP23. For small island states in the Pacific, the perception of threat from stronger and more destructive cyclones, sinking of islands, droughts, sea erosion, loss of land, relocation and loss of culture and identity are all mental constructs articulated and realised through language as a means of reification. These images are shared and collectively crystalised through social media, electronic networks and other forms of modern communication and, in the process, they contribute to the securitisation of the environment and everyday life.

While postcolonial theory is based on the study of inequality of power and exploitation, and securitisation focuses on the conceptualisation of threat through words, the human security approach adds the missing dimension of connectivity between different aspects of life and well-being by defining social, political, economic and environmental issues as security-related by virtue of their impact on human well-being. The case studies demonstrate how various combinations of human security issues such as socioeconomic inequality, justice, competition for power, questionable governance, resources allocation and identity could lead to various stages of individual and group grievances, shimmering conflict and eventually open conflict. The volatile human security issues, which were common in all countries, have continued to worsen over the years.

The point I want to emphasise here is that the use of multiple prisms has the distinctive advantage of providing multiple dimensions to security that single narratives cannot provide. In a region and a world that are changing rapidly and where multiple transformational forces are at play, using multiple narratives is the appropriate way to go.

Colonial experience and security

A major theme that emerged from all three case studies was that most of the security issues were not only internally generated but also built on the issues of the past and replicated themselves over time until they exploded into open hostility. The political conflicts the countries experienced resulted from complex interactions between power relations, inequality in resource ownership and distribution, contestation and protection of identity and unfulfilled collective expectations. The competing players belonged to different ethnicities or classes who constructed cleavages and boundaries based on identities. The boundaries became not only social lines of identity demarcation but also security and battle lines. Most of these security issues had roots in the earlier colonial epoch and, in some cases, even the precolonial era. In Fiji and Solomon Islands, the process of colonial transformation encompassed a complex process of constructing a new imperial state system, resistance to the colonial policies of pacification, introduction of the capitalist mode of production and the imposition of a coercive system of rule. These were to have long-lasting impacts on security in these societies.

Symbolic and functional role of 'ethnicity' in the conflicts

A significant feature of the three case studies is that, while the conflicts were different in relation to their causes, manifestations and impact, ethnicity had a role either as a marker of socioeconomic inequality or as a mobilising force. In Fiji one of the main axes of conflict was between an indigenous group (Taukei) and a dispora group (Indo-Fijians), whereas in Solomon Islands it was between two indigenous groups, although they were from separate islands and tribal affiliations. The conflict in Tonga was quite different in the sense that it was fundamentally between two antagonistic social classes. Moreover, the ethnic factor arose after the riots started when Chinese businesses were attacked, but these were 'collatoral' victims of the main conflict.

The ethnic components of the three case studies were connected to broader issues of socioeconomic disparity, identity, land and political power. Ethnic differences on their own do not automatically invoke conflict, but rather conflict is inspired by the way these differences are linked to socioeocomic inequality and competition for power. In the case of Fiji, the situation was characterised by the division of the economy along ethnic lines with Indo-Fijians controlling commerce and Taukei controlling the land and political power. Socioeconomic grievances by the Taukei after independence culminated in the 1987 conflict and coups, and since then the threat of military takeover has remained part of the country's security narrative. Grievances over land and resources, socioeconomic inequality and lack of opportunities contributed to the intercommunal tension in Solomon Islands. In Tonga, the tension built up over years of pro-democracy protests spilled over into street riots, and some rioters took advantage of the chaos to attack Chinese businesses that they had loathed for some time for taking away business from them. In all these cases of conflicts related to ethnicity, ethnic and political entrepreneurs played a critical role in mobilising people's grivances for political ends.

Responses to conflict

Because the conflicts in the three countries were unique in their own right, the responses to them were somewhat different, although there were some common features, such as the use of traditional means of conflict resolution at the community level. In Fiji, the role of the military was paramount in determining the trajectory of the political process towards democratic elections. This was not the case in Solomon Islands, where the security apparatus of the state was no longer operable and militants took over the security role of the state until the arrival of RAMSI. RAMSI provided some real security muscle to keep the warring militias at bay. In Tonga, they had to call for intervention by the Australian and New Zealand military to quell the situation. In all cases, restoration of stability became the precondition for democratic elections.

At the community level, a range of programs were organised by civil society organisations, churches and other community groups. One of the key factors that distinguished conflict in Fiji and Tonga from Solomon Islands was the fact that, in Solomon Islands, a 'civil war' situation between two militia groups representing two communities took place. Nevertheless, one of the common features of the three case studies is the use of multiple means of peace-building involving a range of stakeholders at the state and community levels.

The international community was more sympathetic to the Tonga and Solomon Islands situations than to Fiji. Australia, the United States and New Zealand imposed sanctions on Fiji and, furthermore, Fiji was suspended from the Pacific Island Forum and the Commonwealth. Instead of weakening Fiji, the sanctions forced Fiji to align itself more strongly with China as well as to build up a more independent and assertive foreign policy aimed at outflanking Australia and New Zealand and making it a minor regional power in its own right. The establishment of the Pacific Islands Development Forum to counter the Pacific Islands Forum, funded by Australia and New Zealand, was part of these geopolitical manoeuvres.

In all three cases of conflict, the ripples spread throughout the region and had different effects. In the case of Fiji, the PICs were initially sympathetic to Fiji after the 1987 and 2000 coups, but this was not so after the coup in 2006. The Pacific Islands Forum tried to send a team to engage with the military government, but Fiji did not take it seriously. The Forum resorted to suspension. In the case of Tonga, Australia and New Zealand, the strongest powers in the region, intervened in the form of military assistance, whereas in the case of Solomon Islands, regional intervention was possible through RAMSI. These interventions show the increasingly regional nature of national conflicts and at the same time the impact of regional security narratives on national conflict resolution.

Security and regime change

In the case of Fiji and Solomon Islands, extralegal regime changes resulted from the conflicts while in Tonga there was potential for a similar situation to occur. Regime change through coups has been an unsavoury part of Fiji's political evolution since 1987, where every coup was followed by a period of calm and then tension as prelude to another coup. In Solomon Islands, the coup in 2000 was part of the larger environment of instability at the time rather than an imitation of the Fiji coup earlier in the same year, as some journalists suggested. In Tonga, it was alleged by the government representative, Lopeti Senituli, that the November 2006 riots were aimed at staging a 'coup', but this did not eventuate.

In the context of the securitisation theory, regime change provides an extreme image of a scenario that must be avoided at all cost. It is associated with images of a collapsed society, anarchy, lawlessness and possible deaths. Although regime change may be 'relatively' peaceful as in the case of Fiji, the thought of a disintegrated, chaotic and lawless society is a powerful psychological deterrent against the use of force as well as a strong incentive for peace-building and conflict resolution. Regime change is an extreme expression of what is possible when human security issues remain unchecked and neglected. Viewed through a postcolonial lens, regime change is seen as a consequence of tension that has its roots in the colonial order. Regime change, and the potential for it, have created new narratives of peace-building in the three communities. As a securitised concept, it provides a psychological marker as a lesson for the future.

Level of violence

The level of violence experienced during the Fiji coups, Tongan riots and Solomon Islands conflict differed considerably. Except for the 2000 coup, when a failed mutiny led to several deaths, the coups in Fiji were relatively bloodless. While there were documented cases of torture and human rights abuse, there was no civil unrest in terms of intercommunal violence of the type witnessed in Rwanda, Kosovo or even Solomon Islands. One of the reasons was that the coups focused largely on competition for state power by elites and the military, and tension was concentrated in the realm of state power. By and large, everyday ethnic relations remained stable, despite some cases of sporadic ethnic violence and intimidation.

This was also the case in Tonga, a very homogenous society. Conflict manifested itself much more vigorously at the realm of state institutions and power. Community relations remained strong amid the riots and burnings. Those who died in the riots were victims of the fire and not of violence. This was not the case in Solomon Islands, where violence revolved around the civil realm. The Malaitans and Guadalcanal communities were in direct confrontation through their respective militia forces and, as a result, hundreds of people were killed. The inability of the state to intervene provided the militia with the self-issued licence to kill, thus worsening the situation considerably.

The contested terrain

This multilayered approach to analysis of the three Pacific case studies testifies to the contested nature of security in the broader theoretical debate. Indeed the competing discourses on security that we examined in Chapter 2 show the diverse ways in which security is framed and articulated. These differences are not to be taken as a basis for creating a hierarchy of reliability of the different modes of framing offered, but as signalling the fact that different approaches have their own legitimate claims, based on their choice of explanatory variables and conceptual justifications. It is probably fair to say that there is no strictly 'right' or 'wrong' way to frame security but rather that there are a range of alternative narratives one can choose from, given particular circumstances.

The debates on security are manifestations of the way in which we interpret the causes, dynamics and consequences of particular types of human behaviour deemed threatening to a particular group or to society as a whole. What is 'threatening' is often constructed in relation to the 'victim/perpetrator' dichotomy, and interpretation of 'threat' depends very much on where one is located in the relationship as well as in the intellectual and ideological lenses of the beholder. For instance, while the notion of 'security as speech act' espoused by the securitisation discourse of the Copenhagen School has been seen as a breakthrough in terms of its ability to redefine the psychological aspect of threat, it has nonetheless been criticised by realists for being too incoherent and idealistic, and by postcolonial theorists for being Eurocentric. These criticisms have not stopped the expanding influence of securitisation and modern security thinking.

The ambiguity and confusion relating to defining security also emanates from this diversity. For instance, while some theories of security, such as human security, have a universalised thrust, others, like the concept of orientalism, are more contextual and are seen as appropriate in particular historical circumstances and in particular places. In addition, some theories (such as securitisation) are classified as formal theories of security whereas some concepts (such as orientalism), which clearly have deep security implications, are not seen as relevant to conventional security framing. This is where a more nuanced, critical and contextualised security approach is important in order to illuminate for us what is relevant without making superficial generalisations that are not applicable in many situations.

The limitations posed by some of the dominant security discourses such as realism, neo-realism and liberalism, among others, are due to their links to particular ideological and geocultural and technical lenses, which often have underpinning interests that exponents hope will serve them. Realism, for instance, was an influential narrative to justify the military build-up and arms race during the Cold War, while securitisation became a more nuanced way of not only redefining the diverse manifestation of security but also identifying the sociopsychological basis of the construction of security. Moreover, security theories should not be seen as strictly independent because, in some cases, there are common strands running through some theories, and there are also areas of overlap. For instance, one of the common threads linking securitisation theory and human security is a shift from identification of generic threats to a more nuanced construction of what constitutes threat, using more dispersed variables.

The increasing dominance of the human security agenda has not necessarily displaced realist and traditional 'hard' or state-centred security thinking. In many ways, rather than 'shifting' the paradigm, as claimed by the UNDP, it has simply absorbed state-centred security into its broad coverage and redefined it as just another random element in the universal basket of human security variables. The numerous criticisms of human security as lacking in coherence and focus have ignited further debates about prioritising threats. US President Donald Trump's disdain for 'liberal' issues and values, including his denial of aspects of human security such as climate change, environmental considerations, accountable democratic governance and ethical politics, poses a major threat to the global human security agenda. His attitude has effectively changed the global power configuration and security dynamics in a major way. To the securitisation school's speech act approach, Trump is himself a security threat because almost everyone—the media, political analysts, world leaders, the general public—talks about him and defines him as such. This has redefined global security dynamics in unprecedented ways, especially when the US president, who is constitutionally the embodiment of US state identity and is to be protected and preserved, is now seen as a security threat to his own country through his alleged political and business dealings with Russia and his perceived lack of integrity.

The securitisation and human security approaches have their shortcomings in terms of providing a reliable framework for understanding the complex realities of 'developing' societies. With its focus on power, ideology, exploitation and the relationship between dominant and subaltern groups, the postcolonial theory tries to rectify these theoretical and analytical deficiencies. Although mainstream political science and international relations does not usually see the postcolonial discourse as a formal security discourse, it does provide a critical approach, which unearths some of the deeper issues of socioeconomic, cultural and political domination that threaten the well-being, identity and survival of subaltern societies.

Capturing diversity of narratives

The use of multiple approaches in this book, especially the postcolonial and human security lenses, to understand some of the dynamics in Pacific societies is an attempt to broaden the analytical paradigm to incorporate diverse perspectives in a highly diverse region. Contrary to dominant stereotypes about a homogeneous entity represented in such romantic notions as 'Pacific identity', 'Pacific way', 'Pacific culture' and 'sea of islands', or articulated in deficit terms such as 'arc of instability' or 'failed states', the case studies show that the three countries have very little in common in terms of sociopolitical security situations. Although they all shared a common 'player' in the form of the British colonial state, the specific historical conditions that shaped the sociopolitical security contours in those countries over the years and that led to political upheaval were very different.

Fiji faced probably the most complex situation because of its multi-ethnic, multireligious and multicultural make-up. Tension was spawned over time by the dynamic and invariable interplay between multiple factors such as resource distribution, intra- and inter-ethnic competition over political power, an ethnically based parliamentary system under the first three constitutions, feelings of insecurity (real and perceived), the role of ethnic entrepreneurs in mobilising ethnonationalism, the politicisation of stereotypes and the military, the political role of the churches and the failure of the state and political leaders to respond effectively to grievances. Ethnicity was often considered the 'primary' factor, but behind the facade of genetics and culture were deeper political and economic interests that constantly constructed and manipulated ethnicity as mobilisation and justificatory leverage.

Tonga's conflict does not involve ethnic diversity but intracommunal class inequality and associated contestation over power. Tonga's hierarchy has three superimposed pyramidal structures, all headed by the King: the traditional chiefly structure of the Tu'i Kanokupolu and Tu'i Tonga lineage; the feudal structure modelled on the British system based on the three tiers of monarch, nobles and commoners; and the constitutional state system, centred on legal political authority and governance. The commoner-based pro-democracy movement has been fighting for democratisation and greater distribution of political rights. Other intersecting variables, such as economic inequality and corruption, fuelled and sparked the riot and arson in November 2006.

In the case of Solomon Islands, paternalistic, unequal and oppressive British development policies and labour policies that encouraged internal migration, land alienation and maldistribution of wealth and resources, nurtured grievances and exploded into open civil war. The conflict was contained by external regional intervention in the form of RAMSI and, with the recent termination of the mandate of the intervention forces and officials, the Solomon Islands Government has now resumed full control of the security of the country.

Despite fundamental differences, a couple of strands seem to connect the three cases. First, they were at some point in their history associated with British colonial rule. Fiji was a Crown colony, Solomon Islands was a protectorate through the British colonial establishment in Fiji, while Tonga was an 'independent' protectorate or 'protected state'. British influence had a significant bearing on the situations in both Fiji and Solomon Islands, especially in relation to socioeconomic development and the political power structure and dynamics, and the effects of these on the security of these countries were profound and long-lasting. While Tonga's political elites had the tendency to mimic British royal symbolism, titles and idiosyncrasies, the actual impact of the British in terms of applied policies was minimal.

The second common thread was ethnicity, although its place in social life and political discourse was very different indeed in each case. In Fiji the two major ethnic groups competing for political power and resources were the indigenous Fijians and Indo-Fijians, a major diaspora group. In contrast, the Chinese, who were 'collateral' victims of both the Tongan and Solomon Islands conflicts, were not major political competitors against the local political elites. Their only 'crime' was their control of local retail businesses, which caused socioeconomic grievances that, over time, metamorphosed into political mobilisation. This was also true in the case of Fiji in respect of Indo-Fijians, where Indo-Fijian retail shops and businesses, which symbolised horizontal inequality, were targeted during the 2000 riots. However, in Fiji, Indo-Fijians were seen by the Taukei as both political and economic threats. The symbiotic relationship between socioeconomic class, ethnicity and politics manifested itself differently in the three different countries. These unique experiences are what this book attempts to capture.

However, it must be noted that these three factors were not part of an interrelated general trend in the Pacific but were, rather, unrelated developments that emanated from specific historical conditions. Nevertheless, it is also relevant to point out here that, as a result of globalisation, regional interactions and the adoption of a common development agenda, including such issues as free trade, there will increasingly be more shared security issues and challenges in the future. The capacity of the different PICs to deal with these challenges differs, and there will be an increasing tendency for both regional approaches and bilateral approaches to be taken, whereby bigger and more resourceful

PICs will need to provide assistance to small ones. The role of New Zealand and Australia, who themselves have entrenched interests, will become more critical in the future.

Rethinking security and empowerment

In a fast-changing and perilous world, perhaps the most critical question that we need to ask is: what are the most empowering and effective responses to security for Pacific peoples? The answer to this is not straightforward for several pertinent and often interrelated reasons.

First, it is not possible to generalise about the universality of various security issues around the Pacific because of the diverse sociocultural, historical and sociopolitical experiences and dynamics of the different communities. The much larger communities in the west are far more heterogeneous than the smaller and more homogeneous communities of the eastern Pacific. Conflict over resources, status and power pervades all communities, but they are manifested in quite different ways. Many of the larger and more resourceful Pacific communities, such as PNG, Fiji and Solomon Islands, face problems associated with commercial appropriation of land resources, while many of the small states do not face the same problems. The level of literacy, health, social support systems and other forms of social protection and associated challenges differ from country to country.

Second, the way security is defined and conceptualised internally by the communities can be at odds with the external definition formulated by others. For instance, land disputes between or within tribal groups in Fiji may be seen from the outside as security threats, but at the same time they are seen by the people involved as ironing out anomalies and correcting imbalances. While lack of luxurious living is usually associated with 'poverty', it is often seen by many villagers as humble, cultural living and being close to nature. In Kiribati and Tuvalu, one of the most challenging social and ideological hurdles for addressing climate change is the perception by ordinary villagers that climate change is part of the divine plan and that humans have no right to alter its course. The appeal to supernatural explanations, either in terms of the intent of the ancestors or the will of the Christian God, is often lauded as an explanation for natural disasters or human misdeeds. These beliefs may run counter to the externally introduced technical and political discourses by the state, civil society organisations, regional institutions and international agencies. Changing perception is not easy, especially when it is rooted in religious beliefs that explain things in terms of divinity, immemoriality and primordiality.

In addition to these forces, the ways in which these threats manifest themselves and affect the communities differ, and the technical capacity of the local communities and the state to respond appropriately differs as well. Some countries, such as Fiji, are more economically advanced than others and are in a position to address some of the security issues more effectively than others.

Given these diverse challenges, addressing and mitigating the security issues in the Pacific needs careful thought and systematic approaches. As we have seen in the cases of Fiji, Tonga and Solomon Islands, political security is linked in complex ways to other human security issues relating to inequality, resource distribution, intergroup perception, feelings of powerlessness and state policies. This means that long-term approaches should encapsulate multiple strategies to address different aspects of security. The different stakeholders, including the state, civil society, faith-based organisations, the private sector and communities, should be involved in a broad collaborative engagement to identify individual security issues and propose ways of collectively addressing these. Because it affects everyone, security should involve a partnership in relation to conceptualisation, response and monitoring. Security partnerships should be inclusive, participatory and consensual:

> The notion of security partnership in this context involves the participatory and mutually agreed process of sustained collective engagement between the state, civil society, private sector and citizens at large in identifying and critically examining security issues, framing responses to security dilemmas and establishing a collective and appropriate process which is sustainable in addressing old and new security challenges. (Ratuva, 2015a: 2)

As we have seen, one of the salient issues pertains to the contending conceptions of security and their various claims over the legitimate approach. Conversations between rival views and approaches are important in creating a consensus. Competing approaches often create conditions for insecurity itself. The seemingly irreconcilable different schools of thought actually have certain things in common, such as the focus on humans and their well-being, yet these are often ignored in favour of differences as a way of imposing intellectual and ideological superiority over one another. Identifying and popularising common strands can be a way forward in a security partnership approach.

In the Pacific, there should be broad partnership at the local, national and regional levels. Different countries have different historical experiences, yet common threads bind them and, increasingly, they share similar security challenges. At the global level, the PICs have exerted themselves quite visibly in drawing the world's attention to their plight. The presidents of Kiribati and Marshall Islands have been vocal internationally about climate change and associated human security issues, and Fiji's convening of the UN Oceans Conference in New York in June 2017 and chairing of COP25 in November 2017 have raised the level of articulation and campaigning for Pacific security for the future. There are indeed obstacles posed by powerful economic and political interests that need to be understood and addressed.

In a world marked by dramatic transformation and conflict, peace-building increasingly becomes an important aspect of life. How secure we are depends very much on how we define security, respond to it and monitor its impact. Security should not be seen as the responsibility of a single group, a single country or a single region. It should be a global responsibility. After all, we are now connected globally, and the painful experience of one becomes a source of collective grief of others.

References

Abrahamsen, R., 2005, 'Blair's Africa: The politics of securitization and fear', *Alternatives: Global, Local, Political*, 30(1): 55–80. doi.org/10.1177/030437540503000103

Adams, R., 2002, *Peace on Bougainville: Truce Monitoring Group*, Victoria University Press, Wellington

Akin, D., 2013, *Colonialism, Maasina Rule and the Origins of Malaitan Kastom*, University of Hawai'i Press, Honolulu

Ali, A., 1972, 'The Fiji general election of 1972', *Journal of Pacific History*, 8: 171–80. doi.org/10.1080/00223334308572230

—— 2008, *The Federation Movement in Fiji, 1880–1902*, iUniverse, Bloomington, IN

Ali, T., 2003, *The Clash of Fundamentalisms: Crusades, Jihads and Modernity*, Verso, London

Allen, M., 2007, 'Greed and grievance in the conflict in Solomon Islands 1998–2003', PhD dissertation, The Australian National University, Canberra

—— 2012, 'Land, identity and conflict on Guadalcanal, Solomon Islands', *Australian Geographer*, 43(2): 163–80. doi.org/10.1080/00049182.2012.682294

Amadae, S.M., 2003, *Rationalizing Capitalist Democracy: The Cold War Origins of Rational Choice Liberalism*, University of Chicago Press, Chicago

Amid, A., 2014, 'Fijian boatmakers to Disney: We want compensation for "Moana"', *The Grinch*. www.cartoonbrew.com/disney/fijian-boatmakers-to-disney-we-want-compensation-for-moana-105257.html (retrieved 8 January 2019)

Anderson, J., and Watson, G. (ed.), 2005, *Securing a Peaceful Pacific*, University of Canterbury Press, Christchurch

Aotearoa Independent Media Center (AIMC), 2006, 'Revolutionary not evolutionary—indymedia activists report from Tonga'. archive.indymedia. org.nz/article/72766/revolutionary-not-evolutionary-%E2%80%93-indymed (retrieved 27 May 2019)

Aradau, C., 2004, 'Security and the democratic scene: Desecuritization and emancipation', *Journal of International Relations and Development*, 7(4): 388–413. doi.org/10.1057/palgrave.jird.1800030

—— 2006, 'Limits of security, limits of politics? A response', *Journal of International Relations and Development*, 9(1): 81–90. doi.org/10.1057/ palgrave.jird.1800073

Ashcroft, B., Griffiths, G., and Tiffin, H., 2013, *Post-Colonial Studies: Key Concepts*, 3rd edn, Routledge, New York

Atkinson, J., 2010, 'China–Taiwan diplomatic competition and the Pacific Islands', *Pacific Review*, 23(4): 407–27. doi.org/10.1080/09512748.2010.495 998

Austin, J.L., 1962, *How to do Things with Words*, Harvard University Press, Cambridge, MA

Australian Broadcasting Corporation (ABC), 2006, 'Tongan pro-democracy movement slams intervention', 19 November. www.abc.net.au/news/2006-11-19/tongan-pro-democracy-movement-slams-intervention/1313148

—— 2014, 'Pacific presidents speak out against Australia's stand on climate change', 13 June. www.abc.net.au/news/2014-06-13/pacific-presidents/5521478

Australian Fair Trade and Investment Network (AFTINET), 2018, 'Pacific Island trade deal diminished without PNG and Fiji', *Scoop World*. www.scoop.co.nz/ stories/WO1805/S00046/pacific-island-trade-deal-diminished-without-png-and-fiji.htm (retrieved 8 January 2019)

Ayoob, M., 1995, *The Third World Security Predicament: State Making, Regional Conflict and the International System*, Lynne Rienner Publishers, Boulder, CO

Ayson, R., 2007, 'The "arc of instability" and Australia's strategic policy', *Australian Journal of International Affairs*, 61(2): 215–31 doi.org/10.1080/ 10357710701358360

Bain, A., 1986, 'Labour protest and control in the gold mining industry in Fiji', *South Pacific Forum*, 3(1): 37–59

Bain, K., 1993, 31 December, 'Obituary: Bishop Patelesio Finau', *The Independent*

Baldwin, D., 1997, 'The concept of security', *Review of International Studies*, 23: 5–26. www.jstor.org/stable/20097464

Baledrokadroka, J., 2003, 'The Fijian understanding of the deed of cession treaty of 1874', MA paper, University of Auckland, New Zealand

—— 2012, 'Sacred kings and warrior chief: The role of the military in Fiji politics', PhD thesis, The Australian National University, Canberra

—— 2016, 'The Fiji military and the 2014 elections', in *The People have Spoken: The 2014 General Elections in Fiji*, ed. S. Ratuva and S. Lawson (pp. 177–89), ANU Press, Canberra. doi.org/10.22459/TPHS.03.2016

Barkawi, T., and Laffey, M., 2006, 'The postcolonial moment in security studies', *Review of International Studies*, 32: 329–52. doi.org/10.1017/S0260210506007054

Barnett, J., 2011, *Human Security*, Oxford University Press, Oxford

Barnett, J., and Waters, E., 2016, 'Rethinking the vulnerability of small island states: Climate change and development in the Pacific Islands', in *The Palgrave Handbook of International Development*, ed. J. Grugel and D. Hammett, Palgrave, London. doi.org/10.1057/978-1-137-42724-3_40

Barnett, M., 2008, *Social Constructivism: The Globalization of World Politics*, Oxford University Press, Oxford

Batley, J., 2017, 'What's the significance of Australia's new security treaty with Solomon Islands?', *The Strategist*. www.aspistrategist.org.au/whats-the-significance-of-australias-new-security-treaty-with-solomon-islands/ (retrieved 14 May 2019)

Battersby, P., and Siracusa, J., 2009, *Globalization and Human Security*, Rowman & Littlefield Publishers, Plymouth, UK

Belshaw, C.S., 1964, *Under the Ivi Tree: Society and Economic Development in Rural Fiji*, Routledge & Kegan Paul, London

Bennett, J., 1987, *Wealth of the Solomons: A History of a Pacific Archipelago, 1800–1978*, Pacific Islands Monographs Series, No. 3, University of Hawai'i Press, Honolulu

—— 2002, 'Roots of conflict in Solomon Islands: Legacies of tradition and colonialism', Discussion paper 2002/5, State, Society and Governance in Melanesia project, The Australian National University, Canberra

Bergreen, L., 2004, *Over the Edge of the World: Magellan's Terrifying Circumnavigation of the Globe*, Harper Collins, London

Berling, T., 2011, 'Science and securitization: Objectivation, the authority of the speaker and mobilization of scientific facts', *Security Dialogue*, 42(4–5): 385–97. doi.org/10.1177/0967010611418714

Bessis, S., 2003, *Western Supremacy: The Triumph*, Zed Books, London

Best, S., 1993, 'At the halls of the mountain kings: Fijian and Samoan fortifications: Comparison and analysis', *Journal of the Polynesian Society*, 102(4): 385–448

Bigo, D., 2000, 'When two become one: Internal and external securitisations in Europe', in *International Relations Theory and the Politics of European Integration*, ed. M. Kelstrup and M.C. Williams (pp. 171–203), Routledge, London

Bilgin, P., 2011, 'The politics of studying securitization? The Copenhagen School in Turkey', *Security Dialogue*, 42(4–5): 399–412. doi.org/10.1177/0967010611418711

Black, C., 1966, *The Dynamics of Modernization: A Study in Comparative History*, Harper & Row, New York

Blaker, J., 1990, *United States Overseas Basing: An Anatomy of the Dilemma*, Praeger, New York

Blanchard, E., 2003, 'Gender, international relations, and the development of feminist security theory', *Signs: Journal of Women in Culture and Society*, 28(4): 1289–1312 doi.org/10.1086/368328

Booth, K., 1991, 'Security and emancipation', *Review of International Relations*, 17: 313–26 www.jstor.org/stable/20097269

Bott, E., 1981, 'Power and rank in the Kingdom of Tonga', *Journal of the Polynesian Society*, 90(1): 7–81

Bourdieu, P., 1977, *Outline of a Theory of Practice*, Cambridge University Press, Cambridge and New York

—— 1984, *Distinction: A Social Critique of the Judgement of Taste*, Routledge, London

—— 1990, *The Logic of Practice*, Polity Press, London

Braithwaite, J., Dinnen, S., Allen, M., and Charlesworth, H., 2010, *Pillars and Shadows: State Building as Peace Building in Solomon Islands*, ANU E Press, Canberra

Brewster, A., 1922, *The Hill Tribes of Fiji*, J.B. Lippincott, Philadelphia

Bromley, M., Cooper, N., and Holtom, P., 2012, 'The UN Arms Trade Treaty: Arms export controls, the human security agenda and the lessons of history', *International Affairs*, 88(5): 1029–48. doi.org/10.1111/j.1468-2346.2012.01117.x

Brooks, D., 2010, 'What is security: Definition through knowledge categorization', *Security Journal*, 23(3): 225–39. doi.org/10.1057/sj.2008.18

Brown, S., 1998, *From Fiji to the Balkans: History of the Fiji Police*, Fiji Police Force, Suva

Brown, T., 2004, 'The role of religious communities in peacemaking: The Solomon Islands', *Anglican Religious Life Journal*, 1: 8–18

Bryar, T., Bello, V., and Corendea, C., 2015, *Promoting Human Security and Minimizing Conflict Associated with Forced Migration in the Pacific Region*, United Nations University, Barcelona

Burke, A., Lee-Koo, K., and McDonald, M., 2016, 'An ethics of global security', *Journal of Global Security Studies*, 1(1): 64–79. doi.org/10.1093/jogss/ogv004

Burt, B., 2001, *Tradition and Christianity: The Colonial Transformation of a Solomon Islands Society*, Harwood Academic Publishers, Amsterdam

Buzan, B., Wæver, O., and De Wilde, J., 1998, *Security: A New Framework for Analysis*, Lynne Rienner Publishers, Boulder, CO

Byrne, P., 2000, 'Solomon Islands peace agreement entrenches ethnic division', World Socialist Web Site, 24 October, www.wsws.org/en/articles/2000/10/solo-o24.html (retrieved 6 May 2019)

Cahill, K. (ed.), 2004, *Human Security for All: A Tribute to Sergio Vieira de Mello*, Fordham University Press and Center for International Health and Cooperation, New York

Call, C.T., 2008, 'The fallacy of the "failed state"', *Third World Quarterly*, 29(8): 1491–1507. doi.org/10.1080/01436590802544207

Calvert, J., 2003 [1858], *Fiji and the Fijians*, vol. 2: *Mission History*, Fiji Museum, Suva

Campbell, I., 1980, 'The historiography of Charles Savage', *Journal of the Polynesian Society*, 89(2): 143–66

—— 2011a, *Tonga's Way to Democracy*, Herodotus Press, Christchurch

—— 2011b, *Worlds Apart: A History of the Pacific Islands*, 2nd edn, Canterbury University Press, Christchurch

—— 2012, 'Statement of evidence of Ian Christopher Campbell on behalf of the plaintiffs', Case number CV 80/2008 (case regarding insurance claims for the 2006 riots in Tonga)

—— 2015, *Island Kingdom: Tonga Ancient and Modern*, Canterbury University Press, Christchurch

Chandler, D., 2012, 'Resilience and human security: The post-interventionist paradigm', *Security Dialogue*, 43(3): 213–29. doi.org/10.1177/0967010612 444151

Chappelle, A.J., 1970, 'Sir Everard im Thurn's policy of individualism for Fijians', *Fiji Society*, 12: 51–68

Chene, M., 2017, 'Solomon Islands: An overview of corruption and anti-corruption', U4 Anti-Corruption Resources Center, Michelsen Institute, Norway

Chomsky, N., 2006, *Failed States: The Abuse of Power and the Assault on Democracy*, Penguin, London

Choong, C., Jayaraman, T., and Kumar, R., 2011, 'The role of remittances in small Pacific Island economies: An empirical study of Fiji', *International Journal of Economics and Business*, 3(5): 526–42

Citizens Constitutional Forum (CCF), 2013, *An Analysis: The 2013 Fiji Government Constitution*, Fiji Constitutional Forum, Suva

Clements, K., Boege, V., Brown, A., Foley, W., and Nolan, A., 2007, 'State building reconsidered: The role of hybridity in the formation of political order', *Political Science*, 59(1): 45–56. doi.org/10.1177/003231870705900106

Clunie, F., 1977, *Fijian Weapons and Warfare*, Fiji Museum, Suva

Collier, P., and Hoeffler, A., 2002, *Greed and Grievance in Civil War*, Policy research working paper, World Bank, Washington, DC

Colony of Fiji, 1876, Ordinance No. XXX, 19 December, Colony of Fiji, Levuka

—— 1906, Fiji Rifle Association Ordinance, Colony of Fiji, Suva

Connell, J., 1981, 'Independence, dependence and fragmentation in the Pacific', *GeoJournal*, 5(6): 583–8. www.jstor.org/stable/41142630

Copeland, D., 1996, 'Economic interdependence and war: A theory of trade expectations', *International Security*, 20(4): 5–41. doi.org/10.1162/isec.20.4.5

Corendea, C., 2012, 'Human security in the Pacific: The climate refugees of the sinking islands', PhD thesis, Golden Gate University School of Law, digitalcommons.law.ggu.edu/theses/32

Corris, P., 1970, 'Passage, port and plantation: A history of Solomon Islands labour migration, 1870–1914', PhD thesis, The Australian National University, Canberra

Court of Appeal, 2009a, 'Court of Appeal Decision on trial of Pohiva, Pulu, Edwards, Uata and Taunisila', Nuku'alofa

—— 2009b, 'Judgement', Tonga Supreme Court paper, 9 September, Tonga

Cox, J., Bhatt, M., Hill, M., and Wedderburn, L., 2017, 'National security implications of climate change: Human security in the South Pacific', Submission to the Senate inquiry into Implications of climate change for Australia's national security, Peacifica, Petersham, NSW

Cox, R., 1996, 'Social forces, states and world orders: Beyond international relations theory', *Millennium—Journal of International Studies*, 10: 126–55 doi.org/10.1177/03058298810100020501

Crean, S., 2009, 'Our Pacific agenda: The opportunity of PACER Plus', speech at Lowy Institute conference, 'Pacific Islands in the World', Brisbane. trademinister.gov.au/speeches/2009/090802_lowy.html

Crocombe, R., 2001, *The South Pacific*, Institute of Pacific Studies, University of the South Pacific, Suva

—— 2005, *Asia in the Pacific Islands: Replacing the West*, Institute of Pacific Studies, Suva

D'Arcy, P., 2003, 'Cultural divisions and island environments since the time of Dumont d'Urville', *Journal of Pacific History*, 38(2): 217–35. doi.org/10.1080/0022334032000120549

d'Hauteserre, A., 2011, 'Politics of imaging New Caledonia', *Annals of Tourism Research*, 38(2): 380–402. doi.org/10.1016/j.annals.2010.09.004

Daly, M., 2009, *Tonga: A New Biography*, University of Hawai'i Press, Honolulu

Darwin, C., 1859, *On the Origin of Species by Means of Natural Selection, or the Preservation of Favoured Races in the Struggle for Life*, John Murray, London

Davies, S., 2017, 'Rememering the human in Asia-Pacific human security', *Australian Journal Journal of International Affairs*, 71(1): 16–19. doi.org/10.1080/10357718.2016.1243224

Dawea, E., and Canon, J., 2017, 'Corruption drives dealings with logging companies in the Solomon Islands', news.mongabay.com/2017/05/corruption-drives-dealings-with-logging-companies-in-the-solomon-islands (retrieved 6 May 2019)

Department of Foreign Affairs and Trade (DFAT), Australia, 2014, 'Development assistance in the Pacific'. www.dfat.gov.au/geo/pacific/development-assistance/Pages/effective-governance-pacific-regional.aspx (retrieved 6 May 2019)

Dobell, G., 2007, 'The arc of instability: The history of an idea', in *History as Policy: Framing the Debate on the Future of Australian Defence*, ed. R. Huisken and M. Thatcher (pp. 85–104), ANU E Press, Canberra

Donnelly, B., 2011, 'Homegrown Australian Muslim terrorist cell', *Australian Islamist Monitor*, 19 June. islammonitor.org/index.php?option=com_content&id=4405:homegrown-australian-muslim-terrorist-cell (retrieved 6 May 2019)

Dorling, D., 2015, *Inequality and the 1%*, Verso, London

Dornan, M., 2013, 'Pacific Islands Development Forum launch in Fiji', Devpolicy. www.devpolicy.org/pacific-islands-development-forum-launch-in-fiji-20130813/ (retrieved 9 January 2019)

Dornan, M., and J. Pryke, 2017, 'Foreign aid to the Pacific: Trends and developments in the twenty-first century', *Asia and the Pacific Policy Studies*, 4: 386–404 doi.org/10.1002/app5.185

Downer, A., 2003a, doorstop interview, Parliament House, 25 June. www.dfat.gov.au/media/transcripts/2003/030625_doorstop.html (retrieved 13 July 2014)

—— 2003b, 'No quick fix for troubled Solomon Islands', *Pacific Islands Report*, 1 August. www.pireport.org/articles/2003/01/08/no-quick-fix-troubled-solomons (retrieved 6 May 2019)

Dumont d'Urville, J., 2003 [1823], 'On the islands of the great ocean', trans. I. Ollivier, A. de Biran and G. Clark, in 'Dumont d'Urville's oceanic provinces: Fundamental precepts or arbitrary constructs?', ed. G. Clark, Special Issue, *Journal of Pacific History*, 38(2): 163–74. doi.org/10.1080/0022334032000120512

Duncan, R., 2008, *Pacific Trade Issues*, Asian Development Bank, Manila

—— 2016, 'Source of growth spurts in Pacific islands economies', *Asia and the Pacific Policy Studies*, 3(2): 351–65. doi.org/10.1002/app5.125

Durodie, B., 2010, 'Human security – a retrospective', *Global Change*, 22(3): 385–90. doi.org/10.1080/14781158.2010.510274

Durutalo, S., 1986, *The Paramountcy of Fijian Interest and the Politicization of Ethnicity*, USP Sociological Society, Suva

Edmond, R., and Smith, V., 2003, *Islands in History and Representation*, Taylor & Francis, London

Edwards, A., and Ferstman, C. (ed.), 2010, *Human Security and Non-Citizens: Law, Policy and International Affairs*, Cambridge University Press, New York

Elbe, S., 2006, 'Should HIV/AIDS be securitized? The ethical dilemmas linking HIV/AIDS and security', *International Studies Quarterly*, 50(1): 119–44. www.jstor.org/stable/3693554

Enloe, C., 1980, *Ethnic Soldiers: State Security in Divided Societies*, University of Georgia Press, Athens, GA

Fanon, F., 1963, *The Wretched of the Earth*, Grove Press, New York

—— 1967, *Black Skin White Masks*, Grove Press, New York

Field, J., 1998, 'Natural and constructed defenses in Fijian fortifications', *Asia Perspective*, 37(1): 32–58. www.jstor.org/stable/42928420

Fiji Constitution Commission, 2012, draft constitution, Fiji Constitution Commission, Suva

Fiji Government, 1955, Army Act, Fiji Government, Suva

—— 1961 (revised 1985), Army Act, Fiji Government, Suva

—— 1966, Fiji Police Act, Fiji Government, Suva

—— 1970, *Fiji Constitution*, Fiji Government, Suva

—— 1990, *The Constitution of the Republic of Fiji Islands*, Fiji Government, Suva

—— 1997, *The Constitution of the Republic of Fiji Islands*, Fiji Government, Suva

—— 2002, *20-Year Development Plan (2001–2020) for the Enhancement of Participation of Indigenous Fijians and Rotumans in the Socio-economic Development of Fiji*, Fiji Government, Suva

—— 2008, *The People's Charter*, Fiji Government, Suva

—— 2013, *The Constitution of the Republic of Fiji*, Fiji Government, Suva

Filer, C., McDonnell, S., and Allen, M., 2017, *Powers of Exclusion in Melanesia. Custom Property and Ideology: Land Transformations in Melanesia*, ANU Press, Canberra

Firth, S., 1987, *Nuclear Playground*, University of Hawaii Press, Honolulu

—— 1989, 'Sovereignty and independence in the contemporary Pacific', *Contemporary Pacific*, 1(1): 75–96. www.jstor.org/stable/23701893

—— 2013, 'New developments in the international relations of the Pacific', *Journal of Pacific History*, 48(3): 286–92. doi.org/10.1080/00223344.2013.812545

Fischer, S., 2013, *A History of the Pacific Islands*, Macmillan Education, London

Fisher, D., 2013, *France in the Pacific*, ANU Press, Canberra

—— 2018, 'New Caledonia votes to stay with France this time but independence supporters take heart', *The Conversation*, theconversation.com/new-caledonia-votes-to-stay-with-france-this-time-but-independence-supporters-take-heart-106329 (retrieved 4 January 2019)

Fisk, E.K., 1970, *The Political Economy of Independent Fiji*, A.H. & A.W. Reed, Wellington

Fisk, E.K. (ed.), 1978, *The Adaptation of Traditional Agriculture: Socio-economic Problems of Urbanization*, Australian National University Press, Canberra

Floyd, R., 2011, 'Can securitization theory be used in normative analysis? Towards a just securitization theory', *Security Dialogue*, 42(4/5): 427–39. doi.org/10.1177/0967010611418712

Fonua, P., 2006, 'One month on: How tension erupted into Tonga's day of mob violence', *Matangi Tonga*, 6 December

—— 2008, 'PM renews public order proclamation for 16th month', *Matangi Tonga*, 30 January

—— 2014, 'Tonga's PM election set for Dec 29', *Matangi Tonga*, 23 October

Foucault, M., 1991, *Discipline and Punish: The Birth of a Prison*, Penguin, London

—— 1998, *The History of Sexuality: The Will to Knowledge*, Penguin, London

Fraenkel, J., 2004, 'The coming anarchy in Oceania? A critique of the "Africanisation" of the South Pacific thesis', *Commonwealth and Comparative Politics*, 42(1): 1–34. doi.org/10.1080/14662040408565567

Fraenkel, J., and Firth, S. (eds), 2007, *From Election to Coup in Fiji: The 2006 Campaign and its Aftermath*, ANU E Press, Canberra

Fraenkel, J., Firth, S., and Lal, B.V., 2009, *The 2006 Military Takeover in Fiji: A Coup to End All Coups*, ANU E Press, Canberra

Fraenkel, J., Madraiwiwi, J., and Okole, H., 2014, *The RAMSI Decade: A Review of the Regional Assistance Mission to Solomon Islands, 2003–2013*. www.eastwest center.org/sites/default/files/filemanager/pidp/pdf/Independent%20RAMSI %20Review%20Report%20Final.pdf (retrieved 6 May 2019)

France, P., 1966, 'The Kaunitoni migration', *Journal of Pacific History*, 1(1): 107–13. www.jstor.org/stable/25167866

—— 1969, *The Charter of the Land: Custom and Colonization in Fiji*, Oxford University Press, Melbourne

Frazer, I., 1990, 'Maasina rule and Solomon Islands labor history', in *Labor in the South Pacific*, ed. C. Moore, J. Leckie and D. Munro (pp. 191–203), James Cook University of North Queensland, Townsville

Fredrickson, G., 2000, *The Comparative Imagination: On the History of Racism, Nationalism and Social Movements*, University of California Press, Berkeley

Fry, G., 1997, 'Framing the islands: Knowledge and power in changing Australian images of "the South Pacific"', *Contemporary Pacific*, 9(2): 148–61. hdl.handle. net/10125/13168

Fry, G., and Kabutaulaka, T. (eds), 2008, *Intervention and State-Building in the Pacific: The Legitimacy of Cooperative Intervention*, Manchester University Press, Manchester

Fry, G., and Tarte, S., 2015, *The New Pacific Diplomacy*, ANU Press, Canberra

Fukuyama, F., 1992, *The End of History and the Last Man*, Avon Books, Los Angeles

—— 1995, 'Reflections on the end of history, five years later', *History and Theory*, 34(2): 27–43. doi.org/10.2307/2505433

Fullilove, M., 2009, 'The case for Australia's UN Security Council bid', Lowy Institute report. www.files.ethz.ch/isn/106873/LPer_FulliloveSept.pdf

Gad, U.P., and Petersen, K.L., 2011, 'Concepts of politics in securitization studies', *Security Dialogue*, 42(4–5): 315–28. doi.org/10.1177/0967010611418716

Gamage, S., 2015, 'Globalization, neoliberal reforms and inequality: A review of conceptual tools, competing discourses, responses and alternatives', *Journal of Developing Societies*, 31(1): 8–27. doi.org/10.1177/0169796X14562126

Gascoigne, J., 2014, *Encountering the Pacific in the Age of Enlightenment*, Cambridge University Press, Cambridge

Geraghty, P., 1994, 'Linguistic evidence for Tongan empire', in *Trends in Linguistics: Language Contacts and Trends in the Austronesian World*, ed. T. Dutton and D. Tryon (pp. 233–49), Mouton de Gruyter, New York

Gillion, K.I., 1962, *Fiji's Indian Migrants: A History to the End of Indenture in 1920*, Oxford University Press, Melbourne

Giroux, H., 2007, *University in Chains: Confronting the Military–Industrial–Academic Complex*, Paradigm, New York

Government of Tonga, 1988a, Emergency Powers Act, Kingdom of Tonga, Nuku'alofa

—— 1988b, Public Order Preservation Act, Kingdom of Tonga, Nuku'alofa

—— 1992, Tonga Defence Services Act, Kingdom of Tonga, Nuku'alofa

—— 2010a, *Constitution of Tonga*, Government of Tonga, Nuku'alofa

—— 2010b, Household and Income Survey, Government of Tonga, Nuku'alofa

Gramsci, A., 1971, *Selection from Prison Notebooks*, Lawrence & Wishart, London

—— 2012, *Selections from Cultural Writings*, Haymarket Books, Chicago

Grant, R., and Newland, K. (eds), 1991, *Gender and International Relations*, Open University Press, Milton Keynes

Green, M.E., 2011, 'Rethinking the subaltern and the question of censorship in Gramsci's prison notebooks', *Postcolonial Studies*, 14(4): 385–402. doi.org/ 10.1080/13688790.2011.641913

Green Climate Fund (GCF), 2017, 'Projects and programmes', www.green climate.fund/what-we-do/projects-programmes

Grynberg, R., 2010, 'Forum runs amok', *Islands Business International Magazine*, November. www.pina.com.fj/print.php?print=news&o=15686685174cd350 482e36e86f678b

—— 2014, 'Pacific Islands Forum meeting—of people and power', 1 August, islandsbusiness.com/archives/item/1191-pacific-islands-forum-meeting-of-people-and-power.html (retrieved 7 May 2019)

Guzzini, S., 2011, 'Securitization as a causal mechanism', *Security Dialogue*, 42(4–5): 329–42. doi.org/10.1177/0967010611419000

Hall, S., 1973, *Encoding and Decoding in the Television Discourse*, Centre for Cultural Studies, University of Birmingham, Birmingham

—— 1996, *The West-and-the-Rest: Discourse and Power in Modernity*, Blackwell Publishers, Cambridge, MA

Hampson, F.O., and Penny, C.K., 2008, 'Human security', in *The Oxford Handbook on the United Nations*, ed. S. Daws and T.G. Weiss, Oxford University Press, New York

Hau'ofa, E., 1975, 'Anthropology and Pacific Islanders', *Oceania*, 45: 283–9

Hayes, P., Zarsky, L., and Bellow, W., 1987, *American Lake: Nuclear Peril in the Pacific*, Penguin, New York

Hempenstall, P., and Rutherford, N., 1984, *Protest and Dissent in the Colonial Pacific*, Institute of Pacific Studies, University of the South Pacific, Suva

Henderson, J., and Watson, G., 2005, *Securing a Peaceful Pacific*, University of Canterbury Press, Christchuch

Henningham, S., 1995, *The Pacific Island States: Security and Sovereignty in the Post-Cold War World*, Macmillan Press, London

Herda, P., 2008, 'Gender, rank and power in 18th-century Tonga: The case of Tupoumoheofo', *Journal of Pacific History*, 22(4): 195–208. doi.org/10.1080/00223348708572568

Herda, P., Terrell, J., and Gunson, N. (eds), 1990, *Tongan Culture and History*, Journal of Pacific History, Canberra

Herman, E.S., and Chomsky, N., 1988, *Manufacturing Consent*, Pantheon Books, New York

Hezel, F., 2013, *Micronesia on the Move*, East West Center, Honolulu

Hocart, A., 1913, 'On the meaning of the Fijian word Turaga', *Man*, 13: 140–3

Hodgson, G., 2004, 'Social Darwinism in Anglophone academic journals: A contribution to the history of the term', *Historical Sociology* 17(4): 428–63. doi.org/10.1111/j.1467-6443.2004.00239

Horowitz, D., 1985, *Ethnic Groups in Conflict*, University of California Press, Berkeley

Hough, R., 2003, *Captain James Cook*, Hodder & Stoughton, Sydney

Hove, K., Kiste, R., and Lal, B. (ed.), 1994, *Tides of History: The Pacific in the 20th Century*, University of Hawaii Press, Honolulu

Howard-Hassmann, R.E., 2012, 'Human security: Undermining human rights?', *Human Rights Quarterly*, 34(1): 88–112. www.jstor.org/stable/41345472

Hunter, R., and Lal, V., 2012, 'Fiji police chief tried to get Bainimarama arrested in NZ', *New Zealand Herald*, 18 February. www.nzherald.co.nz/nz/news/article.cfm?c_id=1&objectid=10786336 (retrieved 7 May 2019)

Huntington, S., 1965, 'Political development and political decay', *World Politics*, 17(3): 386–430. doi.org/10.2307/2009286

—— 1993, 'The clash of civilizations?', *Foreign Affairs*, 72(2): 22–49. doi.org/10.2307/20045621

Huysmans, J., 2006, *The Politics of Insecurity: Fear, Migration and Asylum in the EU*, Routledge, London

—— 2011, 'What's in an act? On security speech acts and little security nothings', *Security Dialogue*, 42(4–5): 371–84. doi.org/10.1177/0967010611418713

Hviding, E., and Baines, G., 1994, 'Community-based fisheries management, tradition and the challenges of development in Marovo, Solomon Islands', *Development and Change*, 25(1): 13–39. doi.org/10.1111/j.1467-7660.1994.tb00508

Jardine, M., 2002, *East Timor: Genocide in Paradise*, Odonian Press, New York

Jenkins, R., 2008, *Rethinking Ethnicity: Arguments and Explorations*, 2nd edn, Sage Publications, London

Jones, R., 2001, 'Introduction: Locating critical international relations theory', in *Critical Theory and World Politics*, ed. R. Jones (pp. 5–10), Lynne Rienner Publishers, London

Jourdan, C., 1995, 'Stepping-stones to national consciousness: The Solomon Islands case', in *Nation Making: Emergent Identities in Postcolonial Melanesia*, ed. R.J. Foster (pp. 127–50), University of Michigan Press, Ann Arbor

Jussim, L., 2012, *Social Perception and Social Reality: Why Accuracy Dominates Bias and Self-fulfilling Prophesy*, Oxford University Press, Oxford

Kabutaulaka, T., 2001, *Beyond Ethnicity: The Political Economy of the Guadalcanal Crisis in Solomon Islands*, Working Paper 01/01, State, Society and Governance in Melanesia Project, The Australian National University, Canberra

—— 2015, 'Re-presenting Melanesia: Ignoble savages and Melanesian alternatives [sic]', *Contemporary Pacific*, 27(1): 110–145. hdl.handle.net/10125/38767

Kaldor, M., 2013, *New and Old Wars: Organized Violence in a Global Era*, 3rd edn, Polity Press, Oxford

Kaliber, A., 2005, 'Securing the ground through securitized "foreign" policy: The Cyprus case', *Security Dialogue*, 36(3): 319–37. doi.org/10.1177/0967010605057019

Kaplan, M., 1995, *Neither Cargo Nor Cult: Ritual Politics and the Colonial Imagination in Fiji*, Duke University Press, London

Kayser, M., Choi, Y., Oven, M., Brauer, S., Trent, R., Suarkia, D., Schiefenhovel, W., and Stoneking, M., 2008, 'The impact of the Austronesian expansion: Evidence from mtDNA and Y chromosome diversity in the Admiralty Islands of Melanesia', *Molecular Biology and Evolution*, 25(7): 1362–74. doi.org/10.1093/molbev/msn078

Keen, D., 2000, 'Incentives and disincentives for violence', in *Greed and Grievance: Economic Agendas in Civil Wars*, ed. M. Berdal and D. Malone (pp. 19–43), Lynne Rienner Publishers, Boulder, CO

Keesing, R., 1978, 'Politico-religious movements and anticolonialism on Malaita: Maasina rule in historical perspective', *Oceania*, 48(4): 241–61. www.jstor.org/stable/40330393

Keesing, R., and Corris, P., 1980, *Lightning Meets the West Wind: The Malaita Massacre*, Oxford University Press, Melbourne

Keown, M., 2005, *Postcolonial Pacific Writing: Representation of the Body*, Routledge, New York

Kingdom of Tonga, 1875, Constitution of the Kingdom of Tonga, Kingdom of Tonga, Nuku'alofa

Lal, B., 1998, *Another Way: The Politics of Constitutional Reform in Post-Coup Fiji*, NCDS Asia Pacific Press, Canberra

—— 2004, *Girmitiyas: The Origins of the Fiji Indians*, Fiji Institute of Applied Studies, Suva

Lamy, S., 2008, 'Contemporary mainstream approaches: Neo-realism and neo-liberalism', in *The Globalization of World Politics: An Introduction to International Relations*, ed. J. Baylis and S. Smith (pp. 114–29), Oxford University Press, Oxford

Lange, D., 2004, 'Nuclear weapons are morally indefensible', *Public Address*, 14 October, publicaddress.net/great-new-zealand-argument/nuclear-weapons-are-morally-indefensible/ (retrieved 7 May 2019)

Laracy, H., 1983, *Pacific Protest: The Maasina Rule Movement, Solomon Islands, 1944–1952*, Institute of Pacific Studies, University of the South Pacific, Suva

Large, J., Austin, R., and International Institute for Democracy and Electoral Assistance (ed.), 2006, *Democracy, Conflict and Human Security*, International Institute for Democracy and Electoral Assistance, Stockholm

Leadbeater, H., 2018, *See No Evil: New Zealand's Betrayal of the People of West Papua*, University of Otago Press, Dunedin

Le Bon, G., 1895, *The Crowd: A Study of the Popular Mind*, T. Fisher Unwin, London

Lerner, D., 1965, *The Passing of Traditional Society: Modernizing the Middle East*, Free Press, New York

Lockwood, V. (ed.), 2003, *Globalization and Cultural Change in the Pacific Islands*, Prentice Hall, New York

Lozada, C., 2017, 'Samuel Huntington, a prophet for the Trump era', *Church and State*, 18 July. churchandstate.org.uk/2017/07/samuel-huntington-a-prophet-for-the-trump-era/

Lucker, V., and Dinnen, S. (eds), 2010, *Civic Insecurity: Law, Order and HIV in Papua New Guinea*, ANU E Press, Canberra

Lynch, J., Ross, M., and Crowley, T., 2002, *The Oceanic Languages*, Curzon Press, London

Lyons, K., 2018, 'Huge increase in Chinese aid pledge to Pacific', *Guardian*, 9 August. www.theguardian.com/world/2018/aug/08/huge-increase-in-chinese-aid-pledged-to-pacific (retrieved 8 May 2019)

McKinnon, D., 2005, 'Foreword', in *Securing a Peaceful Pacific*, ed. J. Henderson and G. Watson (p. xi), University of Canterbury Press, Christchurch

Maclellan, N., 2011, 'Hot potatoes for Pacific trade policies', *Interpreter*, 16 May. www.lowyinstitute.org/the-interpreter/hot-potatoes-pacific-trade-policy (retrieved 7 May 2019)

—— 2015, 'Grappling with the bomb: Opposition to Pacific nuclear testing in the 1950s', Proceedings of the 14th Biennial Labour History Conference (pp. 21–38), ed. P. Deery and J. Kimber, Australian Society for the Study of Labour History, Melbourne

—— 2018, *Grappling with the Bomb: Britain's Pacific H-Bomb*, ANU Press, Canberra

McLeod, L., 2015, *Gender Politics and Security Discourse: Personal–Political Imaginations and Feminism in 'Post-Conflict' Serbia*, Routledge, London

Macnaught, T., 2016, *The Fijian Colonial Experience: A Study of the Neotraditional Order under British Colonial Rule Prior to World War II*, ANU Press, Canberra

Mae, P., 2010, 'Constitutional reforms in Solomon Islands: An analysis of public participation in the reform process', paper presented at conference, Turmoil and Turbulence in Small Developing States: Going Beyond Survival, Sir Arthur Lewis Institute of Social and Economic Studies, University of the West Indies

Maebuta, J., 2012, 'Peace education and peace-building in the Solomon Islands: Disconnected layers', *Security Challenges*, 8(4): 93–104. www.jstor.org/stable/26462894

Manoa, F., 2015, 'The new Pacific diplomacy at the United Nations: The rise of the PSIDS', in *The New Pacific Diplomacy* (pp. 89–98), ed. G. Fry and S. Tarte, ANU Press, Canberra

Marcelles, L., 2011, *From Noble Savage to Colonial Subject: Tahiti in Eighteenth-Century French Literature*, BiblioBazaar, Charleston, SC

Martin, A., 2008, 'The Enlightenment in paradise: Bougainville, Tahiti, and the duty of desire', *Eighteenth Century Studies*, 41(2): 203–16. www.jstor.org/stable/30053536

Martin, M., and Owen, T., 2010, 'The second generation of human security: Lessons from the UN and EU experience', *International Affairs*, 86(1): 211–24. doi.org/10.1111/j.1468-2346.2010.00876

Mason, M., 2015, 'Climate change and human security: The international governance and structures, policies and instruments', in *Handbook on Climate Change and Human Security* (pp. 382–401), ed. M.R. Redcliff and M. Grasso, Edward Edgar, London

Matangi Tonga, 1998, 'Akilisi acquitted on defamation charges', 27 April, matangitonga.to/1998/04/27/akilisi-acquitted-defamation-charges (retrieved 7 May 2019)

Matavesi, L., 2006, Personal film of the 2006 Tongan riots, later used in court cases on damage claims

Matsuda, M., 2012, *Pacific Worlds: A History of Seas, Peoples and Cultures*, Cambridge University Press, Cambridge

Maude, H., 1964, 'Beachcombers and castaways', *Journal of the Polynesian Society*, 73(3): 254–93. www.jps.auckland.ac.nz/document//Volume_73_1964/Volume_73%2C_No._3/Beachcombers_and_castaways%2C_by_H._E._Maude%2C_p_254_-_293/p1

Mearsheimer, J., 2014, *The Tragedy of Great Power Politics*, W.W. Norton & Company, New York

Meleisea, M., 1987, *A History of Western Samoa*, Institute of Pacific Studies, Suva

Mills, C.W., 1959, *The Sociological Imagination*, Oxford University Press, London

Mishra, S., 2011, 'In and out of time: Stagered duration and colonial policy in Fiji', in *Imagined Communities Revisited: Critical Essays on Asia-Pacific Literatures and Cultures*, ed. N. Manaf and M. Quayam (pp. 134–41), IIUM Press, Kuala Lumpur

Moore, C., 2004, *Happy Isles in Crisis: The Historical Causes for a Failing State in Solomon Islands, 1998–2004*, Asia-Pacific Press, Canberra

Moorehead, A., 1990 [1966], *The Fatal Impact, 1767–1840*, Harper Collins, London

Munoz, M.M., 2010, 'Global justice and human security in the context of climate change', *Isegoria* (43): 589–604

Naitoro, J., 2000, *Solomon Islands Conflict: Demands for Historical Rectification and Restorative Justice*, Update papers, Asia Pacific School of Economics and Management, The Australian National University, Canberra

Narayan, J., 1984, *The Political Economy of Fiji*, South Pacific Review Press, Suva

National Committee for Political Reform, 2006, *Report on Tonga's Constitutional Reform*, NCPR, Nukualofa

Nawadra, T., 1995, *Ai matai Malaya*, Fiji Military Forces, Suva

Nay, O., 2012, 'Fragile and failed states: Critical perspectives on conceptual hybrids', paper prepared for 22nd IPSA World Congress of Political Science, Madrid

Nayacakalou, R., 1975, *Leadership in Fiji*, Oxford University Press, Melbourne

Neal, A.W., 2006, 'Foucault in Guantánamo: Towards an archaeology of the exception', *Security Dialogue*, 37(1): 31–46. doi.org/10.1177/0967010606064135

Nelles, W. (ed.), 2003, *Comparative Education, Terrorism, and Human Security Electronic Resource: From Critical Pedagogy to Peace Building?*, Palgrave Macmillan, New York

Newbury, C., 2011, 'History, hermeneutics and Fijian ethnic "paramountcy"', *Journal of Pacific History*, 46(1): 27–57. www.jstor.org/stable/41343775

Newland, L., 2007, 'The role of the Assembly of Christian Churches in Fiji in the 2006 election', in *From Election to Coup in Fiji: The 2006 Campaign and Its Aftermath*, ed. J. Fraenkel and S. Firth (pp. 300–14), ANU Press, Canberra

Newman, E., 2011, 'A human security peace-building agenda', *Third World Quarterly*, 32(10): 1737–56. doi.org/10.1080/01436597.2011.610568

New Zealand Herald, 2006, 'Laughing and looting as Tonga's capital burns', 16 November. www.nzherald.co.nz/nz/news/article.cfm?c_id=1&objectid= 10411218 (retrieved 8 May 2019)

New Zealand Ministry of Foreign Affairs and Trade (NZMFAT), 2012, 'Aid programs'. www.mfat.govt.nz/en/aid-and-development/ (retrieved 8 May 2019)

—— 2014, 'Aid programs'. www.aid.govt.nz/about-aid-programme/aid-statistics/ aid-allocations-201213-201415

—— 2017, 'PACER Plus'. www.mfat.govt.nz/en/trade/free-trade-agreements/ agreements-under-negotiation/pacer/ (retrieved 8 May 2019)

Nicole, R., 2006, *Disturbing History: Resistance in Early Colonial Fiji*, University of Hawai'i Press, Honolulu

Norton, R., 1977, *Race and Politics in Fiji*, University of Queensland Press, Brisbane

Pacific Islands Forum (PIF), 1992, 'Honiara Declaration', www.forumsec.org/ wp-content/uploads/2017/11/HONIARA-Declaration.pdf

—— 1997, 'Aitutaki Declaration on regional security cooperation', Suva. www. forumsec.org/wp-content/uploads/2017/11/AITUTAKI-Declaration.pdf

—— 2000, 'Biketawa Declaration'. www.ramsi.org/wp-content/uploads/2014/ 07/Biketawa-Declaration.pdf

—— 2001, Nasonini Declaration. www.forumsec.org/wp-content/uploads/ 2017/11/Nasonini-Declaration.pdf

—— 2005, *Pacific Plan*, PIF, Suva

—— 2009, 'Human security framework', www.forumsec.org/pages.cfm/political- governance-security/human-security-framework/?printerfriendly=true

Pacific Islands Forum Secretariat, 2018, Forty-ninth Pacific Island Forum, Forum communiqué, PIFS (18)10, 3–6 September, Yaren, Nauru

Pacnews, 2010, 'Pacific trade adviser concerned about independence', 27 January. www.pina.com.fj/index.php?p=pacnews&m=read&o=14332641644b5f8d 56014e4401dcda (retrieved 8 May 2019)

Pacific Islands News Association (PINA), 1998, 'Akilisi Pohiva convicted of defamation in Tonga', 3 April. ifex.org/tonga/1998/04/03/akilisi_pohiva_ convicted_of_defamation/ (retrieved 8 May 2019)

Pareti, S., 2014, 'PACER Plus nears conclusion, says chief trade adviser', *Islands Business,* www.islandsbusiness.com/archives/2016/item/1344-pacer-plus-nears-completion

Paris, R., 2001, 'Human security: Paradigm shift or hot air?', *International Security*, 26(2): 87–102. www.jstor.org/stable/3092123

Parsons, T., 1991 [1951], *The Social System*, Routledge, London

Peck, P., 2010, *Tales from Cannibal Isle: The Private Journals of an Anthropologist in Fiji*, Trafford Publishing, London

Peltonen, H., 2013, *International Responsibility and Grave Humanitarian Crises: Collective Provision for Human Security*, Routledge, Oxford

Perry, N., 2016, '"Moana" a Disney hit, but portrayal irks some in the Pacific', www.stuff.co.nz/entertainment/film/87051108/moana-a-disney-hit-but-portrayal-irks-some-in-the-pacific (retrieved 8 January 2019)

Pettigrew, T.F., and Tropp, L.R., 2006, 'A meta-analytic test of intergroup contact theory', *Journal of Personality and Social Psychology*, 90(5): 751–83. doi.org/ 10.1037/0022-3514.90.5.751

Picciotto, R., Olonisakin, F., and Clarke, M. (ed.), 2007, *Global Development and Human Security*, Transaction Publishers, New Brunswick

Pohiva, A., 2006, July, 'Letter to the General Secretary of the Pacific Island Forum'

—— 2007, 'Tongan Government refused to listen to people', Pacific Islands Report, PIDP East-West Center, Hawaii

Powles, G., 2007, 'Testing tradition in Tonga: Approaches to constitutional change', *Revue Juridique Polynésienne*, 13: 111–42. www.victoria.ac.nz/law/ research/publications/about-nzacl/publications/cljpjdcp-journals/volume-13,-2007/powles.pdf

Prasad, S. (ed.), 1989, *Coup and Crisis: Fiji—A Year Later*, Arena Publishers, Melbourne

Radio New Zealand, 2006a, 'Tonga MP says hundreds brutally beaten by soldiers', 28 November. www.rnz.co.nz/international/pacific-news/166432/tonga-mp-says-hundreds-brutally-beaten-by-soldiers

—— 2006b, 'Tonga passes emergency stop-and-search laws', 17 November. www.radionz.co.nz/news/latest/200611171722/tonga_passes_emergency_stop-and-search_laws

—— 2006c, 'Tongan military dismisses claims of abuse following riots', 29 November. www.radionz.co.nz/international/pacific-news/166449/tongan-military-dismisses-claims-of-abuse-following-riots

RAMSI Media Unit, 2016, 'West Loa youth told to dream big and work hard', 8 November

Ratuva, S., 2003, 'Reinventing the cultural wheel: Restorative justice in multi-ethnic Fiji', in *A Kind of Mending: Conflict and Restorative Justice in the Pacific*, ed. S. Dinnen, Pandanus Press, Canberra

—— 2004, 'Reconceptualizing contemporary Pacific islands states: Towards a syncretic approach', *New Pacific Review*, 2(1): 246–62

—— 2005, 'Political and ethnic identity in a post-colonial communal democracy: The case of Fiji', in *Ethnicity, Class and Nationalism: Caribbean and Extra-Caribbean Dimensions*, ed. A. Allahar (pp. 171–98), Lexington Books, Oxford

—— 2008, 'Australia's new assertiveness in the Pacific: A view from the "backyard"', in *Intervention and State-Building in the Pacific*, ed. G. Fry and T. Kabutaulaka (pp. 87–101), Manchester University Press, Manchester

—— 2010, 'Back to basics: Towards integrated social protection for vulnerable groups in Vanuatu', *Pacific Economic Bulletin*, 25(3): 40–63. hdl.handle.net/2292/14223

—— 2011a, 'The Fiji military coups: Reactive and transformative tendencies', *Journal of Asian Political Science*, 19(1): 96–120. doi.org/10.1080/02185377.2011.568249

—— 2011b, 'The gap between global thinking and local living: Dilemmas of constitutional reform in Nauru', *Journal of Polynesian Society*, 120(3): 241–68. hdl.handle.net/2292/10636

—— 2013, *Politics of Preferential Development: Trans-Global Study of Affirmative Action and Ethnic Conflict in Fiji, Malaysia and South Africa*, ANU Press, Canberra

—— 2014, 'A new regional cold war? American and Chinese posturing in the Pacific', *Asian and Pacific Policy Studies*, 1(2): 409–22. doi.org/10.1002/app5.38

—— 2015a, *Report of the Security Partnership Symposium, Organized by University of Canterbury and UNDP*, University of Canterbury and UNDP, Suva

—— 2015b, 'Triumph of living political martyr likely to ignite fresh Tongan reform hopes', Pacific Scoop, pacific.scoop.co.nz/2015/01/triumph-of-living-political-martyr-likely-to-ignite-tongan-reform-hopes/

—— 2017a, 'Anxiety and diminished hope: The potential impact of Trump's presidency on security in the Pacific islands region', *Round Table: The Commonwealth Journal of International Affairs*, 107: 165–73. doi.org/10.108 0/00358533.2017.1296711

—— 2017b, 'Country review of Tonga', *Journal of Contemporary Pacific*, 29(1): 181–8. doi.org/10.1353/cp.2017.0014

Ratuva, S., and Lawson, S., 2016, *The People have Spoken: The 2014 General Elections in Fiji*, ANU Press, Canberra

Ravuvu, A., 1991a, *The Facade of Democracy: Fijian Struggles for Political Control, 1874 to 1987*, Reader Publishing, Suva

—— 1991b, *Fijians at War*, Institute of Pacific Studies, University of the South Pacific, Suva

Reeves, P., Vakatora, T., and Lal, B., 1996, *The Fiji Islands. Towards a United Future: Report of the Fiji Constitutional Review Commission*, Fiji Government Printers, Suva

Reicher, S., Haslam, S.A., and Rath, R., 2008, 'Making a virtue of evil: A five-step social identity model of development of collective hate', *Social and Personality Psychology Compass*, 2/3: 1313–44. doi.org/10.1111/j.1751-9004.2008.00113.x

Reicher, S., Stott, C., Cronin, P., and Adang, O., 2004, 'An integrated approach to crowd psychology and public order policing', *Policing: An International Journal of Police Strategies and Management*, 27(4): 558–72. doi.org/10.1108/13639510410566271

Reid, A.C., 1990, *Tovata I and II*, Fiji Museum, Suva

Reilly, B., 2000, 'The Africanisation of the South Pacific', *Australian Journal of International Affairs*, 54(3): 261–8. doi.org/10.1080/00049910020012552

Republic of Fiji Military Forces (RFMF), 2012, Republic of Fiji Military Forces submission to the Constitutional Commission (copy in author's possession)

Richmond, O., 2011, 'De-romanticising the local, de-mystifying the international: Hybridity in Timor Leste and Solomon Islands', *Pacific Review*, 24(1): 115–36. doi.org/10.1080/09512748.2010.546873

Rigby, N., Van Der Merwe, P., and Williams, G., 2018, *Pacific Exploration: Voyages of Discovery from Cook's Endeavour to the Beagles*, Bloomsbury Publishing, London

Robertson, R., and Sutherland, W., 2002, *Government by the Gun: The Unfinished Business of Fiji's 2000 Coup*, Zed Books, Sydney

Robertson, R., and Tamanisau, A., 1988, *Fiji: Shattered Coups*, Pluto Press, Sydney

Robie, D., 1996, 'Protests mount over jailing of Tongan journalists', *Green Left Weekly*, 2 October, www.greenleft.org.au/content/protests-mount-over-jailing-tongan-journalists (retrieved 28 May 2019)

Robie, D. (ed.), 1992, *Tu Galala: Social Change in the Pacific*, Bridget Williams Books, Wellington

Roe, P., 2004, 'Securitization and minority rights: Conditions of desecuritization', *Security Dialogue*, 35(3): 279–94. doi-org.ezproxy.canterbury.ac.nz/10.1177/0967010604047527

Rostow, W., 1960, *The Stages of Economic Growth: A Non-Communist Manifesto*, Cambridge University Press, Cambridge

Rotberg, R., 2003, *When States Fail: Causes and Consequences*, Princeton University Press, Princeton

Roth, G., 1953, *Fijian Way of Life*, Oxford University Press, Melbourne

Routledge, D., 1985, *Matanitu: The Struggle for Power in Early Fiji*, Institute of Pacific Studies, University of the South Pacific, Suva

Rustomjee, C., 2016, 'Vulnerability and debt in small states', Center for International Governance Innovation, Waterloo, Canada, Policy Brief No. 83, July

Rutherford, N., 1977, *Friendly Islands: A History of Tonga*, Oxford University Press, Oxford

Ryle, J., 2010, *My God, My Land: Interwoven Paths of Christianity and Tradition in Fiji*, Ashgate, London

Said, E., 1978, *Orientalism: Western Representations of the Orient*, Routledge & Kegan Paul, London

—— 2001, 'The clash of ignorance', *The Nation*, 273(2): 11–14. www.thenation. com/article/clash-ignorance/

Salesa, D., 2017, *Island Time: New Zealand's Pacific Futures*, Bridget Williams Books, Wellington

Salmond, M., 1991, *Two Worlds: First Meetings Between Maoris and Europeans, 1642–1772*, University of Hawaii Press, Honolulu

Salter, M.B., 2007, 'On exactitude in disciplinary science: A response to the network manifesto', *Security Dialogue*, 38(1): 113–22. doi.org/10.1177/ 0967010607075976

Sanday, J., 1991, *The Military in Fiji: A Historical Development and Future Role*, Working paper, Strategic and Defence Studies Centre, The Australian National University, Canberra

Scarr, D., 1968, *Fragments of Empire: A History of the Western Pacific High Commission*, University of Hawaii Press, Honolulu

—— 1984, *Fiji: A Short History*, Allen & Unwin, Sydney

Scruton, R., 2002, *The West and the Rest: Globalization and the Terrorist Threat*, Intercollegiate Studies Institute, Wilmington

Seidman, S., 2008, *Contested Knowledge: Social Theory Today*, Blackwell Publishing, Oxford

Senituli, L., 2005, 'Unfinished business: Democratic transition in Tonga', paper presented to the Pacific Islands Political Studies Association conference, Port Vila

Senituli, L., 2006, 'The attempted coup of 16 November 2006', paper in response to Dr Ana Taufe'ulungaki's paper on the 2006 riots, Nuku'alofa

—— 2017, '16/11: The role of His Majesty's Armed Forces on constitutional reform in Tonga', paper presented to conference on global security organised by International Political Science Association, University of Canterbury, Christchurch

Shani, G., Sato, M., and Pasha, M., 2007, *Protecting Human Security in a Post-9/11 World: Critical and Global Insights*, Palgrave Macmillan, Basingstoke

Sheikh, M.K., 2005, 'Fear for faith: Islamism, security and conflict resolution', master's degree thesis, Department of Political Science, University of Copenhagen

Shinoda, H., 2004, 'The concept of human security: Historical and theoretical implications', *Conflict and Human Security: A Search for New Approches of Peace-building*, IPSHU English Research Report Series No. 19: 5–22

Sils, R., and Katzenstein, P., 2010, *Beyond Paradigms: Analytical Eclecticism in the Study of World Politics*, Palgrave, London

Snyder, J., 2004, 'One world, rival theories', *Foreign Policy*, 145: 52–62. doi.org/10.2307/4152944

Solomon Islands Anglican Communion New Service, 2008, 'Communiqué of the Church of Melanesia: Consultation on reconciliation and peace-building', 6 May. www.anglicannews.org/news/2008/05/communique-of-the-church-of-melanesia-consultation-on-reconciliation-and-peace-building.aspx

Solomon Islands Government, 2000, Townsville Peace Agreement, Solomon Islands Government, Honiara

Solomon Islands Joint Constitutional Congress, 2014, Second 2014 draft for proposed Constitution of the Federal Democratic Republic of Solomon Islands, www.sicr.gov.sb/2nd%202014%20SI%20Constitution%20Draft%20(R)%20pdf%20-%208%205%2014.pdf

Solomon Islands Truth and Reconciliation Commission (STRC), 2012, *Confronting the Truth for a Better Solomon Islands*, Truth and Reconciliation Commission of the Solomon Islands, Honiara

Solomon Star, 2015, 'Church officials end peace-building training', 21 April, www.solomonstarnews.com/news/national/6722-church-officials-end-peace-building-training

Spate, O.H.K., 1959, *Fijian People: Economic Problems and Prospects*, Council paper No. 13 of 1959, Government Press, Suva

Spriggs, M., 1997, *The Island Melanesians*, Blackwell Publishers, Oxford

Spurway, J., 2015, *Ma'afu, Prince of Tonga, Chief of Fiji: The Life and Times of Fiji's First Tui Lau*, ANU Press, Canberra

Staszak, J., 2004, 'Primitivism and the other: History of art and cultural geography', *GeoJornal*, 60: 353–64. unige.ch/sciences-societe/socio/files/7814/0533/5827/Primitivismandtheother_Staszak.pdf

Stavenhagen, A., 1996, *Ethnic Conflicts and the Nation-State*, Palgrave Macmillan, London

Ştefanachi, B., 2011, 'Globalization, development and human security', *Sfera Politicii*, 166: 13–23

Stewart, F. (ed.), 2008, *Horizontal Inequalities and Conflict: Understanding Group Violence in Multi-Ethnic Societies*, Palgrave Macmillan, New York

Stiglitz, J., 2002, *Globalization and Its Discontents*, W.W. Norton & Company, London

Stritzel, H., 2011, 'Security: The translation', *Security Dialogue*, 42(4–5): 343–56. doi.org/10.1177/0967010611418998

Stuff NZ, 2013, 'Tongan Prime Minister's defamation action part of an "ongoing saga"', 17 June. www.radionz.co.nz/international/pacific-news/212970/tongan-prime-minister's-defamation-action-part-of-an-ongoing-saga

Suh, J., Katzenstein, P., and Carlson, A. (eds), 2004, *Rethinking Security in East Asia: Identity, Power, and Efficiency*, Stanford University Press, Stanford

Sutherland, W., 1992, *Beyond the Politics of Race: An Alternative History of Fiji to 1992*, Research School of Asian and Pacific Studies, The Australian National University, Canberra

Swami, N., 2017, 'No threat, says RFMF', *Fiji Times*, 17 July. www.fijitimes.com/story.aspx?id=408883

Swinden, G., 1998, 'The natives appear restless tonight: HMAS *Adelaide* and the punitive expedition to Malaita 1927', in *Maritime Power in the Twentieth Century: The Australian Experience*, ed. D. Stevens (pp. 54–67), Allen & Unwin, London

Sylvester, C., 1987, 'Some dangers in merging feminist and peace projects', *Alternatives*, 12: 493–509. doi.org/10.1177/030437548701200404

Tadjbakhsh, S., and Chenoy, A., 2005, *Human Security: Concepts and Implications with an Application to Post-Intervention Challenges in Afghanistan*, Center for Peace and Conflict Resolution, Institut d'Études Politiques, Paris

Tagicakibau, E., 2018, 'Militarism and masculinity in Fiji', PhD thesis, University of Auckland

Tamate, J., 2013, 'Balancing the scales: The experience of the parties to the Nauru Agreement', PhD thesis, University of Wollongong. ro.uow.edu.au/cgi/viewcontent.cgi?referer=https://www.google.co.nz/&httpsredir=1&article=5085&context=theses (retrieved 9 January 2019)

Taufe'ulungaki, A., 2006, 'Confidential report on the Tongan riots for the University of the South Pacific', unpublished report, University of the South Pacific, Suva

Tawake, S., 2000, 'Transforming the insider–outsider perspective: Post-colonial fiction from the Pacific', *Contemporary Pacific*, 12(1): 155–75. hdl.handle. net/10125/13504

Taylor, O., 2004, 'Human security-conflict, critique and consensus: Colloquium remarks and a proposal for a threshold-based definition', *Security Dialogue*, 35(3): 373–87. doi.org/10.1177/0967010604047555

Thayer, B., 2004, *Darwin and International Relations: On the Evolutionary Origins of War and Ethnic Conflict*, University Press of Kentucky, Lexington

Thomas, N., 1989, 'The force of ethnology: Origins and significance of the Melanesia/Polynesia division', *Cultural Anthropology*, 30: 27–41. www.jstor. org/stable/2743301

Thornley, A., 2002, *Exodus of the iTaukei: The Wesleyan Church in Fiji, 1848–74*, Institute of Pacific Studies, University of the South Pacific, Suva

Tiffany, S., 1980, 'Politics of land disputes in Western Samoa', *Oceania*, 50(3): 176–208. doi.org/10.1002/j.1834-4461.1980.tb01400

Tjalve, V.S., 2011, 'Designing (de)security: European exceptionalism, Atlantic republicanism and the "public sphere"', *Security Dialogue*, 42(4–5): 441–52. doi.org/10.1177/0967010611418715

Turse, N., 2008, *The Complex: How the Military Invades Our Everyday Lives*, Holt Metropolitan Books, New York

United Nations, 1979, Convention on the Elimination of all Forms of Discrimination Against Women, United Nations, New York

United Nations Development Program (UNDP), 2007, *Human Security Consultations Report*, UNDP, Suva

—— 2010, *Millenium Development Goals Report*, UNDP, New York

—— 2016, 'UNDP peace-building program launched in the Solomon Islands', 15 July. www.pacific.undp.org/content/pacific/en/home/presscenter/press releases/2016/07/15/new-un-peacebuilding-programme-launched-in-the-solomon-islands.html (retrieved 9 May 2019)

United Nations Educational, Scientific and Cultural Organization (UNESCO), 2014, 'Solomon Islands case study in education, conflict and social cohesion', Bangkok. www.unicef.org/eapro/17_PBEA_Solomon_Islands_Case_Study.pdf (retrieved 9 May 2019)

Van der Grijp, P., 2014, *Manifestations of Mana: Political Power and Divine Inspirations in Polynesia*, Lit Verlag, Berlin

Van der Vat, D., 1992, *The Pacific Campaign: The US–Japanese Naval War 1941–1945*, Simon & Schuster, New York

Von Tigerstrom, B., 2007, *Human Security and International Law: Prospects and Problems*, Hart Publishing, Oxford

Vuori, J., 2008, 'Illocutionary logic and strands of securitization: Applying the theory of securitization to the study of non-democratic political orders', *European Journal of International Relations*, 14(1): 65–99. doi.org/10.1177/1354066107087767

Waddington, D., and King, M., 2005, 'The disorderly crowd: From classical psychological reductionism to socio-contextual theory—the impact on public order policing strategies', *Howard Journal of Criminal Justice*, 44(5): 490–503. doi.org/10.1111/j.1468-2311.2005.00393

Wæver, O., 1995, 'Securitization and desecuritization', in *On Security*, ed. R.D. Lipschutz (pp. 46–86), Columbia University Press, New York

—— 2010, 'Taking stock of a research programme: Revisions and restatements of securitization theory', paper presented at the annual convention of the International Studies Association, New Orleans, 17–20 February

Wainwright, E., 2003, *Our Failing Neighbour: Australia and the Future of the Solomon Islands*, Australian Strategic Policy Institute, Canberra

Wallerstein, I., 1989, *The Modern World-System*, vols 1–3, Academic Press, New York

Wallis, J., 2015, 'The South Pacific: "Arc of instability" or "arc of opportunity"?', *Global Change, Peace and Security*, 27(1): 39–53. doi.org/10.1080/14781158.2015.992010

Wallis, J., Jeffery, R., and Kent, L., 2015, 'Political reconciliation in Timor Leste, Solomon Islands and Bougainville: The dark side of hybridity', *Australian Journal of International Affairs*, 70(2): 159–78. doi.org/10.1080/10357718.2015.1113231

Waterhouse, J., 1866. *The king and people of Fiji*, Wesleyan Conference Office, London

Waterhouse, J., 1997, *The King and People of Fiji*, Pasifika Press, Wellington

Webel, C., and Johansen, J., 2012, *Peace and Conflict Studies: A Reader*, Routledge, London

Wilkins, T., 2010, 'The new "Pacific century" and the rise of China: An international perspective', *Australian Journal of International Relations*, 64(4): 381–405. doi.org/10.1080/10357718.2010.489993

Williams, M., and McDuie-Ra, D., 2018, *Combatting Climate Change in the Pacific: The Role of Regional Organizations*, Palgrave Macmillan, London

Williams, M.C., 2003, 'Words, images, enemies: Securitization and international politics', *International Studies Quarterly*, 47(4): 511–31. www.jstor.org/stable/3693634

—— 2011, 'The continuing evolution of securitization theory', in *Securitization Theory: How Security Problems Emerge and Dissolve*, ed. T. Balzacq (pp. 212–22), Routledge, London

Williams, T., 1858, *Fiji and the Fijians: The islands and their inhabitants*, A. Heylin, London

Williams, T., 1982, *Fiji and the Fijians: The Islands and Their Inhabitants*, vol. 1, Fiji Museum, Suva

Wirrick, P., 2008, 'Restricting the freedom of movement in Vanuatu: Custom in conflict with human rights', *Journal of South Pacific Law*, 12(1): 76–83. www.paclii.org/journals/fJSPL/vol12no1/pdf/wirrick.pdf

Wood, A.H., 1938, *A History and Geography of Tonga*, Wilton & Horton, Auckland

Wood-Ellem, E., 1999, *Queen Salote of Tonga: The Story of an Era*, Auckland University Press, Auckland

Xuetong, Y., 2009, 'Defining peace: Peace vs security', *Korean Journal of Defence Analysis*, 16(1): 201–19. doi.org/10.1080/10163270409464062